Critical Transnational
Feminist Praxis

SUNY Series, Praxis: Theory in Action
Nancy A. Naples, editor

Critical Transnational
Feminist Praxis

EDITED BY

AMANDA LOCK SWARR

AND

RICHA NAGAR

Cover image of Ananya Dance Theatre's performance provided
by Ananya Dance Theatre.

Published by State University of New York Press, Albany

Printed in the United States of America

For information, contact State University of New York Press, Albany, NY
www.sunypress.edu

Production by Ryan Morris
Marketing by Michael Campochiaro

Library of Congress Cataloging-in-Publication Data

Critical transnational feminist praxis / edited by Richa Nagar and Amanda Lock Swarr.
        p.   cm. — (praxis: theory in action)
    Includes bibliographical references and index.
    ISBN 978-1-4384-2937-3 (hardcover : alk. paper) — ISBN 978-1-4384-2938-0 (pbk. : alk. paper)
    1. Feminism—Cross-cultural studies. I. Nagar, Richa. II. Swarr, Amanda Lock.
    HQ1121.C69 2009
    305.4201—dc22

                                                                            2009008531

10   9   8   7   6   5   4   3   2   1

Contents

Illustrations

Acknowledgments

When a work is a product of more than a decade of journeying together, it is very difficult to name and thank every single individual or institution that has shaped our ideas and efforts. While it is not possible to name everyone who has directly or indirectly molded our vision and work, we would like to acknowledge with deepest gratitude those who have been most critical in sowing the seeds of this volume, nourishing it, and bringing it to fruition.

It was a Graduate Research Partnership Program grant from the University of Minnesota in 2001–2002 that first allowed us to extend our intellectual partnership beyond an advisor-advisee relationship and begin an exciting research partnership. A Mellon Postdoctoral Fellowship in the Humanities and support from the Department of Women's Studies at Barnard College of Columbia University (2003–2005) and from the Department of Women Studies at the University of Washington (since 2005) have allowed Amanda Swarr to continue her collaboration with Richa Nagar. A residential fellowship for Richa from the Center for Advanced Study in the Behavioral Sciences at Stanford along with a grant from the College of Liberal Arts at Minnesota in 2005–2006 allowed us the space and time to plan the workshop Towards a Transnational Feminist Praxis and to enjoy the beautiful environs *on the hill* as we completed the initial draft of the paper that evolved into the introduction to this volume.

The workshop Towards a Transnational Feminist Praxis, where the idea for this book finally crystallized, was hosted at the University of Minnesota on September 15–16, 2006 by the Institute for Global Studies (IGS) with generous support from the Interdisciplinary Center for the Study of Global Change (ICGC) and a cosponsorship from the Department of Gender, Women, and Sexuality Studies. This workshop provided the platform to begin the dialogues that now find expression in *Critical Transnational Feminist Praxis*. The idea for the workshop first emerged in spring 2005 in a series of conversations with Laura Sayles (IGS) and Karen Brown (ICGC). We could not have undertaken this workshop without Laura Sayles's intellectual engagement and meticulous planning; Klaas van der Sanden's creative, careful, and experienced organizing; and Allison Lindberg's dedicated attention to detail. The photo exhibit organized by Alondra Espejel and her colleagues at the Minnesota Immigrant Freedom Network, and the jointly organized events and activities with the Ananya Dance Theatre and the Resource Center of the Americas, profoundly enriched the workshop. Last, but not least, we are grateful that a workshop organized by the South Asia Center, the Simpson Center for the Humanities, the Departments of Women Studies and Geography at the University of Washington, Seattle, and the Interdisciplinary Arts and Sciences at the University of Washington, Bothell gave the two of us the opportunity to merge the comments of the contributors into the last chapter of this volume.

We would like to thank all those who participated in the workshop as authors, presenters, and dancers: M. Jacqui Alexander, Deborah Barndt, Karen de Souza, Chandra Talpade Mohanty, Obioma Nnaemeka, Linda Peake, Geraldine Pratt, Rachel Silvey, Reena, Richa Singh, Surbala, and the members of Ananya Dance Theatre, including Ananya Chatterjea, Shannon Gibney, Omise'eke Natasha Tinsley, and Hui Niu Wilcox. Eight feminist scholars from the University of Minnesota served as discussants for these papers and provided invaluable feedback: Rose Brewer, Karen Brown, Susan Craddock, Jigna Desai, Kale Fajardo, Karen Ho, Amy Kaminsky, and Naomi Scheman. We would also like to thank those who could not participate as authors or discussants during the workshop but joined us as contributors later on: Danielle Bouchard, Sam Bullington, Piya Chatterjee, and Diane Detournay. The lively engagement and challenging questions from the students, community workers, and other members of the audience have continued to give momentum to many of our ideas long after the conclusion of the workshop.

The journey from the 2006 workshop at Minnesota to *Critical Transnational Feminist Praxis* has been marked by a series of meaningful partnerships. We thank Larin McLaughlin, our editor at SUNY Press, for her enthusiastic engagement and support of this collaboration, and Andrew Kenyon and Ryan Morris for smoothing our path throughout the long process of production. We would also like to thank David Faust, Louise Fortmann, Elaine Haig-Widner, Carol Langdon, Joel Wainwright, David Allen, Judy Howard, Chi-ming Yang, Abdi Samatar, Priti Ramamurthy, Sharad Chari, Karen Falconer Al-Hindi, and Pamela Moss for their intellectual generosity and support at crucial junctures in the making of this book.

And then there are those of you whom we have lived and breathed and argued and learned with in the more intimate and vulnerable spaces of our personal and political lives: Bass John, Conny, Phumla, Midi, Theresa, Dawie, Juan, Tee, Barbara, Jessica, Dan, Frank, Kathleen, Fred, Val, Gabe, Karla, Zach, Maribeth, Declan, Maa (Vibha Nagar), Babuji (Sharad Nagar), Medha, Tarun, Dumdi, Deeksha, "Namarashi," and *sathis* of Sangtin. As inadequate as words are, we want to say *tahe dil se shukriya* to you for embracing us during all those times when rules of academic productivity do not sit so well with the commitments we have made to you. *Hamba kahle* to those we have lost along the way.

—AMANDA LOCK SWARR AND RICHA NAGAR

Introduction

Theorizing Transnational Feminist Praxis

RICHA NAGAR AND AMANDA LOCK SWARR

Arundhati Roy follows in the traditions of Nehru, Gandhi, and many others. She is . . . using her position as an artist to fight for those who do not have a voice and is prepared to suffer the consequences. . . . These are qualities worthy of the highest praise.
  —Kevin Baker, quoted in *The Guardian*, Friday, March 8, 2002

The global left media celebrates Arundhati Roy as one of the most influential Third World activists resisting U.S. empire. Such celebration, however, does not mean that Roy's intellectual voice and her political analyses have emerged in isolation from the struggles of activist communities—particularly, the Narmada Bachao Andolan—where she has learned many political lessons and developed her analytical frameworks as a part of collectives and movements. In other words, the limelight bestowed on a single activist does not change the reality that all activism is collectively constituted. It is the community of struggle that turns an activist into a hero; the labor of the activist cannot be abstracted from the community.

In much the same way, all academic production is necessarily collaborative, notwithstanding the individualized manner in which authorship is claimed and assigned and celebrity granted to academics as isolated knowledge producers. Undergraduate classrooms, graduate seminars, workshops, conferences, academic peer reviews, and fieldwork-based knowledge production are all examples of the everyday collaborative spaces and tools through which academics create knowledges and learn to speak to various communities inside and outside of academia. These spaces are also excellent reminders of an inherent contradiction that exists in the U.S. academic establishment: the system relies on the rhetoric and vitality of intellectual *communities*, while at the same time privileging a structure of *individual* merits and rewards

1

that is premised on a denial and dismissal of the collaborative basis of all intellectual work produced within the institution. This general tendency in the U.S. academy is made more pronounced by a celebrity culture where an internalized need to present oneself as an individual academic star often translates into a drive to abstract and generalize, frequently in opposition to those who are seen as immersed in "grounded struggles."

The assumptions and fallacies of a model based on the notion of an individual knowledge producer in academia (feminist studies included) are useful starting points for an interrogation of three sets of dichotomies critical to rethinking the meanings and possibilities of feminist praxis: individually/collaboratively produced knowledges, academia/activism, and theory/method. Such interrogation can also serve as a meaningful entry point from which to consider the relationships between local and global as well as to revisit the politics of authenticity, translation, and mediation with an explicit aim of extending ongoing conversations about the meanings and possibilities of transnational feminist engagements.

This volume is an initial step in what we see as our long-term collaborative journey with one another and with collaborators in other academic and nonacademic locations (e.g., Swarr and Nagar 2004; Nagar and Swarr 2004; Bullington and Swarr 2007; Sangtin Writers [and Nagar] 2006) to reflect on the meanings and implications of these three dichotomies in relation to transnational feminist praxis. We note two phenomena that have been in mutual tension. On the one hand, growing interests in questions of globalization, neo-liberalism, and social justice have fuelled the emergence and growth of transnational feminisms in interdisciplinary feminist studies. On the other hand, ongoing debates since the 1980s over questions of voice, authority, representation, and identity have often produced a gap between the efforts of feminists engaged in theorizing the complexities of knowledge production across borders and those concerned with imagining concrete ways to enact solidarities across nations, institutions, sociopolitical identifications, and economic categories and materialities.

We reconceptualize collaboration as an intellectual and political tool to bridge this gap, with possibilities that exceed its potential as a methodological intervention. We suggest that interweaving theories and practices of knowledge production through collaborative dialogues provides a way to radically rethink existing approaches to subalternity, voice, authorship, and representation. Although such concepts as *transnational feminist studies* are sometimes invoked as if a subfield with shared meanings and assumptions exists, we suggest that the two phenomena noted here have constituted transnational feminisms as a diverse and diffuse field where hierarchies and practices pertaining to knowledge production have been unevenly treated in theoretical interventions. We argue for a transnational feminist praxis that is critically aware of its own historical, geographical, and political locations, even as it is invested in alliances that are created and sustained through deeply dialogic and critically self-reflexive processes of knowledge production and dissemination. We actively resist celebrity/expert politics while recognizing the limits of this resistance.

In this introduction, we first consider key approaches to the transnational by interdisciplinary feminist scholars in U.S. and Canadian academia. Next, we discuss these inquiries into the transnational in relation to practices of knowledge production by examining the interstices of the three sets of dichotomies identified: academic/activist, theory/method, and individual/collaborative. Finally, we analyze two texts published in the 1990s that have become canonical in transnational feminist studies to explore the manner and extent to which they address these concerns and to identify some critical points of engagement and departure that might broaden and deepen the imaginaries and practices associated with political dialogues and intellectual production across borders. These three points of inquiry allow us to grapple with the ways in which collaborative praxis is marginalized in dominant institutional spaces of the academy and to imagine how such praxis can become a rich source of methodological *and* theoretical interventions and agendas that can begin the process of identifying and re/claiming those spaces. In the last section, we situate our arguments in relation to the process, structure, and specific contributions that have come together in the making of this volume.

The *Transnational* of Transnational Feminisms

Generally speaking, the popularization and embracing of transnational feminisms as a discourse in feminist/women's and gender studies has coincided with a commitment to address the asymmetries of the globalization process. Yet, it would be incorrect to suggest that the term *transnational* has the same salience in South Africa, India, Egypt, or Brazil as it does in U.S. and Canadian academic feminist studies. Similar to concepts of "women of color" feminisms (e.g. The Combahee River Collective 1982), "third world" feminisms (e.g., Mohanty et al. 1991), "multi-cultural" feminisms (e.g., Shohat 1998), "international" feminisms (e.g., Enloe 1990), and "global" feminisms (e.g., Morgan 1984), *transnational* as a descriptor has emerged out of certain historical moments in the U.S. and Canadian academy. It is important to acknowledge, therefore, the ways in which the deployments of transnational feminisms continue, or depart from, the intellectual and political legacies of women of color/third world/multicultural/international/global feminisms. At the same time, however, it is critical to be aware of the limits engendered by the overuse of *transnational*. Indeed, as Inderpal Grewal and Caren Kaplan argue, the term *transnational* "has become so ubiquitous in cultural, literary and critical studies that much of its political valence seems to have become evacuated" (2001: 664). This makes it necessary to consider briefly the various deployments of the idea of the transnational and how they feed visions of feminist praxis and collaborative knowledge production.

In a discussion of transnational sexuality studies, Grewal and Kaplan (2001) specify at least five kinds of foci where the term *transnational* has gained currency: (a) in theorizing migration as a transnational process; (b) to signal the demise or irrelevance of the nation-state in the current phase of globalization; (c) as a synonym for *diasporic*; (d) to designate a form of postcolonialism; and (e) as an alternative to the problematic of the global and the international, articulated primarily by Western or Euro-American second-wave feminists as well as by multinational corporations, for which "becoming global" marks an expansion into new markets.

It is in this last sense that we are concerned with the idea of transnational feminisms in this chapter—as a conceptual framework that strives to liberate itself from the political and intellectual constraints of international feminisms and global feminisms. Whereas international feminisms are seen as rigidly adhering to nation-state borders and paying inadequate attention to forces of globalization, global feminisms have been subjected to critical scrutiny for prioritizing northern feminist agendas and perspectives and for homogenizing women's struggles for sociopolitical justice, especially in colonial and neocolonial contexts.[1]

In the North American academy, transnational feminisms emerged, in part, from postcolonial critiques and introspection that is often linked to the writings of authors such as Mohanty (1986), Lazreg (1988), and Trinh (1991), who highlighted the contradictions and dangers inherent in a feminist project where "difference" is only allowed to unfold according to external standards and within an external frame of reference. "Under these circumstances," wrote Marnia Lazreg,

> the consciousness of one's womanhood coincides with the realization that it has already been appropriated in one form or another by outsiders, women as well as men, experts in things Middle Eastern. In this sense, the feminist project is warped and rarely brings with it the potential for personal liberation that it does in this country [U.S.] or in Europe. (1988: 81)

These and similar works critiqued the hegemony of a monolithic notion of "Third World women" as passive victims and underscored the need to highlight Third World women's activism and agency, as well as to recast the category of Third World women to imagine new forms of transnational solidarities and collaborations (Mohanty 1986). The result was a series of exciting academic interventions where questions of modernity, emergence and circulation of global identities, transnational formations, and the relationships between the local and global became topics of sustained debate and discussion in a continuously emerging field of transborder feminisms.

At the same time, we suggest that considerations of the specific ways in which particular transnational collaborations and solidarities can be articulated, enacted, mediated, translated, and represented in and across the borders of the northern academy—as well as the consequences, losses, gains, and possibilities of such imaginaries and practices— have remained largely peripheral or implicit in these discussions. Similarly, these conversations have not sufficiently grappled with the goals, agendas, and visions of different forms of transnational solidarities and collaborations as facilitated and constrained by specific institutional spaces and practices. We seek to create more spaces for a critical interrogation of these issues.

As a working definition that tries to bring these questions to the forefront, we propose that transnational feminisms are an intersectional set of understandings, tools, and practices that can: (a) attend to racialized, classed, masculinized, and heteronormative logics and practices of globalization and capitalist patriarchies, and the multiple ways in which they (re)structure colonial and neocolonial relations of domination and subordination; (b) grapple with the complex and contradictory ways in which these processes both inform and are shaped by a range of subjectivities and understandings of individual and collective agency; and (c) interweave critiques, actions, and self-reflexivity so as to resist a priori predictions of what might constitute feminist politics in a given place and time.

Instead of investing ourselves in claiming feminism, then, we suggest that grounding feminisms in activist communities *everywhere* is a means to interrogate all forms of implicit and explicit relations of power (e.g., racist/ classist/casteist), and to contest those power relations through ongoing processes of self-critique and collective reflection. This definition can serve as a starting point for refiguring the three sets of dichotomies we have identified, with an explicit aim of inserting and specifying collaborative praxis in theorizations of transnational feminisms.

Refuting Individualism and Reclaiming Collaborative Praxis

Marginalization of praxis has been a recurring theme in academic discussions. Generally speaking, praxis is understood as the processes of mediation through which theory and practice become deeply interwoven with one another. It is often traced back to Paulo Freire's (1993 [1970]) concept of liberation as praxis—that is, the cycle of action, reflection, and action through which human beings work to transform their worlds. In feminist engagements, the idea of situated knowledges has provided an important focus for reflections on praxis and on the mutually constitutive nature of the intellectual and the political. For those immersed in the challenges of transnational feminisms, such reflections have frequently revolved around the limits and possibilities of writing, as well as positionality, intellectual and political accountability, and representation. Here we revisit some key approaches to these questions with an eye toward the manner in which the dichotomies of academia/activism, theory/method, and individualism/collaboration have been confronted, problematized, or retained in these engagements.

Vexed questions about the theoretical absence and empirical presence of the Other, the authority and privilege of the writer and the representer, and the provisional nature of all knowledge, have been most intensely debated in the context of postcolonial critiques of ethnographic knowledge production. These critiques, in turn, intersect with broader critiques of the manner in which social scientific and humanities knowledges are produced in and from the ivory towers of academia, and the exclusions that emanate from this process. Two broad themes can be discerned in these critiques. The first relates to the dichotomy between academic intellectuals and sources/subjects of knowledge. It has been argued that academics tend to speak to problems constituted by their disciplines, which limits the relevance of academic knowledges to struggles on the ground (Dreze 2002; Messer-Davidow 2002). Furthermore, this disjuncture between disciplines and what is labeled as "the ground" is exacerbated by researchers from the North who tend to read "over the shoulders of natives," not "alongside natives" with the result that hidden experts are always at the top of the hierarchy of knowledge production (Crapanzano 1986, quoted in Lassiter 2005: 5).

The second theme in these critiques pertains to the isolated realms of theory, method, and knowledge dissemination. Historian Tom Bender (1998) argues that a categorical distinction between production and popularization of knowledge accelerates professionalism while ignoring how diffusion of knowledge is a central part of making knowledge(s). This distinction is intimately connected with—and has played a role in constituting and perpetuating—the separation of (a) theory from method and (b) research processes from research products. The end result is a compartmentalization of questions pertaining to praxis and intellectual and political accountability (Enslin 1994; Poitevin 2002).

Feminist scholars' attempts to engage with these two themes have led to the development of three specific practices:

1. *Engagement with positionality and reflexivity*, where the concept of positionality refers to the ways in which a researcher's position in terms of gender, race, class, among other categories, shapes the content of research and critical self-reflexivity becomes a tool to produce a description of that positionality;

2. *Representational experiments* that seek to interrupt the researcher's own authority by incorporating or juxtaposing multiple "voices";

3. *Enacting accountability*, which for many interdisciplinary social scientists has translated into such practices as sharing of interview transcripts, life histories, and finished academic products with informants/subjects; and which has involved wide-ranging engagements with questions of how to write for multiple audiences, and of mediation, translation, and reception.

Although these practices have advanced feminist engagements with dilemmas of representation in several ways, each practice also suffers from serious limitations. First, approaches to positionality often assume transparent reflexivity in ways that the very desire to "reveal" multiple, complex, and shifting positionality of the researcher freezes identities and social positions in space and time, foreclosing an analysis of the manner in which identities and locations of those who produce knowledges are constituted and negotiated in and through the process of knowledge production itself (Rose 1997; Nagar and Geiger 2007).

The second practice of creating representational experiments seeks to operationalize self-reflexivity by challenging the idea of a master narrative or authoritative accounts and by experimenting with genres. However, it runs the risk of becoming what Johannes Fabian (1990) refers to as a regrouping of "anthropologists" to save the representer's privileges—a critique that can be applied more broadly to academics than merely those who carry the burden of anthropology. To put it another way, dialogic motifs in academic writing do not necessarily advance dialogues with so-called research subjects/subalterns. Rather, they often reproduce these distinctions, and run the risk of being dismissed by some academics as atheoretical narratives.[2]

Finally, the practice of accountability through such means as sharing interview transcripts, life stories, and academic products is a worthy goal that has the potential of advancing dialogues, but given the institutional and time constraints faced by academics in an environment of "accelerated professionalism" (Bender 1998), it rarely finds the legitimacy, encouragement, or resources that it deserves to prosper as a rigorous practice.

With respect to the understanding of praxis that we want to elaborate here, perhaps the most important limitation shared by all of the three approaches mentioned here is that although each attempts to engage with subjects on the ground, the hierarchy of knowledge producers and knowledges remains intact. The status of the academic researcher as the "true intellectual thinker" remains undisturbed, along with the hierarchies that elevate theory, research, and academic knowledge production to a higher plane than method, outreach, community-based conversations, and nonconventional academic writing. Not only does this hierarchization relegate the nonacademic collaborators to the second tier of knowledge production, it also automatically labels as "methodology," "activism," "atheoretical," or "unscholarly" most efforts that seek to destabilize or advance academic frameworks on the basis of dialogues and conversations outside academia. This hierarchy is further reinscribed by class; for instance, even when funding is available in academic settings for activist-academic partnerships, the academics' agendas and methodologies remain dominant in almost all cases (Barndt 2007).

This inevitable process of hierarchization serves to reinforce the three dichotomies named at the outset—between academics and activists; between theory and method; and between individual and collaborative processes of knowledge making. Looking at the relationships among these categories simultaneously—of the individual, the academic, and the theoretical, on the one hand, and of the collaborative, activist, and methodological on the other—suggests how dialogic praxis is pushed to the margins. At best, the critique that emerges through praxis gets reduced to another form of representational device or labeled as "participatory action research," and, in the process, gets bureaucratically controlled or abstracted from its embeddedness in lived struggles. At worst, academic gatekeepers discount such critique as "activism" and relegate it to a community outreach activity on the individual academic's *curriculum vitae* or annual report. And we are left again with a recurring problem: academic knowledges that dominate and languages that exclude, to safeguard the closed interpretive communities that have become constantly shrinking fiefdoms forbidden to the uninitiated (Said 2002).

By framing the challenge of collaborative praxis in terms of three dichotomies, we do not want to duplicate the problems that inhabit the binary of global and local. Local and global are often imagined in ways such that, rather than being seen as mutually constitutive and permeable constructs, the global is viewed as an oppressive network of power structures and the local becomes an innocent victim. The local also becomes a pure source of oppositional consciousness and a space of resistance to the global. In strikingly parallel ways, there is a danger of constructing the "academic" as the "global" and the "activist" as the "local," and of similarly conflating the "collaborative" and the "methodological" as victims of individually produced knowledges and theories.

Our argument for dismantling the three dichotomies, then, is not about a simple reversal of hierarchies and systems of valorization. Rather, we suggest that transnational collaboration should become a dynamic construct through which praxis can acquire its meaning and form in a given place, time, and struggle. Like our collaborators in this volume, we resist the inclination to position transnational feminisms as some teleological end result of progress narratives. Instead, we work within a crisis of representation that relies on critical transnational feminism as inherently unstable praxis whose survival and evolution hinge on a continuous commitment to produce self-reflexive and dialogic critiques of its own practices rather than a search for resolutions or closures—not to reproduce exercises in narrow "navel-gazing" but always in relation to overlapping hegemonic power structures at multiple temporal and geographic scales.

Revisiting *Scattered Hegemonies* and *Feminist Genealogies*

As a way to generate new conversations that are committed to envisioning and advancing transnational feminist praxis, we want to reconnect our focus on praxis and knowledge production with current theorizations of transnational feminisms. We begin by considering two texts that are often viewed as canonical in defining and conceptualizing transnational feminisms: Inderpal Grewal and Caren Kaplan's *Scattered Hegemonies: Postmodernity and Transnational Feminist Practices* (1994) and M. Jacqui Alexander and Chandra Talpade Mohanty's *Feminist Genealogies, Colonial Legacies, Democratic Futures* (1997). The decade following their respective publications has not lessened their influence in scholarship and pedagogical contexts. How do these two texts approach questions of collaboration in transnational feminist theory?

Scattered Hegemonies intends to problematize feminist theory and consider the usefulness of "postmodernity." Grewal and Kaplan's central questions are: "(1) What kinds of feminist practices engender theories that resist or question modernity? [and] (2) How do we understand the production and reception of diverse feminisms within a framework of transnational social/cultural/economic movements?" (1994: 2–3). For these two authors, decentering feminism and allowing for multiplicities is critical. They suggest that analyses of the relationship of "scattered hegemonies"—defined as "the effects of mobile capital as well as the multiple subjectivities that replace the European unitary subject"—to gender relations will serve to reduce generalizing northern dominance (Grewal and Kaplan 1994: 7).

Feminist Genealogies, by comparison, addresses feminist approaches to colonialism and possibilities of feminist democracy and "aims to provide a comparative, relational, and historically based conception of feminism, one that differs markedly from the liberal-pluralist understanding of feminism, an inheritance of the predominantly liberal roots of American feminist praxis" (Alexander and Mohanty 1997: xvi). Their articulation of feminist praxis is particularly relevant to our discussion here:

> To talk about feminist praxis in global contexts would involve shifting the unit of analysis from local, regional, and national culture to relations and processes across cultures. Grounding analyses in particular local, feminist praxis is necessary, but we also need to understand the local in relation to larger, cross-national processes. (Alexander and Mohanty 1997: xix)

Alexander and Mohanty push us to move toward a transnational vision of praxis itself that allows us to understand not only their articulation of this concept, but their analysis of the ways praxis necessarily works with processes that move through and beyond the global/local dichotomy.

Clearly, there are substantive differences between these two texts in the intentions of their respective projects. The subjects of each of these books also differs; while Grewal and Kaplan's collaborators focus primarily on published texts, the contributions that constitute *Feminist Genealogies* are concerned primarily with authors' involvements with activist movements. In terms of our present concerns, both volumes disrupt the divides between academia and activism and between theory and method. However, it is in considering the individual/collaborative divide that we find the most relevant differences between these texts. Grewal and Kaplan "believe that we must work collaboratively to formulate transnational feminist alliances" (1994: 1) and forged alliances with one another and with the volume's contributors to form a "writing community." Furthermore, their own activist work has informed their understandings of gender and geopolitics. They inform the reader, "Many of our close allies are not necessarily represented by essays in the collection but their work with us in study and writing groups is reflected in these pages" (Grewal and Kaplan 1994: 2). These collaborations influence the text in deep ways; as Grewal and Kaplan state, "Rather than attempt to account for or definitively circumscribe either 'theory' or 'practice,' the essays in this collection engage political and narrative strategies as they proliferate in transnational cultures" (1994: 28).

Alexander and Mohanty similarly collaborate with the volume's authors, while at the same time highlighting their accountability to the communities with whom they produce both activism and knowledge(s). They write: "In collaborating with the authors, each other, and other sisters and comrades over the years, we have come to know the critical importance of figuring out our communities to which we are accountable" (1997: ix). Alexander and Mohanty (1997: xiii) further suggest that, through their process of working together, "we now know that our best ideas are produced through working and thinking together." *Feminist Genealogies* attempts to intervene into the space of praxis while taking the notion of collaboration in a different direction than that articulated in *Scattered Hegemonies*. Alexander and Mohanty (1997: xx) write:

Individual analyses are grounded in the contemporary crisis of global capitalism, suggesting that these particular contexts are the ones which throw up very specific analytic and political challenges for organizations. Here, no false dichotomy exists between theory and practice. We literally have to think ourselves out of these crises through collective praxis and particular kinds of theorizing.

This collective commitment to "think ourselves out of these crises" returns us to the dichotomous constructions that have concerned us in this chapter. It challenges us to ask whether the hierarchical relations between theory and method and the oversimplified dichotomy of academia and activism can be subverted through intellectual productions that refuse to separate the two. In the instance of *Feminist Genealogies*, "the sustained and collective work that has gone into producing it is itself a reflection of a way of doing politics, a mode of organizing that interrupts the more pervasive 'professionalized' production of scholarship. . . .In other words, all the authors connect their work to feminist communities in struggle—their work flows from this connection" (Alexander and Mohanty 1997: xx). However, as Ella Shohat points out in *Talking Visions*, a less-cited but similarly crucial contribution to what she terms "multicultural feminisms," the reality that connections, borders, and passports are under surveillance is a constant reminder that some connections are easier to make than others in a world "simultaneously undergoing globalization and fragmentation" (1998: 15).

How does contemporary scholarship within this increasingly codified field help us to redefine the boundaries of *transnational feminist collaboration* when all three of these terms are highly contested? In their more recent work, Kaplan and Grewal frame their interventions as operating within a "transnational feminist cultural studies" framework (2002). For them, this approach offers "an interdisciplinary site [that] can provide a space for critique and production of new sites of knowledge" (2002: 67). In this chapter, and in this volume more generally, our claim is that transnational feminist studies is a necessarily unstable field that must contest its very definition in order to be useful. As M. Jacqui Alexander pointed out, ". . . the very category of the transnational—which has itself been put to multiple uses—*continues to be haunted by relativist claims that effectively reinscribe dysfunctional hierarchies* and obscure the ways in which national and transnational processes are mutually, though unequally, imbricated" (2005: 183, emphasis added). This reinscription is at the heart of the paradoxes of transnational feminisms. Perhaps we can take heed of Butler's (1993) earlier cautions and recent discussions of queerness (Eng et al. 2005) that remind us that queer studies, when operating ideally within its own principles of self-critique, can never fully be articulated or defined. Along similar lines, we suggest that (a) transnational feminist collaboration must be critically interrogated as we simultaneously work to define it as a set of slippery and contingent terms, and (b) that this should be done not with the primary purpose of generating new debates in narrowly defined academic circles, but to forge the kind of connections that Chatterjee (2009) invites us to imagine,

> connections [that] chafe against the *realpolitik* of geopolitical mappings [so that] . . . we/i might begin to conceive of hemispheric linkages within the deepest epistemic and affective logics of empire and violence. Then, we/i can conceive the shared cosmologies of suffering which bring together a displaced mother from New Orleans with another mother from an Indian plantation, each mourning her dead child. One is dead from the impacts of state violence and neglect, the other from starvation. Perhaps our task as activist/scholars is to tie the threads of such connected suffering, across spaces of embodied difference, with ethical purpose and reflection. Perhaps, then, we can *together* mourn, hunger *and* create global knowledges—*global literacies*—in the service of social transformation, compassion and justice. (146, emphasis in original)

Extending the Discussion

Attending to these conceptual complications, this volume provides a systematic discussion of the possibilities of collaborations that consciously combine
struggles for sociopolitical justice with feminist research methodologies,
thereby extending the meanings and scope of transnational feminist theory
and practice. This collection emerges from a twelve-year-long intellectual
partnership between the editors that has included our own collaborations
as feminist teachers, students, and coauthors in the U.S. academy, as well
as dialogues between us about our respective engagements with grassroots
activists and struggles in India and South Africa. As we worked through
the debates about feminist theories and methods in U.S. academia and their
intersections (or absences thereof) with the ongoing debates in the sites of
our feminist activism, research, and creative work in the global South, we
often found ourselves mingling questions of access to drinking water with
those of access to antiretroviral drugs, and the languages and spaces of
"empowerment" and poverty with those of intimacies and sexualities.

Throughout these conversations, however, we kept returning to the
productive but troubling relationships between academia and activism, to
the contradictions of the growth of "transnational feminisms," and to the
dilemmas we found in our own North/South collaborations. Paradoxically,
however, the spaces to address these concerns in our graduate and undergraduate classrooms seemed to be forever shrinking despite the emergence
of a feminist studies professoriate in the global North, on the one hand, and
the rise of transnational feminist discourses, on the other.

From these ruminations evolved the idea of organizing a two-day workshop on transnational feminist praxis. This workshop, held at the University
of Minnesota in fall 2006, featured eight papers authored by feminist scholars
in the North American academy who have been thoroughly immersed in
questions pertaining to collaborative praxis. The papers were circulated
beforehand and each was assigned to a scholar from the University of
Minnesota whose own research interests intersected with the paper, and
who provided careful reading and critical commentary on the paper, before
opening up the discussion in a public forum (attended mainly by graduate
students and scholar activists). In addition, the authors also spent time
learning about each other's political and intellectual trajectories. These
conversations sowed the seeds of new partnerships, and the participants
decided to develop the papers into chapters for a collaborative volume. Each
paper presented at the workshop was exchanged with and reviewed by two
other contributors to the collection, while four new chapters were added in

the process of making this volume, at least in part, because of the conversations that the workshop triggered. The following questions animated our initial inquiry:

- What forms can transnational feminist collaboration take and what limits do such forms pose?
- What are the relationships among collaboration and transnational feminist theories in creating new spaces for political and intellectual engagements across North/South and East/West divides?
- Can collaborative practices consciously combine struggles for intellectual empowerment and socioeconomic justice while also attending to the problem of how northern academic engagements inevitably produce "difference"?

What finally emerged from these dialogues was a set of chapters that addresses the complexities and challenges of multiple forms of collaboration: across geographical, linguistic, and socioeconomic borders; between activists and academics; and across institutions and "fields" of feminist academics and NGO workers.

The chapters of this volume collectively suggest that collaboration is not merely a set of concrete strategies or models with ethical dilemmas and conceptual difficulties that must be addressed and attended to. On the contrary, collaboration itself poses a theoretical challenge to and potential for rethinking transnational feminist frameworks by creating new spaces for political and intellectual initiatives beyond disciplinary borders, academic/artistic/activist divides, and North/South dichotomies. At the same time, the authors resist an impulse to celebrate collaboration as a panacea and remind us that for collaborative praxis to retain its critical edge and radical potential, collaboration itself must be subjected to continuous critical scrutiny so that it can oppose the paralyzing effects emanating from the institutionalization of both academia and activism.

As conversations unfolded among the contributors to this volume, the objectives herein came to be threefold. The first was to conceptualize feminist collaboration as an intellectual and political practice that allows us to grapple with the possibilities and limitations of theory as praxis and insists upon problematizing the rigid compartmentalization that separates research from pedagogy, academic from activist labor, and theorizing from organizing and performative arts. Our second goal was to combine theories and practices of knowledge production through collaborative dialogues that invite us to rethink dominant scholarly approaches to subalternity, voice, authorship, and representation. Last, but not least, the contributors sought to explore how feminist approaches to collaboration can allow us to articulate transnational feminist frameworks and to simultaneously create new spaces for political and intellectual initiatives across socioeconomic, geographical, and institutional borders. Our collective efforts to reconceptualize transnational feminist collaboration in this volume consider how collaborative praxis is marginalized in dominant institutional spaces of the academy, while also imagining the ways in which such praxis can become a rich source of theoretical *and* methodological interventions and agendas that can begin the process of identifying and re/claiming those spaces.

Part 1 of this volume, Decolonizing Transnational Feminisms, takes up paradoxes of language and meaning that concern all of its contributors. This section opens with M. Jacqui Alexander and Chandra Talpade Mohanty's critical exploration of the category of *the transnational*, interrogating the genealogy of this category in women's and LGBTT/queer studies in the U.S. and Canadian academy.[3] As part of their larger project to think through the political and epistemological struggles that are embedded in radical transnational feminist praxis, the authors analyze the work that this category does in particular feminist contexts; its complex relationship to colonial, neocolonial, and imperial histories and practices on different geographical scales; and the specific material and ideological practices that constitute the transnational at this historical juncture and in the U.S. and Canadian sites we as feminist thinkers occupy ourselves. To those who embrace the label of *transnational feminism*, Alexander and Mohanty pose the crucial question: when is the transnational a normativizing gesture and when does it perform a radical decolonizing function? In the next chapter, Jigna Desai, Danielle Bouchard, and Diane Detournay approach this same problematic by suggesting that we must see the working definitions of transnational feminisms as necessarily open and contingent, rather than as static and prescriptive. The authors explicate *praxis* and propose that transnational feminist praxis and collaboration must be understood as critically compromised and embedded within their very sites of analysis and critique. For these authors, understanding transnational feminism as having completed its intellectual mission is a mistake; rather, transnational feminism should provide a self-critique and means for understanding rather than codifying globalism.

If all knowledge is embodied in dialogue, then the dimensions of what must constitute the specific politics of accountability, representation, and positionality must also emerge through the particularities of a given collaborative process. At the same time, a commitment to collaborative praxis also requires a serious critical reflection on who is or is not deemed to be a legitimate knowledge producer, which spaces, institutions, and languages get included or excluded from practices of knowledge making, and with what results. In part 2 of this volume, Dialogical Journeys, the authors continue to engage with the challenges posed in part 1 of the book, but framed in terms of political and intellectual journeys that continue to evolve through dialogues marked by continuous self-critique, unlearning, and relearning.

The section begins with Geraldine Pratt's chapter authored in collaboration with the Philippine Women Centre of BC and Ugnayan ng Kabataang Pilipino sa Canada/the Filipino-Canadian Youth Alliance. They reflect on the practices by which they attempt a reversed flow of knowledge from activists to expert and how this involved moving from a national to transnational frame of reference. Sam Bullington and Amanda Lock Swarr also unsettle hierarchies of knowledge production by considering the authors' navigation of their ten-year relationship with each other and with South African LGBT rights and HIV/AIDS treatment access activists. Both of these chapters present different sorts of dialogic exchanges, examining what it has meant to cultivate often contentious and complicated multiple collaborations over space and time, while interrogating the meanings of collaboration and building trust in historically exploited communities.

Linda Peake and Karen de Souza's contribution investigates the dialogic journeys of their political, intellectual, and emotional labor as collaborators, working over the last fifteen years in the Guyanese women's organization, Red Thread. Focusing primarily on questions of race, institutional location, and NGOization of development, the authors explore the feminist production of knowledge; the links between activism, social change and research; and dimensions of power that speak to silences within Red Thread. The Sangtin Writers—Reena, Richa Nagar, Richa Singh, and Surbala—delve into the same themes, but rather than centering on the distinction between academic and activist labor, they participate in the coproduction of dialogical/dialectical relationships between theory and practice, the lettered and the unlettered, and the fields inhabited by people's movements, NGOs, and academic scholars in analyzing the political transformation of Sangtin, an organization conceptualized as an NGO for rural women's empowerment. The authors of this chapter map the archaeology of Sangtin's evolution into a peasants' and laborers' movement and reflect on the ways that this shift throws up larger questions pertaining to women's issues, feminist politics, and transnational collaborations.

Part 3 of the volume critically engages questions of transnational feminisms and praxis through a thematic focus on Representations and Reclamations. The section opens with reflections by Omise'eke Natasha Tinsley, Ananya Chatterjea, Hui Niu Wilcox, and Shannon Gibney on Ananya Dance Theatre's production *Duurbaar: Journeys into Horizon*. During the Transnational Feminist Praxis workshop in September 2006, participants attended this performance, which was followed by a discussion that centered on the themes of praxis, intersectionality, representation, embodiment, and funding. The dialogue that started in this space eventually resulted in the dancers' coauthored chapter for this collection. In it, the authors highlight how this choreography articulates a form that, while still recognizable in a South Asian aesthetic, resituates itself as it settles in different bodies and is deconstructed and hybridized to tell a complex, diasporic story. The writers claim that it is only through the constant negotiation of interpersonal relationships, a deep investment in learning each other's histories, a shared political vision, and plenty of sweat labor that collaboration and artistry can be created.

Similarly highlighting difficulties of artistic representation and collaboration, Deborah Barndt reflects on the VIVA! project that has engaged partners from four NGOs and four universities in Panama, Nicaragua, Mexico, the United States, and Canada in a collaborative research process focused on community arts and popular education processes. Recognition of the tension between embodied practice in community arts and a pervasive use of disembodied technologies to document and discuss this practice leads the VIVA! partners to imagine a model that envisions research as historical and cultural reclamation. In the final chapter of the book, Rachel Silvey returns us to the question of normativizing versus radical functions of transnational feminisms by reminding us that transnational praxis is characterized by a complex politics of representation, privilege, and positionality, and always runs the risk of unwittingly reinforcing the deeply problematic power relations that it seeks to disrupt. Focusing on a collaborative film project based in Indonesia and the United States, Silvey reconsiders definitions of feminist research, pedagogy, and outreach, while reflecting on the often conflicting agendas that different actors invest in reinforcing and challenging specific representations. Analysis of the complex possibilities and limitations of dance, the arts, and film as processes, products, and pedagogies are elements of both defining and undefining transnational feminist praxis.

Throughout this collection, the engagements of the contributors variously echo Alexander and Mohanty's critical call to grapple with the necessity of moving "away from the academic/activist divides . . . to think specifically about destabilizing such binaries through formulations of the spatialization of power and to recall the genealogy of public intellectuals, radical political education movements, and public scholarship that is anchored in cultures of dissent" (Alexander and Mohanty, this volume, 26). At the same time, the contributors point out the dangers of reifying collaboration or alliance work and turning it into a universalism or a panacea. The point here is not to encourage a codification or institutionalization of collaboration in the same ways that both intersectionality and the notion of transnational are being codified and disciplined. For collaboration to remain a dynamic and generative concept, it is critical to retain the incoherent, contingent, and contextual nature of such praxis. It is not that there should not be any room for individually produced knowledges and theorizations in transnational feminist enterprise—it is more that such enterprise will remain incomplete and impoverished in the absence of the kinds of collaborative spaces that we are seeking to open. Claiming more spaces for dialogic praxis necessitates constant renegotiations and retheorizations of power through alliances, languages, and critiques that disrupt dominant logics and imaginaries—not simply by resisting the celebration of the "expert," but also by creating radicalized practices for institutional transformations and sociopolitical justice.

Notes

We would like to acknowledge the support of the Center for Advanced Study in the Behavioral Sciences at Stanford where we wrote the first version of this chapter in 2006. Since then, we have benefited from comments of participants in the Feminist Studies Colloquia Series and the "Towards Transnational Feminist Praxis" workshop at the University of Minnesota and the "Collaborative Research and Praxis" workshop at the Simpson Center for the Humanities at the University of Washington. We would especially like to thank Deborah Barndt, Amy Brandzel, Sam Bullington, Sharad Chari, David Faust, Priti Ramamurthy, Naomi Scheman, and Joel Wainwright for their close readings of and valuable feedback on earlier versions of this chapter.

1. Our analysis of the deployment of *transnational* overlaps with the five intellectual foundations of transnational studies identified by Khagram and Levitt (2008: 2): empirical transnationalism, methodological transnationalism, theoretical transnationalism, philosophical transnationalism, and public transnationalism. However, we also insist on blurring and complicating the borders that place empiricism, method, theory, philosophy, and public/private in clearly separate domains.

2. It is interesting to note that labeling scholarship as "atheoretical" is taken to be a much more serious charge than deeming it irrelevant to "action."

3. The contributors to this volume make different choices about the acronyms to describe lesbian, gay, bisexual, transgendered, transsexual, intersexed, and queer communities. We follow their respective formulations here.

Works Cited

Alexander, M. Jacqui. 2005. *Pedagogies of Crossing: Meditations on Feminism, Sexual Politics, Memory, and the Sacred*. Durham and London: Duke University Press.

Alexander, M. Jacqui, and Chandra Talpade Mohanty. 1997. "Introduction: Genealogies, Legacies, Movements." In M. Jacqui Alexander and Chandra Talpade Mohanty, eds., *Feminist Genealogies, Colonial Legacies, Democratic Futures*. New York: Routledge. xii–xlii.

Barndt, Deborah. 2007. Personal Communication.

Bender, Thomas. 1998. "Scholarship, Local Life, and the Necessity of Worldliness." In Herman Van Der Wusten, ed., *The Urban University and Its Identity*. Boston: Kulwer Academic Publishers. 17–28.

Bullington, Sam, and Amanda Lock Swarr. 2007. "Negotiating Feminist Futures: Transgender Challenges and Contradictions of a Ph.D. in Feminist Studies." In Hokulani Aikau, Karla Erickson, and Jennifer L. Pierce, eds. *Feminist Waves, Feminist Generations: Life Stories of Three Generations in the Academy, 1968–1998*. Minneapolis: University of Minnesota Press.

Butler, Judith. 1993. *Bodies That Matter: On the Discursive Limits of "Sex."* New York: Routledge.

Chatterjee, Piya. 2009. "Transforming Pedagogies: Imagining Internationalist/Feminist/Antiracist Literacies." In Margo Okazawa-Rey and Julia Sudbury, eds., *Activist Scholarship: Antiracism, Feminism, and Social Change*. Boulder: Paradigm Publishers.

The Combahee River Collective. 1982. "A Black Feminist Statement." In Gloria T. Hull, Patricia Bell Scott, and Barbara Smith, eds., *But Some of Us Are Brave: Black Women's Studies*. Old Westbury, NY: The Feminist Press. 13–22.

Dreze, Jean. 2002. "On Research and Activism." *Economic and Political Weekly* 37(9): 817.

Eng, David L., with Judith Halberstam and José Esteban Muñoz. 2005. "What's Queer About Queer Studies Now?" *Social Text* 84–85, 23(3–4): 1–17.

Enloe, Cynthia. 1990. *Bananas, Beaches, and Bases: Making Feminist Sense of International Politics*. Berkeley: University of California Press.

Enslin, Elizabeth. 1994. "Feminist Practice and the Limitations of Ethnography." *Cultural Anthropology* 9: 537–568.

Fabian, Johannes. 1990. "Presence and Representation: The Other and Anthropological Writing." *Critical Inquiry* 16(4): 753–772.

Freire, Paulo. 1993 [1970]. *Pedagogy of the Oppressed*. New York: Continuum.

Grewal, Inderpal, and Caren Kaplan. 2001. "Global Identities: Theorizing Transnational Studies of Sexuality." *GLQ* 7(4): 663–679.

Grewal, Inderpal, and Caren Kaplan. 1994. "Introduction: Transnational Feminist Practices and Questions of Postmodernity." In Inderpal Grewal and Caren Kaplan, eds., *Scattered Hegemonies: Postmodernity and Transnational Feminist Practices*. Minneapolis: University of Minnesota Press. 1–36.

The Guardian. 2002. "Roy's Feminine Virtues." *The Guardian*, Friday, March 8. http://www.guardian.co.uk/theguardian/2002/mar/08/guardianletters3. Accessed on August 28, 2008.

Kaplan, Caren, and Inderpal Grewal. 2002. "Transnational Practices and Interdisciplinary Feminist Scholarship: Refiguring Women's and Gender Studies." In Robyn Weigman, ed., *Women's Studies on Its Own: A Next Wave*

Reader in Institutional Change. Durham and London: Duke University Press. 66–81.

Khagram, Sanjeev, and Peggy Levitt. 2008. "Constructing Transnational Studies." In Sanjeev Khagram and Peggy Levitt, eds., *The Transnational Studies Reader: Intersections and Innovations.* New York and London: Routledge. 1–18.

Lassiter, Luke. 2005. *The Chicago Guide to Collaborative Ethnography.* Chicago: University of Chicago Press.

Lazreg, Marnia. 1988. "Feminism and Difference: The Perils of Writing as a Woman on Women in Algeria." *Feminist Studies* 14(1): 81–107.

Messer-Davidow, Ellen. 2002. "Feminist Studies and Social Activism." Paper presented at the Feminist Studies Colloquium Series, Department of Women's Studies, University of Minnesota, Minneapolis, U.S.A., September 30.

Mohanty, Chandra Talpade. 1986. "Under Western Eyes: Feminist Scholarship and Colonial Discourses." *Boundary 2* XII/XIII (1, 3): 333–358.

Mohanty, Chandra Talpade, Ann Russo, and Lourdes Torres, eds. 1991. *Third World Women and the Politics of Feminism.* Bloomington and Indianapolis: Indiana University Press.

Morgan, Robin. 1984. *Sisterhood Is Global: The International Women's Movement Anthology.* Garden City, NY: Anchor Press/Doubleday.

Nagar, Richa, and Amanda Lock Swarr. 2004. "Organizing from the Margins: Grappling with 'Empowerment' in India and South Africa." In Joni Seager and Lisc Nelson, eds., *A Companion to Feminist Geography.* London: Blackwell. 291–304.

Nagar, Richa, and Susan Geiger. 2007. "Reflexivity, Positionality and Identity in Feminist Fieldwork Revisited." In Adam Tickell, Trevor Barnes, Eric Sheppard, and Jamie Peck, eds., *Politics and Practice in Economic Geography.* London: Sage. 267–278.

Poitevin, G. 2002. *The Voice and the Will: Subaltern Agency: Forms and Motives.* New Delhi: Manohar and Centre de Sciences Humaines.

Rose, Gillian. 1997. "Situating Knowledges: Positionality, Reflexivities and Other Tactics." *Progress in Human Geography* 21(3): 305–320.

Said, Edward W. 2002. "Opponents, Audiences, Constituencies and Communities." In Edward W. Said, ed., *Reflections on Exile and Other Essays.* Cambridge: Harvard University Press. 118–147.

Sangtin Writers [and Richa Nagar]. 2006. *Playing with Fire: Feminist Thought and Activism Through Seven Lives in India.* New Delhi: Zubaan [and Minneapolis: University of Minnesota Press].

Shohat, Ella, ed. 1998. *Talking Visions: Multicultural Feminism in a Transnational Age.* New York: The MIT Press.

Swarr, Amanda Lock, and Richa Nagar. 2004. "Dismantling Assumptions: Interrogating 'Lesbian' Struggles for Identity and Survival in India and South Africa." *SIGNS: Journal of Women in Culture and Society* 29(2): 491–516.

Trinh T. Minh-ha. 1991. *Woman, Native, Other: Writing Postcoloniality and Feminism.* Bloomington: Indiana University Press.

PART I

Decolonizing Transnational Feminisms

Cartographies of Knowledge and Power

Transnational Feminism as Radical Praxis

M. JACQUI ALEXANDER AND CHANDRA TALPADE MOHANTY

This essay is one moment in the process of almost two decades of thinking, struggling, writing, and working together in friendship and solidarity as immigrant women of color living in North America. Each of us has been involved in collaborative work in and outside the academy in different racial, cultural, and national sites—and we have worked together in scholarly, curricular, institutional, and organizing contexts. For us, this collaboration, over many years and in these many sites, has been marked by struggle, joy, and the ongoing possibility of new understandings and illumination that only collective work makes possible.[1]

More than a decade ago, we embarked on a feminist collaborative project that resulted in the collection *Feminist Genealogies, Colonial Legacies, Democratic Futures* (Routledge 1997). Its main purpose was to take account of some of the most egregious effects of the political economic impact of globalization, what we called then capitalist recolonization—the racialized and gendered relations of rule of the state—both its neocolonial and advanced capitalist incarnations, and to foreground a set of collective political practices that women in different parts of the world had undertaken as a way of understanding genealogies of feminist political struggles and organizing. Our methodological task here was quite steep for the inheritance of the "international" within women's studies, particularly its U.S. variant, provided little analytic room to map the specific deployment of transnational that we intended *Feminist Genealogies* to encapsulate, especially since we saw that the term *international* had come to be collapsed into the cultures and values of capitalism and into notions of global sisterhood. How, then, could we conceptualize transnational to take globalization seriously while at the same time not succumb to the pitfalls of either free market capitalism or free market feminism?

Feminist Genealogies drew attention to three important elements in our definition of the transnational: 1) a way of thinking about women in similar contexts across the world, in different geographical spaces, rather than as all women across the world; 2) an understanding of a set of unequal relationships among and between peoples, rather than as a set of traits embodied in all non-U.S. citizens (particularly because U.S. citizenship continues to be premised within a white, Eurocentric, masculinist, heterosexist regime); and 3) a consideration of the term *international* in relation to an analysis of economic, political, and ideological processes that would therefore require taking critical antiracist, anticapitalist positions that would make feminist solidarity work possible (1997: xix).

In the decade since the publication of *Feminist Genealogies*, there has been a proliferation of discourses about transnational feminism, as well as the rise of transnational feminist networks.[2] Within the academy, particular imperatives like study abroad programs in different countries, the effects of Structural Adjustment Programs on public education globally, the (now lopsided) focus on area studies in geographical spaces seen as crucial to knowledge production post 9/11, and the rise of new disciplines like terrorism studies and security studies can all be read as responses to globalization that have concrete transnational contours. Transnational studies in the academy often dovetail with more radical impulses in social movements, and given the place of transnational feminist studies in the academy at this moment, we have embarked on another large collaborative project, this time seeking to map a genealogy or archeology of the transnational in feminist and LGBTT/queer studies in the United States and Canada.

To this end we pose a set of questions that can probe the definitions of transnational feminism in relation to globalization (local/global/regional) and the operation of the categories of gender, race, nation, sexuality, and capitalism. We want to explore what the category of the transnational illuminates—the work it does in particular feminist contexts—the relation of the transnational to colonial, neocolonial, and imperial histories and practices on different geographical scales, and finally we want to analyze the specific material and ideological practices that constitute the transnational at this historical juncture and in the U.S. and Canadian sites we ourselves occupy. When is the transnational a normativizing gesture—and when does it perform a radical, decolonizing function? Are cultural relativist claims smuggled into the transnational in ways that reinforce binary notions of tradition and modernity?

A number of feminist scholars have distinguished between the categories of global, international, and transnational. Suzanne Bergeron (2001), for instance, argues that globalization is the condition under which transnational analysis is made possible. The transnational is connected to neoliberal economics and theories of globalization—it is used to distinguish between the global as a universal system, and the cross-national, as a way to engage the interconnections between particular nations. Feminist scholars have also defined the transnational in relation to women's cross-border organizing (Mindry 2001), and as a spatialized analytic frame that can account for varying scales of representation, ideology, economics, and politics, while maintaining a commitment to difference and asymmetrical power. Radcliffe et al. (2003), for instance, connect the transnational to the neoliberal through exchanges of power that impact indigenous communities across the globe. Felicity Schaeffer-Gabriel (2006) defines the current form of economics in relation to ideologies of masculinity, examining what she refers to as the "transnational routes of U.S. masculinity."

Our own definitions of transnational feminist praxis are anchored in very particular intellectual and political genealogies—in studies of race, colonialism, and empire in the global North, in the critiques of feminists of color in the USA, and in studies of decolonization, anticapitalist critique, and LGBTT/queer studies in the North and the South. Our use of this category is thus anchored in our own locations in the global North, and in the commitment to work systematically and overtly against racialized, heterosexist, imperial, corporatist projects that characterize North American global adventures. We are aware that this particular genealogy of the transnational is specific to our locations and the materiality of our everyday lives in North America. Here our interest lies in the connections between the politics of knowledge, and the spaces, places, and locations that we occupy. Our larger project, then, is an attempt to think through the political and epistemological struggles that are embedded in radical transnational feminist praxis at this time.

For this chapter, however, we focus on a particular part of this larger project. Drawing on an analysis of the contemporary U.S. academy and on core women's and gender studies and LGBTT/queer studies syllabi, we attempt a preliminary map of the institutional struggles over transnational feminist praxis, specifically, the politics of knowledge construction in women's studies and LGBTT/queer studies in the U.S. academy. Given the privatization and restructuring of the U.S. academy, the hegemony of neoliberalism and corporate/capitalist values and free market ideologies, the increasingly close alignment of the academy with the "war on terror" and the U.S. imperial project, we ask questions about the objects of knowledge involved in women's and gender studies and LGBTT/queer studies. Beginning with a broad mapping of the U.S. academy as a major site in the production of knowledge about globalization and the transnational, we move on to an analysis of the ethics and politics of knowledge in the teaching of transnational feminism. The two fundamental questions that preoccupy us are: What are the specific challenges for collaborative transnational feminist praxis given the material and ideological sites that many of us occupy? And, what forms of struggle engender cultures of dissent and decolonized knowledge practices in the context of radical transnational feminist projects? We believe that at this historical moment it is necessary to move away from the academic/activist divides that are central to much work on globalization, to think specifically about destabilizing such binaries through formulations of the spatialization of power and to recall the genealogy of public intellectuals, radical political education movements, and public scholarship that is anchored in cultures of dissent. Such work also requires acute ethical attentiveness. In addressing herself to the African Studies Association in 2006, Amina Mama (2007: 3) speaks of the need for developing scholarship as a "critical tradition premised on an ethic of freedom." She goes on to define this: "Such scholarship regards itself as integral to the struggle for freedom and holds itself accountable, not to a particular institution, regime, class, or gender, but to the imagination, aspirations, and interests of ordinary people. It is a tradition some would call radical, as it seeks to be socially and politically responsible in more than a neutral or liberal sense." Thus, one of the major points of our analysis is to understand the relationship between a politics of location and accountability, and the politics of knowledge production by examining the academy as one site in which transnational feminist knowledge is produced, while examining those knowledges that derive from political mobilizations that push up, in, and against the academy ultimately foregrounding the existence of multiple genealogies of radical transnational feminist practice.

The U.S. Academy: Mapping Location and Power

The U.S. academy is a very particular location for the production of knowledge. Within a hegemonic culture of conformity and surveillance, many of us experience the perils of being in the U.S. academy. At a time when women's and gender studies, race and ethnic studies, queer studies, and critical area studies run the risk of co-optation within the neoliberal, multiculturalist, corporatist frame of the academy, we bear a deep responsibility to think carefully and ethically about our place in this academy where we are paid to produce knowledge, and where we have come to know that the spatiality of power needs to be made visible and to be challenged. One of the questions we want to raise, then, is whether it is *possible to undo* the convergence between location and knowledge production. Put differently, can transnational feminist lenses push us to ask questions that are location specific but not necessarily location bound? If we take seriously the mandate to do collaborative work in and outside the academy, the kind of work that would demystify the borders between inside and outside and thereby render them porous rather than mythically fixed, it is imperative that the academy *not* be the only location that determines our research and pedagogical work; that we recognize those hierarchies of place within the multiple sites and locations in which knowledge is produced, and we maintain clarity about the origin of the production of knowledge and the spaces where this knowledge travels. And this mandate in turn requires the recognition that knowledge is produced by activist and community-based political work—that some knowledges can only emerge within these contexts and locations. Thus, in not understanding the intricate and complex links between the politics of location, the geographies and spatialities of power, and the politics of knowledge production we risk masking the limits of the work we do within the academy and more specifically their effects on the kinds of pedagogic projects we are able to undertake in the classroom. We attempt to clarify and address some of these links in the second half of this essay. Our intention here is not to reinforce or solidify an academic/activist divide, although we are well aware that these divides exist. It is rather to draw attention to different academic and activist sites as differentiated geographies of knowledge production. Thus, we want to be attentive to the spatialities of power and the ways in which they operate in and through the academy, as well as within political movements whose identities are not constituted within it.

In North America, the binary that distinguishes the "academy" from the "community" or the academic from the activist, that has also made it necessary to pen the qualification "activist scholar," has assisted in the creation of apparently distinct spaces where the former is privileged over the latter. This process of binary/boundary making is also a fundamental way to (re)configure space and to mask the power relations that constitute that reconfiguration. We can think of this binary as spatial in that it has its own cartographic rules, which according to Katherine McKittrick, "unjustly organize human hierarchies *in place* and reify uneven geographies in familiar, seemingly natural ways" (McKittrick 2006: xiv). Given over two decades of neoliberalism, privatization, and the accompanying commodification of knowledge that marks academies across the globe, the cartographic rules of the academy necessarily produce insiders and outsiders in the geographies of knowledge production. On the one hand, such cartographic rules draw somewhat rigid boundaries around neoliberal academies (the academy/community divide), and on the other they normalize the spatial location of the academy as the epitome of knowledge production. So what are these cartographic rules that normalize the position of the academy at the pinnacle of this knowledge-making hierarchy? Among them are the making of white heterosexual masculinity consonant with the identity of the institution against which racialized and sexed others are made, imagined, and positioned as well as the diffusion of ways of knowing that are informed by the fictions of European Enlightenment rationality, which heighten political contestation from those knowledges that are made to bear an oppositional genealogy and are rendered marginal once they travel inside the academy. These rules are reinforced through an ideological apparatus that creates the academy/community divide in the first place and that is itself an element in the deployment of power while attempting to conceal that power through other border patrol strategies such as academic-community partnerships and the creation of various offices of community relations; devising strategies of governance that delimit the kind of scholar and the kind of scholarship deserving legitimation, which are at odds with the very community with which it has established relations.[3] These cartographic rules are crucial since they create a hierarchy of place and permit the binary to operate as a verb, demarcating the spurious divide between academy and community while at the same time masking the creation of the divide. We say spurious here not because the creation of boundaries does not have serious effects in creating insiders and outsiders along lines similar to those created by the state, for instance, but because the practices of power within the academy bear close resemblance to the practices of power deployed by its allies such as the state and global capital that participate both materially and ideologically in its day-to-day operation. Ultimately these rules promote a spatial segregation that constructs the "community" as a hyper-racialized homogeneous space; and it is usually not just *any* community but one that has been subject to forced dispossession. This community may or may not be the same as grassroots mobilizations that derive from many sources. To make visible, then, these racialized geographies of dispossession with their own imperatives that do not rely on the academy for self-definition even as the academy summons them, and reifies them in that summoning, in the service of the formation of its own identity is a crucial strategy. This gesture assists us in demystifying the cartographic rules, fragmenting the hierarchy of place that would make them an undifferentiated mass in relation to the academy and thus in identifying the operation of the very idea of the spatialization of power that points to the social formation of multiple uneven spaces, which individually and together make up the power/knowledge matrix. Who resides in which spaces? Who belongs and whom are rendered outsiders? Who is constituted as the knowledgeable and the unknowledgeable? Which knowledges and ways of knowing are legitimized and which are discounted? Settling these questions stands at the core in making hierarchies of place.

This power/knowledge matrix that creates insiders and outsiders, those who know, and those who cannot know, has of course been challenged in multiple spaces by edu-activists. Two examples of political movements that challenge the cartographic rules consolidated by neoliberal, privatized academies include CAFA (The Committee on Academic Freedom in Africa) and the Italian Network for Self-Education founded in 2005. CAFA, founded in 1991, mobilized North American students and teachers in support of African edu-activists fighting against World Bank–initiated Structural Adjustment Programs (SAPs) aimed at dismantling autonomous African university systems. Arguing that these SAP initiatives were part of a larger attack on African workers, and that they functioned as recolonization projects, CAFA drew attention to the inexorable dismantling of African higher education resulting in the shift of knowledge production *elsewhere* from international NGOs training technocrats under the "African Capacity Building" initiative to U.S. international and study abroad programs. Similarly, the Italian Network for Self-Education was formed in 2005 as a result of a mass mobilization of over 150,000 people in response to the restructuring of academic labor by the Italian parliament. Challenging the spatialization of knowledge and expertise within disciplines, faculties, and the logic of neoliberal university systems, the network claims to traverse the division between teaching and research, education and metropolitan production, and theory and praxis. The self-education movement deconstructs traditional modes of knowledge production and research, unsettling the taken-for-granted cartographic binary of the university/metropole, potentially serving as a device for social transformation.[4] Thus, the spatialities of power that anoint the academy as the pinnacle of knowledge are demystified and profoundly challenged by CAFA and the Network for Self-Education.

For our purposes, however, and in order to wrestle with the gendered, racialized, and sexualized spatialization of power, we would have to come to terms with what McKittrick (2006) calls its material physicality, which, in the context of this chapter, pertains to our own formulations of the objects of transnational feminist analysis and the potential cartographic rules of syllabi, the spaces where colonialism and race dovetail with the practices of empire, where the academy consorts with state and corporatist projects and where oppositional practices take hold in ways that bend those cartographic rules or make them situationally irrelevant to the practices of hegemonic power. Those physical spaces include: the detention center; the army, the navy, and other institutions of the military-industrial complex; the institutions of state; the corporation, the factory, the export processing zones, the warehouse for secondhand clothing, the home, the brothel; the capsized boat, makeshift homes, the desert; the neighborhood, the street, NGOs, cross-border networks; the university, the boardroom, the classroom.[5] The question we want to ask then is, under what conditions, and for what purpose do particular spaces become dominant in the construction of the transnational?

Almost two decades ago, Jonathan Feldman, Noam Chomsky, and others analyzed the role of the academy in what was then referred to as the military-industrial complex (Feldman 1989). In 2008, the academy continues to figure prominently in the consolidation of Empire, the corporatization of knowledge, and the operation of the national security state. Most visibly, it aids in the surveillance and policing functions of the state via the USA Patriot Act of 2001, which calls for international students, scholars, and their dependents on F and J visas to be registered on SEVIS, a web-based data collection and monitoring system created to link the academy to the Department of Homeland Security, consulates, and embassies abroad, ports of entry into the United States, and other state agencies. The intimate connections between scientific knowledge, corporate power, and profit have now been examined by many scholars.[6] And the earlier discussion of CAFA and the Network for Self-Education points to radical educational movements that challenge the corporatization of the academy and its varied geographies of power in different national spaces.

The social organization of knowledge in the academy, its structures of inquiry, and discipline-based pedagogies are inevitably connected to larger state and national projects. And this is nowhere more palpable as in the mobilization of various disciplines, beyond area studies, to assist the state in the consolidation of empire.[7] They engender their own complicities as well as practices of dissent. Just as privatized academies engender capitalist, market-based citizenship, they also encode stories of the U.S. nation—a presumably "democratic" nation that is simultaneously involved in the project of Empire building. One important aspect of a radical transnational feminist project then involves looking at the way curricula and pedagogies mark and become sites for the mobilization of knowledge about the transnational. In what follows we examine syllabi in women's and gender studies (WGS), and in LGBTT/queer studies, in an attempt to understand the deployment of the transnational. Given our focus on the spatialization of power, we look especially at how those WGS and LGBTT/queer studies syllabi that deploy the transnational organize a set of cartographic rules that define how knowledge production operates in the academy. We look at syllabi in terms of the racial and gendered spatialization of power. This suggests questions like what kinds of hierarchies of place and space get set up; how power gets configured and reiterated; where do teachers locate feminism and queer sexuality in relation to these larger processes of colonialism and imperialism; the organization and presence of the academy and grassroots activism, political mobilizations, and so forth. Put differently, in what ways do syllabi bend or reinforce normative cartographic rules?

The Politics of Feminist Knowledge: Curricular Maps and Stories

The ethics and politics of crossing cultural, geographical, and conceptual borders in feminist and LGBTT/queer pedagogies in the context of the transnational is a crucial element in analyzing the interface of the politics of knowledge and location in the academy. How we teach transnational feminism in women's studies is crucial in analyzing the struggles over knowledge and power both within the U.S. academy and outside its fictive borders. The way we construct curricula and the pedagogies we use to put such curricula into practice tell a story—or tell many stories of gendered, racial, and sexual bodies in work and home spaces, prisons and armed forces, boardrooms and NGOs, local and transnational organizations, and so on. We suggest that these "stories" are also anchored in cartographic rules that encapsulate differentiated and hierarchical spatialities, thus foregrounding the links between sites, location, and the production of knowledge about the transnational. "Stories" are simultaneously "maps" in that they mobilize both histories and geographies of power. Thus, just as we suggested there are cartographic rules that normalize the position of the academy in the knowledge hierarchy earlier, we now explore whether similar rules are encoded and normalized in the curriculum, specifically in the syllabi we analyze.

We analyze thirteen core syllabi from WGS and LGBTT/queer studies curricula at a variety of colleges and universities in the United States in terms of these stories and maps. The sample syllabi we chose were from large state universities; private, elite universities; small liberal arts colleges;

and smaller state schools.[8] Each of the syllabi gesture toward transnational feminist praxis in some form or another, and most seem to anchor the core curriculum in women's and gender and LGBTT/queer studies. We suggest that an examination of the core curriculum can help us understand the politics of knowledge and the spatialities of power in the cross-cultural construction of feminist and LGBTT/queer studies in the U.S. academy, and to ask questions about the academy as a site for such knowledge production. This analysis allows us to see what it is students are being asked to know within these disciplines at this historical moment, what knowledge is being generated within introductory and upper-level classrooms—those spaces where explicitly oppositional knowledges are being produced. It also allows us to make preliminary connections between the politics of location, differentiated spatializations, and the production of knowledge.

Some of the larger analytic questions we might then ask include: how precisely is the transnational deployed in the core curriculum in relationship to racial and colonial histories and geographies, and to the relationship of the local and global? And what happens with the transnational when it encounters women of color, for instance, or queer communities of color? What productive tensions and contradictions are visible when the transnational emerges? And finally, what cartographic rules pertaining to the transnational can be made visible in this analysis of syllabi? In what ways are curricular stories also curricular maps? And finally, are there convergences and/or divergences in the ways that these transnational maps intersect with the spatialization of power in the academy as a whole?

Specifically, we analyzed six syllabi designated as core introductory courses and seven upper-level courses in the interdisciplinary fields of women's and gender and LGBTT/queer studies. Examples of these include Introduction to Women's and Gender Studies, Introduction to LGBTT/Queer Studies, and Introduction to Feminist Studies. We were interested in understanding what categories (e.g., gender, race, nation, sexuality, etc.) animate the transnational, the work it is being called upon to do in the curriculum, the particular histories and spatialities (colonial, neocolonial, imperial) it mobilizes, and the practices that are seen to constitute transnational feminism.

While our selection of these syllabi was intentional, purposive one might say, in that our explicit focus was the transnational, we should also note that there were many upper-level seminars devoted to an exploration of "urgent contemporary issues" of gender or of sexuality in which there was a curious elision of the transnational within the United States, pushing it to operate only elsewhere, outside of the geopolitical borders of the U.S. nation-state.[9] This paradoxical duality of marked absence on the one hand

and of hyper-presence on the other might leave no way for students to negotiate the circuits of travel between the local and the global, or to intuit the precise ways in which the local is constituted through the global. Still, we have to leave open the possibility that such linkages are indeed made. We might, for instance, talk about this particular curricular strategy as the cartographic rule of the transnational as always "elsewhere." This "elsewhere" rule thus suggests a separation of the spaces of the local/national and the transnational.

Overall, the interweaving of the categories of racialized gender and sexuality as well as the attention to non-U.S. feminist geographies was impressive. In many of these courses, there was a marked shift from the ways in which racialized and cross-cultural knowledges were being produced in WGS courses in the1970s and 1980s. Unlike in most WGS curricula from the 1970s and 1980s, women of color texts, queer texts by men and women of color from different parts of the world, and texts by "Third World" women are central in the syllabi we analyzed. Yet there were many paradoxes. In the case of LGBTT/queer studies, one of the most complex of the introductory syllabi exposed students to the lives and experiences of U.S. queer communities of color, linking these with racialized colonial histories of immigrant and native communities, and the contemporary effects of globalization. The central actors in this narrative were thus queers of color and the conceptual movement of the course mapped sexuality studies in relation to colonialism, racial formation, nation-states, and finally to globalization. Paradoxically, however, the central "stories" remained U.S.-centric with the USA being defined as a multicultural, multiracial nation in the most interesting of these syllabi. Here is yet another cartographic rule then, one that constructs a hierarchy of place within the transnational: the U.S.- or Eurocentric organization of the syllabus. However, this is very different from the "elsewhere" rule in that it suggests a connectivity of the spaces of the local/national, and the transnational, but always in terms of a hierarchy of place wherein Euro-America constitutes the norm.

Genealogies of sexuality studies remain largely U.S.-centered in otherwise multiply layered courses. Thus, while racial and colonial histories were often threaded through the courses, these histories remained focused on the United States or Europe. In one Introduction to LGBTT/Queer Studies, designed as an introduction to the academic interdisciplinary field itself, the syllabus drew on the now familiar canon of theorists of sexuality (Foucault, Sedgwick, Butler), yet again mobilizing Euro-American histories of sexuality while referring to the lives and experiences of queer communities of color.

This paradox of foregrounding subjects of color as agents while reproducing a white Eurocentric center has another effect in that the transnational
can be deployed in normative rather than critical terms. In one upper-level
seminar, the story of the syllabus was to map the impact of globalization on
different women in different parts of the world.[10] Marking this difference is
clearly important since it moves us away from thinking of globalization as a
homogenous or homogenizing project. Yet the emphasis on democratization
and equality as a way to understand feminist mobilizations among Islamic,
Latin American, or African feminists seemed to perform an odd theoretical
move that wished to export democracy and equality from the United States
to these different parts of the world. Ironically, the syllabus carried a great
deal of resonance with earlier formulations of a global sisterhood, though
it did so in terms that were ostensibly different: the terms of "multiple feminisms." Indeed residing underneath these multiple feminisms was cultural
relativism that housed two interrelated elements. One was the creation of a
geographic distance through which an absolute alterity was constructed. It
was only through greater proximity to the United States and the inherited
categories of the West that women's experiences were most intelligible. The
other, implied in the first, was the spatial creation of an *us* and *them* so that
Islamic, Latin American, or African feminism could neither be understood
relationally nor could they be positioned to interrogate the kinds of feminist
mobilizations deployed in the West.[11] The place of Western knowledge was
reconsolidated all over again. Here, too, while spatial connectivities are
mobilized, there is a clear hierarchy in place.

Our analysis suggests several important trends. First, in spite of its link
to racial and colonial histories, the transnational is made to inhabit very
different meanings and emerges at different junctures and in different spaces
in the overall story of the syllabi we examined. Second, in the introductory
courses to gender and sexuality where the writings and theorizations of
U.S. women of color and non-Western women's movements were central,
the stories these syllabi dealt with were of complex feminisms anchored in
different racial communities of women and queers. However, not only were
U.S. and Eurocentric histories mobilized, for instance, the linear periodiza-
tion of first-, second-, and third-wave feminisms, but also very visible were
the genealogies of feminist thought that once again foregrounded narratives
of European liberal, socialist, and postmodern theory. Cartographically,
then, the transnational was either placed elsewhere or positioned Eurocentrically or within the United States as theoretically normative.

Transnational feminism also emerged in all of these courses in relation to
singular and often isolated categories and contexts. Thus, for instance, it was

made visible only in relation to discussions of work and globalization, or human rights, or gay diasporas, or cross-border mobilizations. The majority of the readings and topics in the syllabi remained U.S.-centric. Thus, transnationalism might emerge, for instance, only in relation to queer diasporas and the effects of globalization, with only two out of fourteen weeks devoted to "gay diasporas and queer transnationalism," rendering it an exceptional or theoretical option. In other words, the "local" remained intact, and somewhat disconnected from cross-border experiences. Transnationalism was then anchored only outside the borders of the nation (the "elsewhere" rule). Thus, it seems that the transnational has now come to occupy the place that "race" and women of color held in women's studies syllabi in the 1990s and earlier. We have now moved from white women's studies to multiracial women's studies (in the best instances), but the methodology for understanding the transnational remains an "add and stir" method, and the maps that are drawn construct the transnational as spatializing power either "elsewhere" or as within the United States and/or Europe.

Thus, a focus on diaspora, globalization, and colonial discourse as well as on feminist and LGBTT/queer communities in different national contexts often seems to stand in for what the courses describe as a "transnational perspective." Transnationalism, if identified at all, is understood only in the context of contemporary globalization, or in some rare cases, with nationalisms and religious fundamentalisms that fuel cross-border masculinist and heterosexist state practices. Given our interest in the politics of knowledge and the place of transnational feminisms in the academy, we were especially intrigued by the fact that none of these introductory courses raised questions about the ethics of cross-cultural knowledge production, or about the academy at all. This curious absence of the academy as the space many of us occupy every day, given the larger political battles that often shape our curricula and pedagogy seems all the more problematic from the point of view of understanding the spatiality of power in terms of the academy and its relationship to other institutions of rule like the state, and corporate interests. After all, being attentive to the ethics of knowledge production requires bringing questions of identity, epistemology, and method to the forefront of our scholarship and teaching. If the academy as a political space is absent from our syllabi, even as experience remains central to feminist thinking, surely there is a major contradiction here. We may be erasing our own experiences (and the profoundly material effects of our locations) at our own peril. For instance, as Amina Mama (2007: 6) argues, "our intellectual identities—and the ethics that we adopt to guide our scholarly practices—are informed by our identifications with particular communities and the values they uphold." Thus, if we take the connections between the politics of knowledge and the politics of location (identity) and of space seriously, we may need to take on broad institutional ethnography projects that allow a materialist understanding of academic spaces as mobilizing and reproducing hegemonic power. While some courses touched on urgent transnational issues like HIV/AIDS, and war and militarism, there was no mention of the U.S. imperial project or, say, the prison industrial complex as a site of analysis or feminist debate, thus begging the question of what particular (transnational) issues women's and gender studies and LGBTT/queer studies curricula speak to in the world we now occupy. Interestingly then, syllabi may serve unwittingly to reinforce and even naturalize the university/community divide in terms of hierarchies of location, identity, and sites of knowledge.

One upper-level seminar, however, was notable in terms of its explicit engagement with some of the ethical conundrums associated with cross-cultural comparison, which seemed crucial in light of its attention to the methodological politics of doing cross-cultural work. The story of this syllabus was a complex one, attempting to map the ways in which sex, sexuality, and gender operated within local and global processes that are at once transnational since the rapid dispersal of peoples and reading and inter-pretive practices operated everywhere. Within the construction of "queer diaspora" and the making of queer historiography, the social actors were specific communities that included cultures of two-spirit, cross-dressing women in U.S. Civil War; the *fa'afafine* of Samoa; and gay, lesbian, and trans-gender communities in different geographies, thus resisting the impulse to create a queer universal subject, and engendering a map that was attentive to different spatializations in the construction of sexualities. The syllabus asked explicit questions about when comparisons were useful or when they participated in reproducing the kind of discursive violence that comes with imposing U.S. social categories on cultural configurations that were not U.S. based. It was also interested in having students see themselves as intel-lectuals with ethical responsibilities: "What is our responsibility," it asked, "as students of gender and sexuality studies to be aware of the politics of making 'queer' travel?" Thus, this particular syllabus also engaged partially with the U.S. academy as a contested site in the production of knowledge.

Finally, all of the upper-level seminars we examined signaled the trans-national through some political economic pressures of globalization, diaspora, and migration. Importantly, racial and colonial histories marked the transnational in all instances. For example, in one course the story of transnational feminism was one in which the politics of women of color in the United States was linked to feminist movements among "Third World" women, attempting to map genealogies of feminism by asking how these feminisms had reshaped mainstream U.S. feminist praxis. While racialization functioned primarily in relationship to women of color, transnational feminist theory seemed hesitant, however, to engage women of color or "Third World Women" as sexual subjects or interpolated within sexualized projects pertaining to the state and/or global capital. Most often gender and sexuality were positioned either as theoretical strangers or distant cousins, once again reinforcing a separation of constructs of race and sexuality in the organization of knowledge about transnational feminisms.

This distancing of sexuality from questions of transnational feminism or rather the practice of deploying an uninterrogated heterosexuality within transnational feminist analyses both cedes the domain of sexuality to LGBTT/queer studies and renders an incomplete story of the ways in which the racialized gendered practices of neoimperial modernity are simultaneously sexualized. Some of the methodological cues for probing these links have been laid out by Jacqui in earlier work, where she stages a political conversation between transnational feminism and sexuality studies by examining the complicity of state and corporate practices in the manufacture of heterosexual citizenship and nation-building structures practices as seemingly disparate as welfare, structural adjustment, and discursive legal practices such as Domestic Violence in the Caribbean, the Defense of Marriage Act, and the Don't Ask Don't Tell policy of the U.S. military.[12] She suggests one possible analytic strategy by bringing these practices into ideological and geographical proximity to one another and by foregrounding heterosexual regulatory practices as those of violence. Thus, she is able to bring sexuality within the racialized gendered practices of the state and capital both within and across formations that have been separately designated as colonial, neocolonial, and neoimperial and conceive of the transnational across a wide range of ideological, political, economic, and discursive practices straddling multiple temporalities and multiple interests. This question about the connectivity of multiple though unequally organized geographies, temporalities, and interests bears on the question that is at the heart of our consideration, that is the relationship between the politics of location and the politics of knowledge production and who is able, that is, legitimized, to make sustainable claims about these links. And it raises additional questions about the analytic and political consequences of deploying an either/or framing: either connectivity or separation. Hierarchies of space and place mark what we have called the cartographic rules of the transnational in the syllabi we examined. Thus, while the transnational as elsewhere signals the spatial separation of sites of knowledge, the transnational as U.S. or Eurocentric signals connectivity, but on the basis of a hierarchical spatialization of power

Multiplying Radical Sites of Knowledge

Let's now consider the antiviolence and political mobilizations to abolish prisons that dovetail with antiglobalization and antimilitarization campaigns. Activists in these global networks have examined how punishment regimes, including the prison, are intimately linked to global capitalism, neoliberal politics, and U.S. economic and military dominance (Sudbury 2005). More specifically, however, it is the incarceration of increasing numbers of impoverished women of color that enables us to track the links between neoliberal privatization, the U.S. export of prison technologies, organized militarization, dominant and subordinate patriarchies, and neocolonial ideologies. As Sudbury argues, "Women's testimonies of survival under neoliberal cutbacks, border crossing, exploitation in the sex and drug industries, and life under occupation and colonial regimes provide a map of the local and global factors that generate prison as a solution to the conflicts and social problems generated by the new world order" (2005: xiii). One of those social problems is the massive migration of impoverished women and men from the global South instigated by neoliberal globalization, who are now disproportionately criminalized together with Indigenous and Aboriginal women from Canada and the United States to Australia.

Sudbury's collection, *Global Lockdown*, is significant for thinking through these relationships refracted through the transnational spatialization of power for several reasons. First, it is located within critical antiprison and antiviolence projects such as Critical Resistance, the Prison Activist Resource Center, the Arizona Prison Moratorium Coalition, and Social Justice. Second, the contributors to the collection, in Sudbury's words, are "intellectuals both organic and intellectual, former prisoners, political prisoners, activists, women in recovery, former sex workers, immigrants and indigenous women" (xi), who by virtue of their differentiated locations point to the gaps that ensue when political struggle is not attentive to connectivity. Third, to take seriously the insights of differently positioned intellectuals is not to argue that prison intellectuals or sex workers have knowledge too; rather it is to say that their location engenders an epistemic advantage that researchers not similarly positioned have been unable to mobilize. It helps us to explain why scholars "have yet to locate race, citizenship and national status at the center of the prison boom" (xviii). And fourth, it enacts different border crossings of geography and the nation-state; of time and the continued, albeit discontinuous, traffic between the colonial, the neocolonial, and the imperial; among and between different colonized spaces; of different yet related political mobilizations at the center of whose praxis is the labor of building connectivity not only to upset the cartographic rules that would position the prison and the brothel as separate and unrelated spaces and the women within them only as "objects of scholarly study and state reha-bilitation" (xxiv) but to redraw and therefore reiterate through practice the connectivity of those spaces and ultimately of the political struggles that make that connectivity possible. What then is the ethical responsibility of the teacher in the university classroom who wishes to teach about global-ization and privatization, militarization and the racialized gendered global lockdown?

If to talk about space is to talk also about geography, then to talk about geography is to talk also about land and the fierce contestations over land that are at the center of both neoimperial and colonial land appropriation. And if we think the ways in which the colonial traffics in the neoimperial, then it becomes possible to delineate the many ways in which white settler colonization continues to be an important dimension of the spatialization of power at this very moment in history. It also explains why struggles for sovereignty and the retrieval of stolen lands figure so centrally in Aboriginal, First Nations, and Indigenous politics.

Aboriginal, First Nations, and Indigenous activists and scholars together have written and organized at the fragile border between the master histo-ries of legislated inclusion and the always disappeared, the twin ideological companions of the material practices of genocide. Locating this matrix within the context of white supremacy, Andrea Smith (2006: 68) has argued that "[the logic of genocide] holds that indigenous peoples must disappear. In fact they must *always* be disappearing in order to allow non-indigenous peoples' rightful claim over this land." In *Conquest*, Smith pulls from the lived experiences of Native Women to draw links between this disappearance and the organization of a colonial patriarchy that deployed sexual violence against Native women—and other women of color—who were and continue to be positioned as "rapable," and "violable," in much the same way in which land is appropriated, raped, and violated. In this formulation, it is not so much the elsewhere cartographic rule that is at work—*elsewhere* as in outside the boundaries of modernity—but rather absence, that "present absence," as Kate Shanley (cited in Smith 2006) calls it, which in this ideo-logical script has presumably no knowledge to possess. Thus, fashioning political struggles in ways that refuse these contradictory divides provides

insight into how and why struggles for sovereignty and for land are simultaneously political, physical and spatial, metaphysical and spiritual.[13] Of course
one central question that emerges here has to do with the ways in which
that disappearance in the colonial and imperial geography travels within the
academy and manifests as negligible numbers of Native students, teachers,
and administrators and, as significantly, their disappearance in curricular and
other pedagogical projects in the classroom.[14]

We noted earlier that the hierarchies of place position a "community"
that is racially homogeneous and otherwise undifferentiated. But mapping
community from an understanding of the differentiated and heterogeneous
colonial spaces of "containment, internment and exile" (Burman 2007: 177)
creates the possibility of a deeper and more nuanced understanding of
the subjects who are positioned to stand outside of modernity, presumably outside of citizenship, displaced from land in the same way that, for
instance, the "deportable subject," the "admissible subject," "the present
absent subject," the suspect subject are positioned by the state against the
exalted national subject (the term is Thobani's) within the segregated landscape of transnational modernity. It is the *combined* work of activists and
scholars that has brought these meanings to our understanding of occupied
territory within white settler states.

Thinking through the outlines of a radical feminist project at a time
when U.S. imperialism, genocide, incarceration, militarization, and empire
building have significantly deepened is both tough and necessary.[15] While a
"multiple feminisms" pedagogical strategy may be more analytically viable
than the "Euro-American feminism as the normative subject" of feminist and
LGBTT/queer studies curricula, the specter of cultural relativism remains
intact. Transnational feminist solidarities and ethical cross-cultural comparisons attentive to the histories and hierarchies of power and agency cannot
be premised on an "us and them" foundation. Our conceptual foci would
need to shift and that might be possible when different cross-border practices, spaces, and temporalities are brought into ideological and geographic
proximity with one another in ways that produce connectivity and intersubjectivity (albeit a tense or uneven one) rather than an absolute alterity.
We would need to be attentive to how we think the object of our research,
for what the antiprison/antiglobalization mobilizations suggest is that solidarity work provokes us to pay close attention to the spaces of confinement
that warehouse those who are surplus or resistant to the new world order
(Sudbury 2005: xii). "Multiple feminisms" would need to be anchored in
ways of reading that foreground the ethics of knowledge production and
political practices across multiple borders—both those that are hypervisible

and those that are somewhat invisible—within hierarchies of domination and resistance. And questions of responsibility and accountability need to be central to this pedagogy, as do ethnographies of the academy as sites of struggle and contested spaces of knowledge.

What might a map of a radical, nonnormative transnational feminist solidarity pedagogy that is attentive to the genealogies and spatializations of power across multiple borders look like? Clearly syllabi are crucial spaces for thinking the reconfiguring of knowledge, spatial practices, and for respatializing power. So perhaps the first element in this map making is making the underlying epistemological assumptions visible and tracking that visibility throughout the life of the course. This requires making three interrelated moves. The first is to demystify and destabilize the old cartographic binaries set up by the academy and by the pedagogic and spatial practices within our syllabi so that we can think about the transnational, specifically transnational feminism, by looking at the ways cultural borders are crossed and the way hierarchies of place are normalized. The second attends to the hyperracialization and sexualization of the various "elsewheres." Precisely because the academy fetishizes these elsewheres in the service of its own identity formation, race and sex must be central to our thinking about the transnational. And the third would require that we ask very specifically what kinds of border crossings we want and what are their ethical dimensions? This is a tough question, for it has to do not necessarily with the question that there are, according to Richa Nagar, "varying forms of knowledge evolving in specific places," but more crucially, "what we are in a position to do in producing knowledge, namely, constitute ourselves as political actors in institutions and processes both near and far" (2006: 154). Fundamentally, then, we are talking about breaking the "epistemological contract" (the term is Sylvia Wynter's [1995]) that consigns the hierarchy of space and positions only those at the top as capable of producing and disseminating that knowledge. And breaking that epistemological contract would necessarily entail disinvesting these academic identities from the will to power, moving beyond a liberal "policy neutral" academic stance to actively developing a radical ethic that challenges power and global hegemonies.

This map requires that we take space and spatialization seriously. To think the transnational in relation to the inherited uneven geographies of place and space would require holding in tension questions of power, gender, race, and space. Who resides where and what kinds of knowledges do these residencies generate? We would examine those oppositional spatial politics that are not in the first instance invested in reconstituting insides and outsides, the citizen and noncitizen. The spatial links that the transnational makes visible need always to be emphasized so as not to reinscribe the normative cartographic rule of the transnational as elsewhere and therefore recycle colonial cartographies that support the mandate for conquest. It is these politics of spatialization, with their attendant ethical imperatives, that allow us to understand colonial/imperial racial and sexual underpinnings of border crossings "without losing ourselves" or privileging an elsewhere. Location matters in this model of a feminist solidarity transnationalism.[16] And we can learn how to be location specific without being location bound.

Based on this analysis then, our earlier definitions of the transnational in *Feminist Genealogies* would need to wrestle with the following: 1) the links between the politics of location, the spatiality of power, and that of knowledge production; 2) the physicality and materiality of space in terms of contestation over land; 3) a sharper focus on the ethics of the cross-cultural production of knowledge; and 4) a foregrounding of questions of intersubjectivity, connectivity, collective responsibility, and mutual accountability as fundamental markers of a radical praxis. Indeed it is the way we live our own lives as scholars, teachers, and organizers, and our relations to labor and practices of consumption in an age of privatization, and hegemonic imperial projects that are at stake here.

Clearly the world has undergone major seismic changes that might have been difficult to imagine almost a decade ago. It may well be that the contradictions between the knowledges generated in the classroom and those generated within grassroots political mobilization have been more sharpened given the increased institutionalization of oppositional knowledges and the increased embeddedness of the academy within the imperial militaristic projects of the state. And yet it's clear to us that without our respective involvement in political work outside (and sometimes in the in-between spaces within) the academy, it would be almost impossible to navigate the still contested spaces we occupy within it, spaces where we are called upon to be consistently attentive to our spiritual and psychic health. And so we continue to do this work across the fictive boundaries of the academy, constantly wrestling with its costs, and knowing that the intellectual, spiritual, and psychic stakes are high, but believing that it is imperative to engage in the struggles over the production of liberatory knowledges and subjectivities in the belly of the imperial beast.

Notes

Many thanks to Richa Nagar, Amanda Lock Swarr, Linda Peake, Jigna Desai, and Katherine McKittrick for invaluable feedback on this essay.

1. We are now situated in academic contexts in the USA and Canada, although much of our work emerges from in our location in the U.S. academy for over two decades.
2. See especially Valentine Moghadam, *Globalizing Women* (2005). We should also note that the transnational is not always already a radical category or one that speaks to a transformative or liberatory praxis.
3. Witness the struggle of women of color faculty denied tenure at the University of Michigan, Ann Arbor (Conference on Campus Lockdown: Women of Color Negotiating the Academic Industrial Complex, Ann Arbor, 15 April 2008); witness also the struggle over the inclusion of "scholarship in action" as part of tenure and promotion guidelines at Syracuse University (2007–2008).
4. Silvia Federici and George Caffentzis, "CAFA and the 'Edu-Factory,'" contribution to the edu-factory online discussion, 5 June 2007, and "Rete per l'Autoformazione, Roma" edu-factory discussion, 11 March 2007. Chandra was part of this discussion in 2007. For more information contact info@edu-factory.org.
5. In this materialist reading we do not pose the question about whether the sacred cajoles us into thinking space differently. To think about the sacred in relationship to space and to bending these cartographic rules, see McKittrick and Woods's (2007: 4) discussion of the Atlantic Ocean as a "geographic region that . . . represents the political histories of the disappeared," and at the same time a place of the unknowable. Coupling this tension between the "mapped" and the "unknown," they suggest that "places, experiences, histories and people that 'no one knows' do exist, within our present geographic order."
6. See Chandra's earlier work (Mohanty 2003: chap. 7), where she argued for an anticapitalist feminist project that examines the political economy of higher education, defining the effects of globalization in the academy as a process that combines market ideology with a set of material practices drawn from the business world. See also Jacqui's examination of the curricular effects of academic downsizing, the failures of normative multiculturalism and liberal pluralism, and the critical imperatives we face at this moment to teach for justice (Alexander 2006: chaps. 3 and 4).
7. See, among others, Sunera Thobani (2007).
8. Many thanks to Jennifer Wingard for research assistance for this project. Most of the research for this essay was conducted in early 2006, and the syllabi we analyze were all accessed electronically. We deliberately chose not to use our own syllabi, or even to discuss the curricula at our own institutions.
9. This was true of all the syllabi, except for an introductory course to LGBTT/queer studies, in which colonial, immigrant, and native histories of queers of color indicated a recognition of the transnational within the United States without identifying it as such (the terms used here were diaspora and globalization).
10. Often, globalization was used to signify the transnational, and sometimes the terms were used to signal the same phenomena.
11. See Alexander (2006: chap. 5) for a detailed discussion of cultural relativism in the context of the transnational feminist classroom.
12. See Alexander's chapter five, "Transnationalism, Sexuality, and the State: Modernity's Traditions at the Height of Empire" (2006).
13. Winona LaDuke (2005); Pinto (2003).

14. See "Diversity in Academe," *The Chronicle of Higher Education*, 26 September 2008, Section B; Smith (2005); Ward Churchill and Winona LaDuke (1992); Sarah Deer, "Federal Indian Law and Violent Crime," in Smith (2006: 32–41).

15. In Chandra's earlier work (2003: chap. 9) describing three pedagogical models used in "internationalizing" women's studies, she suggested that each of these perspectives was grounded in particular conceptions of the local and the global, of women's agency, and of national identity, and that each curricular model mapped different stories and ways of crossing borders and building bridges. She also suggested that a "comparative feminist studies" or "feminist solidarity" model is the most useful and productive pedagogical strategy for feminist cross-cultural work, claiming that it is this particular model that provides a way to theorize a complex relational understanding of experience, location, and history such that feminist cross-cultural work moves through the specific context to construct a real notion of universal *and* of democratization rather than colonization. It is this model that can put into practice the idea of "common differences" as the basis for deeper solidarity across differences and unequal power relations.

16. We are indebted to Katherine McKittrick for this formulation.

Works Cited

Alexander, M. Jacqui. 2006. *Pedagogies of Crossing: Meditations on Feminism, Sexual Politics, Memory, and the Sacred*. Durham: Duke University Press.

Alexander, M. Jacqui, and Chandra Talpade Mohanty. 1997. *Feminist Genealogies, Colonial Legacies, Democratic Futures*. New York: Routledge.

Bergeron, Suzanne. 2001. "Political Economy, Discourses of Globalization, and Feminist Politics." *Signs* 26(4): 983–1006.

Burman, Jenny. 2007. "Deportable or Admissible? Black Women and the Space of 'Removal,'" in Katherine McKittrick and Clyde Woods, eds., *Black Geographies and the Politics of Place*. Toronto: Between the Lines. 177–192.

Churchill, Ward, and Winona LaDuke. 1992. "Native North America: The Political Economy of Radioactive Colonialism." In M. Annette Jaimes, ed., *The State of Native America: Genocide, Colonization and Resistance*. Boston: South End Press. 241–266.

Davies, Carole Boyce. 2007. "Towards African Diaspora Citizenship." In Katherine McKittrick and Clyde Woods, eds., *Black Geographies and the Politics of Place*. Toronto: Between the Lines.14–45.

Deer, Sarah. 2006. "Federal Indian Law and Violent Crime." In Incite! Women of Color Against Violence, ed., *Color of Violence: The Incite! Anthology*. Cambridge, MA: South End Press. 32–41.

"Diversity in Academe." *The Chronicle of Higher Education*, 26 September 2008. Section B.

Feldman, Jonathan. 1989. *Universities in the Business of Repression: The Academic-Military-Industrial Complex in Central America*. Boston: South End Press.

LaDuke, Winona. 2005. *Recovering the Sacred: The Power of Naming and Reclaiming*, Toronto: Between the Lines.

Lawrence, Bonita, and Enakshi Dua. 2005. "Decolonizing Antiracism." *Social Justice* 21(4): 120–138.

Mama, Amina. 2007. "Is It Ethical to Study Africa? Preliminary Thoughts on Scholarship and Freedom." *African Studies Review* 50(1): 1–26.

McKittrick, Katherine. 2006. *Demonic Grounds: Black Women and the Cartographies of Struggle.* Minneapolis: University of Minnesota Press.

McKittrick, Katherine, and Clyde Woods, eds. 2007. *Black Geographies and the Politics of Place.* Toronto: Between the Lines.

McKittrick, Katherine, and Linda Peake. 2005. "What Difference Does Difference Make to Geography?" In Neil Castree, Ali Rogers, and Douglas Sharman, eds., *Questioning Geography.* Oxford: Blackwell. 39–54.

Mindry, Deborah. 2001. "Nongovernmental Organizations, 'Grassroots,' and the Politics of Virtue." *Signs* 26(4): 1187–1211.

Moghadam, V. M. 2005. *Globalizing Women: Transnational Feminist Networks.* Baltimore, MD: Johns Hopkins University Press.

Mohanty, Chandra Talpade. 2003. *Feminism Without Borders: Decolonizing Theory, Practicing Solidarity.* Durham: Duke University Press.

Nagar, Richa. 2006. "Postscript: NGOs, Global Feminisms, and Collaborative Border Crossings." In Sangtin Writers and Richa Nagar, *Playing with Fire: Feminist Thought and Activism Through Seven Lives in India.* Minneapolis: University of Minnesota Press. 132–155.

Pinto, V. Oliveira. 2003. "The Lessons of Candomblé, The Lessons of Life." In M. Jacqui Alexander, Lisa Albrecht, Sharon Day, and Mab Segrest, eds., *Sing, Whisper, Shout, Pray! Feminist Visions for a Just World.* Fort Bragg, CA: EdgeWork Books. 704–708.

Radcliffe, Sarah A., Nina Laurie, and Robert Andolina. 2003. "The Transnationalization of Gender and Reimagining Andean Indigenous Development." *Signs* 29(2): 387–416.

Rodriguez, Dylan. 2006. *Forced Passages: Imprisoned Radical Intellectuals and the U.S. Prison Regime.* Minneapolis: University of Minnesota Press.

Schaeffer-Gabriel, Felicity. 2006. "Planet-Love.com: Cyberbrides in the Americas and the Transnational Routes of U.S. Masculinity." *Signs* 31(2): 331–356.

Smith, Andrea. 2005. *Conquest: Sexual Violence and American Indian Genocide.* Cambridge, MA: South End Press.

Smith, Andrea. 2006. "Heteropatriarchy and the Three Pillars of White Supremacy: Rethinking Women of Color Organizing." In Incite! Women of Color Against Violence, ed., *Color of Violence: The Incite! Anthology.* Cambridge, MA: South End Press. 68.

Sudbury, Julia, ed. 2005. *Global Lockdown: Race, Gender, and the Prison-Industrial Complex.* New York: Routledge.

Thobani, Sunera. 2007. *Exalted Subjects: Studies in the Making of Race and Nation in Canada.* Canada: University of Toronto Press, Inc.

Wynter, Sylvia. 1995. "Breaking the Epistemological Contract on Black America." *Forum NHI* 2(1): 41–57 and 64–70.

‹ 2 ›

Disavowed Legacies and Honorable Thievery

The Work of the "Transnational" in Feminist and LGBTQ Studies

JIGNA DESAI, DANIELLE BOUCHARD, AND DIANE DETOURNAY

Our aim in this essay is to examine the central debates of transnational feminism, treating it as a contested field of inquiry shot through with disagreements and productive tensions. How has the field congealed around certain keywords and concepts? How is our understanding of it being forged in particular arenas and via certain disciplines? This questioning is critical to the work of transnational feminism, not the least because the question of knowledge production itself has been a central facet (both implicitly and explicitly) of feminist analysis. Multiple feminisms have sought to interrogate the link between power and knowledge as a critical component of their critiques—questions regarding feminist knowledge production, raised by disciplinary and interdisciplinary scholars alike, have named the imperial, capitalist, and racist genealogies of feminism itself. This commitment to interrogating the mode, location, meaning, and impact of knowledge has a long legacy within critical race feminism, postcolonial feminism, and transnational feminism. Transnational feminism has revitalized these discussions by focusing primarily on a particular domain of inquiry, namely on intersubjective relations of power as they affect collaborative knowledge production. And in doing so, it has advanced a line of inquiry that emphasizes a specific set of questions, primarily ones regarding 1) the social acts of individuals as they negotiate their locations within institutional and state apparatuses and 2) the geopolitics of knowledge production. In order to do this, transnational feminists have sought to *map* the processes and cartographies of knowledge production most literally. Thus the language of the discipline of geography has come to dominate analyses of knowledge production, as transnational feminists use metaphors of cartography, boundaries, and border crossings to capture the complexities of working through difference and material inequalities. This phenomenon of spatializing relations of power is one that, like all knowledge production, enables significant critiques and imaginaries, and indeed many of the contributors to this volume find this analytic particularly helpful (see in this volume Pratt et al., Barndt, and Silvey). But it also forecloses other possibilities for understanding the work of theory and praxis, the relationship between the two, and what transnational feminism's commitment to either or both might be.

We approach these questions regarding transnational feminist knowledge production from a different perspective and interdisciplinary framework. Our scholarship is primarily located in the humanities and reflects, therefore, a different set of questions. For us, this is not merely about pitting one set of transnational feminist scholars against another, but rather engaging differently with the debates in the field. We do so below by focusing on several concepts that have become "keywords" within transnational feminist discourse. While analysis of the micro-dynamics of specific transnational feminist projects is surely important, we also see the need for an examination of how the transnational and the feminist come to be available to the university as objects of knowledge. It is via such an examination that transnational feminism as a field of inquiry and critical practice might be able to address questions regarding intellectual and political responsibility in a way that looks carefully at the disciplinary languages that make our work possible and that on some level we must rely on, whether or not we are located "inside" or "outside" of the university.

Despite the different path we wish to chart, we see our analysis as aligned with questions asked by other contributors to this volume. In "Cartographies of Knowledge and Power: Transnational Feminism as Radical Praxis," M. Jacqui Alexander and Chandra Talpade Mohanty point to the necessity of tracing a genealogy of the transnational, in both feminism and LGBTQ studies:[1]

> We want to explore what the category of the transnational illuminates—the work it does in particular feminist contexts—the relation of the transnational to colonial, neocolonial, and imperial histories, and practices on different geographical scales, and finally we want to analyze the specific material and ideological practices that constitute the transnational at this historical juncture and in the U.S. and Canadian sites we ourselves occupy. When is the transnational a normativizing gesture—and when does it perform a radical, decolonizing function? (24)

This proposal is important for several reasons. Perhaps most crucially, it suggests a shift in emphasis away from the individual scholar's or feminist's capacity for self-reflexivity and toward the enabling structures, paradigms, and assumptions of the concepts that many of us working in this area of inquiry use. Thus in the rest of this essay, we take up this project by considering the work done by the "transnational" in relation to the other key concepts with which it often appears: collaboration, theory, praxis, and the university.

First and foremost, we seek to engage an analysis of the work done by invocations of the "transnational" for disciplinary projects themselves and thus to the very criteria by which certain feminist projects are validated as such and others are not, rather than simply to individual practices of transnational feminism and whether or not they are "valid." While the term has become increasingly popular in the last decade, replacing "global feminism" and "international feminism," it has also become increasingly broad. We are not suggesting that it has become diluted and therefore that we should return the term to its "original meaning," if that were even possible. Rather, we offer that the "transnational" has come to serve as a catch-all and umbrella term within feminism by purporting to include and synthesize an increasing number of critiques without attention to the contradictions and complexities between them. "Transnational feminism" supposedly can and does do it all. In this volume, Alexander and Mohanty and Nagar and Swarr note that, among its many meanings, the "transnational" functions to reference migratory, mobile, and other global phenomena, hence it functions as an empirical descriptive, for example, of diasporic subjects, rather than as a mode of critique. More importantly, even as a form of critique, transnational feminism often functions prescriptively in that it is seen to both encompass and move beyond other "previous" feminisms. In this teleological approach, the transnational is problematically evoked as having yoked together and integrated anticapitalist, multicultural, globalist, postcolonial, and now anti-imperialist critiques. The potential elasticity of transnational feminism is not necessarily an issue. What raises concern, however, is the proposed interchangeability of each of these critiques and transnational feminism's supposed ability to reconcile and address them all when they themselves may not cohere. Consequently, the "transnational" has come to define our current moment as "beyond"—that is, feminism is understood to have evolved and arrived at a singular resolution of both its own and the university's problems of knowledge production.

What happens to Third World feminisms, to women of color feminisms, to black feminisms, to diasporic feminisms (to name a few of the bodies of

theory that have sought to interrogate the intersections of racial formation, sexuality, empire, capitalism, and colonialism) with the advent of the
transnational? It is important to theorize the distinctions between these
approaches (rather than pose them as having been transcended) as well as
where they may cohere (rather than pose them as the same) in order to
level a continuing critique of the "global" within feminism. Global feminism has been critiqued by many scholars for the ways in which it poses
difference as a quality that marks certain ("other") objects and subjects, and
that it is the goal and duty of the implicitly U.S.-based scholar to translate
for inclusion in "our" general knowledge about women. The transnational
may replicate these problems insofar as it is used to reference a generalized racial, international, and anthropological difference, a difference that
is supposed to preexist the subject constitution of the scholar. Yet when
conceived as a critical approach to the legacy of globalism, transnational
feminism might at least allow us to acknowledge the continuing problem
of certain concepts and practices that have been difficult (perhaps impossible) to give up. Thus refusing to collapse these different political and
intellectual movements into each other might allow us to address some of
transnational feminism's disavowed legacies. Transnational feminism is often
seen to subsume women of color feminism in that the latter is proposed to
be attentive to race, gender, and perhaps nation. However, we may argue
that women of color feminisms, like postcolonial feminism, have not been
resolved and transcended by transnational feminism. For example, woman
of color feminist scholarship is now making clear its theorizations of transnationality—as a case in point, Indigenous and Chicana feminisms argue that
they are transnational feminisms (but transnational feminism is itself not
identical to Chicana or Indigenous feminism). This implies that the two are
not collapsible and identical but are heterogeneous, irreducible, and related.
Other scholars charge that the emphasis on transnationalism often evacuates
an emphasis on race; hence, the parameters of the relation between different
feminisms require further articulation and clarification.

　　The question of the transnational is similarly significant in sexuality and
LGBTQ studies, where it is primarily used as an empirical term denoting the
diasporic or migratory. Counter to this use, we ask what might constitute a
transnational queer critique. In reading the transnational as related to migration or diasporas and centering itself in the United States, transnational
LGBTQ studies often holds up diasporic queers or U.S.-based queers of color
as paradigmatic subjects and leaves U.S.- or Eurocentric privilege unnamed
and unacknowledged. Unlike transnational feminism, this critique rarely
raises questions about its epistemological frameworks, privileged location,

or its mobility. Hence, it replicates the earlier problematics associated with global feminism and global gay studies in producing certain kinds of self-realized subjects, who are located in the West as it simultaneously ignores the contributions of postcolonial feminism to critiques of Eurocentrism and U.S.-centrism. Alternatively, we may seek not to privilege diasporic queer subjects, but to place multiple sexualities and heteronormativities into question. Transnational queer critique, like feminism, must ask questions about its proliferation and circulation and its production of the global universal subject. More specifically, what may be needed as part of our LGBTQ and sexuality studies is not the codification and canonization of queer racialized and diasporic subjects, but broader and multiple engagements with questions about how identities, theories, and epistemologies are produced, exchanged, marketed, and given value within multiple global, imperial, and colonial circuits. Furthermore, we must expand our discussions of transnationality and sexualities by raising questions about heteronormativity and development; race, empire, and deviance; the state and neoliberalism; capital and migration; queerness and transnational cultural production in order to make visible the complex local and global processes in which sexualities must be understood. In part, this may call for an epistemological and political economy of queerness that questions and decenters the U.S. and places queer studies into question in relation to transnational feminism, postcolonial feminism, and women of color feminism.

As with any set of intellectually informed practices, transnational feminism owes its conditions of possibility to a variety of institutional formations, concepts, and theoretical trends. This is not all bad per se, but recognizing this does open up to question the idea that transnational feminism has simply moved beyond "past" problems, as well as the idea that such a movement beyond is what would make transnational feminism effective or important. For example, we might point to the rise of the "transnational" as a category of analysis not solely or originally in feminism, but also in economic theories that have not necessarily themselves been critical of capitalism. It has also been taken up in both the social sciences and the humanities as a counter to postcolonial studies, which has been seen by many as not "material" enough (that is, as more directly allied with cultural studies and literary work). It is not the use of the transnational to think about the problems of other concepts that we wish to call into question, but rather the use of the transnational as a transcendental concept that itself remains out of reach of such questioning. Here we can see the disciplinary work that the transnational has been made to do in feminist and LGBTQ studies, marking off different areas of inquiry and methods as opposed to each other (for example, the positing of women of color feminism as simply national or postcolonial studies as insufficiently political).

Along the same lines, we might also call attention to how transnational feminism steps into a set of conflicts regarding the place and legitimacy of women's studies in the university, providing women's studies with a unity and direction and with a project to call its own. In other words, transnational feminism can be seen as offering a particular response to what has been constituted as a "crisis" in women's studies. This "crisis" is not singular or coherent, but is configured in multiple and conflicting ways. For some, the institutionalization of women's studies, and its increasing resemblance to other disciplines, is met with the sense that it failed to remain true to its mission of critiquing academic structures of knowledge. Women's studies, as the narrative goes, emerged to name and compensate for the exclusions performed by traditional disciplines; in this sense, it was founded upon a deep skepticism and antagonism toward a disciplinarity that it has now betrayed. At another level, the "crisis" is also related to the loss of "woman" as an object of analysis, and the difficulty of establishing the significance of the discipline in the face of this loss. The recent sweep of departments renaming themselves Gender Studies is perhaps the most visible attempt to demarcate a field of study that will right the wrongs of "women " and establish the institutional uniqueness of the discipline (see Robyn Wiegman 2002).[2] The substitution of "women" with "gender" is a move that claims new ground, and in so doing, professes to leave the troubles that plagued the discipline firmly circumscribed within its old territory. Lastly, the demand (from within and without) that women's studies perform interdisciplinarity produces a general confusion regarding the project and methods of a women's studies curriculum, resulting in coursework that offers a mix of disciplinary methods without pledging alliance to any single one (see Sabina Sawhney 2002). While these tensions are familiar and well rehearsed, they are useful to recall here precisely because they suggest that the arrival of transnational feminism and its overwhelmingly warm reception take place within a specific set of institutional pressures.

Within the context of such debates, collaborative praxis is often invoked in ways that purport to offer women's studies the opportunity to claim a distinct methodology, rather than one culled from other disciplinary sites. Moreover, this method reaffirms the position of women's studies as an extra-institutional site within the academy that, rather than being caught up in reaffirming its own foundations, is turned toward the outside. Collaboration, in privileging cooperation, promises to bridge the fractures and disagree-ments among the conflicting academic projects brought together under the umbrella of women's studies, and to present a united front that is askew to other disciplines. Thus in the same way that transnational feminism functions as a teleological theoretical destination for the project of feminism, collaboration is often configured as the teleological methodology of feminism. The point in raising this concern is neither to suggest that there is a problem with collaboration itself nor to take away from the crucial work of individual collaborative projects. By putting into question the authority of the academic intellectual and the interests and purpose of knowledge production, collaboration offers a critique of institutionalized knowledge production and seeks to imagine other possibilities for academic work. In this sense, collaboration emerges from a critique of the university and the academic as sovereign knower. Yet while many authors are attentive to the dangers of reifying divisions between "activist" and "academic," collaboration still often emerges as *the* (singular) method that will finally dismantle the boundaries of the university. It is this understanding of collaboration as providing a "solution" to the tricky problems of institutionality that we seek to interrogate. As a model of knowledge production that attends to the needs and interests of those situated "outside" the academy, collaboration promises to make the academy more democratic by providing access to a particular kind of "global knowledge." Therefore, collaboration also works within the university's demand for the inclusion of marginalized difference, even as it seeks to challenge the ways in which this project is often undertaken (i.e., without actually dismantling the opposition between subjects and objects of knowledge). In privileging the collective over the individual, moreover, the imputed structure of collaboration implicitly relies upon a logic of inclusion. The community that is imagined here, in contrast to the one underlying appeals to global sisterhood, is endowed with the ability to better recognize difference, and to identify points of similarity without reverting to a homogenizing form of transhistorical solidarity. Collaboration, it is supposed, can better account for and represent difference. The plurality that such a model subscribes to is one of difference as empirical fact, which posits that past exclusions can be compensated through more adequate representation. This approach to difference is problematic precisely because it presumes there is a proper meaning to difference, one that exists prior to and outside of representation, that collaboration can work to uncover; under this logic, the problem with global and international feminism is that they merely misrecognized difference. Instead, we propose that transnational feminism might want to put into question an approach to difference that takes "accuracy" as the measure of its success.

Generally, the call for collaborative work is one that importantly functions as an imperative to move beyond the self, to be responsible to an other, and thereby make the university have meaning beyond its immediate self. But by always looking "beyond" the academy for its sources of engagement, collaboration promises to disentangle the academic intellectual from the mandates of the university and the demands of disciplinarity.[3] While it is perhaps not stated so directly, the woman from the global South emerges as the central figure to be collaborated with by transnational feminism. As the emblem of the "most oppressed" and therefore the "most outside," the figure of the woman from the global South promises to finally complete the quest for and responsibility to difference. Postcolonial feminism has long sought to critique the ways in which the woman from the global South stands for the "material" and the "real" within feminist scholarship, but her status as the privileged knower for transnational feminism replicates the problem of representation that has been the central object of this critique. For example, Gayatri Spivak (1988) has pointed out how leftist intellectuals, masquerading as "nonrepresenters," conceal their indebtedness to colonial relations of power by calling upon the oppressed to articulate the truth of their experience. Appeals to collaboration, then, might also work within the university's mandate to "recognize" difference by offering up the voice of the marginalized woman. Again, the point here is not to critique collaboration as a method, but rather to think critically about the ways in which it is inserted and called forth by a globalized academe in line with a more general call to collaboration by the neoliberal university. In the spirit of confronting intellectual knowledge production's complicity with structures of marginalization, we suggest that transnational feminism must contend with the legacies of the model of collaboration that it (perhaps implicitly) prescribes.[4]

Collaboration is often posited as an ideal model for democratic community and exchange by transnational feminism, which works to guard democracy itself from scrutiny. We suggest that the collapsing of collaboration into a notion of democratic community needs to be questioned. The collective context promises to free the individual from the trappings of her positionality in order to "see" and draw connections to the experiences of others. This conceptualization of community, then, is one where plurality is representable to itself and difference is adequately accounted for. Such an idealized democratic community, moreover, is implicitly composed of sovereign, willful, and fully self-conscious individuals who recognize themselves as a community and agree upon the terms of their membership. Therefore, collaboration is premised upon a certain transcendence of antagonism and conflict, which offers up community as a harmonious unity. While individual examples of collaboration overwhelmingly emphasize dissonance and antagonism, the larger point that we want to make is that recognizing conflict might not in itself be an adequate response to our concerns, precisely because it still operates within a logic of accounting for, or representing, difference. In other words, the dictum of "agreeing to disagree" is still a mode of consensus, and one that the university importantly relies upon to "include" and legislate the difficult articulation of difference and representation.

If we are to engage with critiques of representation as productive, rather than merely inhibiting, we must search for alternatives to the presumption of community as founded upon a coming to terms with difference. For instance, we might begin by questioning the very drive to offer a more proper, a more totalizing, and a more "just" representation by leaving no one unaccounted for. Naming inclusion as the final objective, as our argument suggests, demands an empirical understanding of difference and poses the task of representation as one of providing an accurate reflection of "reality." Rather than conceptualizing democratic exchange as merely transparent and communicative, we suggest that transnational feminism put into question the notion of a "common" that is achieved through mutual understanding. A different way to conceptualize community, following Jacques Rancière (1999), would be to entertain the possibility of a dispute.[5] To "give up" on finding a solution for exclusion, then, might lead transnational feminism to finally do away with the possibility of resolution altogether. A feminist community whose very existence is premised upon a dispute is one whose ability to encompass the whole will never be complete. Instead, this is a community whose "common" is the contention over the presumption of anything shared.

As a keyword that functions in close connection with "collaboration," the invocation of "praxis" in transnational feminism might also be looked at for its relationship with a teleological model of knowledge production as well as a model of community that emphasizes the "agreement to disagree." Alexander and Mohanty (chapter 1 in this volume) urge an attention to such questions in their close readings of syllabi. Methodologically, reading syllabi as a set of texts illuminates how scholars define, theorize, and practice their discipline. In other words, syllabi are treatises on how we as theorists and practitioners of feminist and LGBTQ studies think about and construct our field. In this regard, feminist and queer pedagogies are not only sites of transnational feminist praxis and theory, but may tell us something about the common ways in which "practice" and "theory" are defined and the disciplinary work that such definitions do. Syllabi are often structured chronologically or teleologically, following a developmental narrative. However, we also hope that the theory and practice of pedagogy itself may undermine this teleology by disrupting the narrative of development and culmination that, in collapsing theory and practice, proposes to resolve feminism's relationship to the real. For us, the project of transnational feminism, like teaching, is not about getting beyond, per se, and can never be complete, as it both succeeds and fails continually. In other words, its project cannot be decided upon once and for all by a description of how things "really are," which would close down further inquiry into how objects and subjects of knowledge are brought into being (through specific conceptual and material processes, in particular relationships of power). Pedagogy itself constantly reminds us that critical readings are always necessary and in need of being redone, relearned, and rewritten and that knowledge and its production are in a constant state of being contested, analyzed, and reformulated.

In that spirit, we inquire into the role the notion of praxis plays within transnational feminism to conceptualize it as distinctly different from other modes of knowledge production. As defined by the *Oxford English Dictionary*, praxis is "conscious, willed action, *esp.* (in Marxist and neo-Marxist thought) that through which theory or philosophy is transformed into practical social activity; the synthesis of theory and practice seen as a basis for or condition of political and economic change" ("Praxis," *OED* online, def. 1). Therefore, praxis is located firmly within the realm of "action," and encompasses *both* theory and practice within itself. Following a teleological narrative, praxis marks a "step beyond" theory, and indicates the action whereby knowledge is translated into having "material" implications. Praxis, then, announces itself as resolutely *political*, directly involved in effecting social change, and positions itself as outside, or distinct from, institutionalized knowledge that is caught up with the concerns of disciplinarity. In this sense, the invocation of praxis as code word for an "activist knowledge" that itself goes unquestioned may set up a kind of hierarchy of scholarship within feminist and LGBTQ studies: theory is posed as institutional and problematic, praxis as the extra-institutional answer to our conundrum. We are skeptical of this implicit definition of praxis not because we question the value of work done with and by individuals and organizations that have been actively excluded from the institution of the university; rather, precisely in order to challenge the university's understanding of its goals and aims and the ways that these produce social hierarchy, we believe that it is necessary to put into question the common positing of theory and praxis as in opposition. This is not the least because this opposition has a long history in Western thought, and has undergirded particular understandings of knowledge production and the subject that many have pointed out and critiqued: the idea that individuals produce knowledge through a willful self-consciousness by using language as a tool is foremost among them.

That the tradition of metaphysics has itself relied so heavily on the opposition of praxis to theory leads us to question its use as one of the primary characteristics ascribed to the transnational, particularly because this may actually reinvest the transnational with an implicit hierarchy not only of what kind of scholarship qualifies as feminist, but of knowledge producers and those about whom knowledge is produced. The racial and colonial legacies of this hierarchy have been noted by many a scholar. As such, the privileging of praxis does not straightforwardly contribute toward the dismantling of "theory" and "practice" as categories that organize and define academic scholarship. Rather, any invocation of "praxis" also necessarily participates in reinscribing such an opposition. This opposition, moreover, relies upon other concepts, such as "action." In other words, "action" does not have an unmediated meaning, but is rendered legible and coherent in relation to a constellation of other concepts. Thus rather than trying to decide where to draw the line between theory and praxis, we might redirect our attention toward the questions of why and how the investment in drawing such a line arises in the first place, and what other kinds of assumptions this line might rely upon. In this sense, the call to activism that is implicit within the celebration of praxis might also perform a particular disciplining of women's studies (see Robyn Wiegman 2003). The focus on activism, for example, positions the project of women's studies outside the boundaries of the academy, and reaffirms its status as an exceptional discipline. At the same time that the university devalues knowledge that is produced outside of its purview, the role of activism within women's studies has a different lineage of its own. Within the discipline, the privileging of "activism" has worked to define what counts as social change, and which kinds of endeavors are more committed to pursuing a just world.

Such a consideration of how the concepts of theory, practice, praxis, and activism do work for transnational feminism necessarily leads us to think critically about how we understand the institution of the university and what its relationship is to "other" institutions, social formations, and intellectual practices. In their theorization of transnational feminism's intervention in the university, Alexander and Mohanty seek "to understand the relationship between a politics of location and accountability, and the politics of knowledge production by examining the academy as one site in which transnational feminist knowledge is produced, while examining those knowledges that derive from political mobilizations that push up, in, and against the academy ultimately foregrounding the existence of multiple genealogies of radical transnational feminist practice" (26). Thus, they seek to locate academic knowledge production in relation to other knowledge productions. However, this move can also function to simply reverse the binary and privilege outside knowledges, rather than seeking to question the relationship and power between the two. In order to follow up on Alexander and Mohanty's crucial proposal for transnational feminism to take up a strong critique of the university, we suggest that this critique does not have to rely on an inside/outside binary, but can be based in an alternative paradigm that acknowledges and names the specific modes of production of both academic and nonacademic knowledges. On the one hand, to think through the importance of different forms of knowledge and knowledge production it seems important to actually address their particularities; whereas if we were to leave the nonacademic as a term that itself goes unquestioned, it becomes emptied of content. On the other hand, the distinction between academic and nonacademic is not itself transparent or simply a description of how things are. That is, it might serve as a prescriptive, particularly insofar as this very binary is a product of university knowledge production in its dominant mode. Calling this binary into question is important not simply because it allows an increased porosity of borders, but because it reveals the way that the "inside" and "outside" rely on each other. In other words, embracing this unquestioningly leads us to define the university as a discrete, circumscribable system—which may be not so distinct from how the university thinks of itself. Questioning our own model of the university would allow us to at once problematize the university's relationship with other institutions—thus also putting into question whether the distinction between the academic and nonacademic is actually productive for those of us who do wish to critique accepted modes of knowledge production—while at the same time exposing the supposed sovereignty of the university as the falsehood that it is. Changing the university might be better effected by an approach that seeks to find the tensions and fissures within the university itself, while acknowledging the impossibility of any scholar to completely disinvest from its problems. The question at stake is not that of how, as members of the university, we participate in the goal of achieving a more perfect representation of the until-now-excluded, but rather that of what work is done by the very presumption that we could either on the one hand have the ability to achieve such an inclusion, or on the other hand, willfully and completely detach ourselves from the tricky representational mandates of the institution.

Insofar as it allies itself with the nonacademic and plays the role of the outside, transnational feminism often claims to be *central* to the university. We thus suggest that transnational feminism needs to advance a critique of the way the university itself has articulated an investment in the "nonacademic," variously coded as the real, the material, and the political. In its fetishization of difference as what lies somewhere "out there," it proposes an empiricist approach that claims to simply be seeing more clearly what is (implicitly) already there. The university's invocation of the transnational provides a description of a state of things, which are themselves coded for in the language of capital, economics, and geopolitics. And it is prescriptive in the sense that it measures the value of feminist work itself on the basis of how well it is able to take account of some predefined reality, a world increasingly characterized by global difference. Indeed, the impetus behind much postcolonial, Third World, and transnational feminist work has been to critique this globalist approach to difference; global feminism is problematic not because it fails to recognize difference, but because it posits difference as a kind of real thing that preexists representation. But insofar as it works to account for as much difference as possible, transnational feminism may follow the structure of global feminism. Collaboration plays a crucial role here in establishing transnational feminism's progress away from monolithic and Eurocentric accounts of women's experience. In other words, the knowledge produced by transnational feminism is claimed to avoid such pitfalls precisely because it is the product of collaboration. However, the unstated assumption remains that it is still the task to represent, and thus the "more" elsewheres are featured, the better. As a result, transnational feminism may remain indebted to global feminism in ways that still need to be thought and traced out.

In addition to the increasing influence of national security interests on academic knowledge production, we propose that the university's relationship to global capital and the nation-state is expressed in a variety of different disciplinary sites, including not only the sciences and the professional disciplines, but also the social sciences and humanities. Not only do the state and the law bring the interests of global capital to bear on the university; the disciplines themselves and the various work undertaken in their name also produce the concepts and material conditions that support the spread of global capital. In that sense, perhaps none of us can exempt ourselves from the workings of global capital—to attempt to do so shuts down the possibility of continuing to be able to critique them. Thus an understanding of how modern neoliberal universities produce and manage racial and global difference is crucial to transnational feminism. Consequently, transnational feminism must vigilantly critique normative multiculturalisms as well as normative internationalism, transnationalism, and globalism. In thinking about what form this critique might take, we suggest that it must be aware of the neoliberal university's interests in difference, and particularly the inclusion of difference through the invocation of the transnational. The university's call for inclusion of "global difference" is not simply benevolent and aimed at redressing past crimes of exclusion, but is necessary to the expansion of its global purview and sovereignty. Serving as a generalized reference to some sort of difference, the university's accumulation of knowledges of the transnational reinstates a center/periphery model of globality. Thus when transnational feminism describes itself as important because it introduces into the U.S. university forgotten or overlooked knowledges, ironically the U.S. state and capitalism go unquestioned as the U.S. becomes recentered as both the origin point of transnational knowledge and a kind of figural reference point grounding the definition of "anything else"; it proposes to simply gather up transnational otherness (which is defined as non-U.S. difference) (see Gayatri Spivak 2003). Furthermore, both the U.S. and the university are defined as self-present and internally coherent, thus barring inquiry into the possibility of seeing them as constituted in difference (which would then allow us to challenge the authority accrued from the covering over of this originary difference). This understanding of the university raises two related issues. The first is the necessity of recognizing that feminist knowledge production within the university may itself forward the university's neoliberal and imperialist interests. The second is that the U.S. must remain some component of our understanding of transnational feminism. That is, transnational feminist critique might work against the paradigm of the U.S. as center and origin of the production of knowledge about "non-U.S. difference," instead attempting to highlight how the "inclusion" of transnational difference itself is one of the key ways in which the U.S. (and the U.S. university) constructs itself as having a discrete, sovereign identity in the first place. This would hold open to question the role of the "U.S." as a concept in arguments about the politics of knowledge production.

By way of a conclusion, how do we, in the end, understand transnational feminist and queer critique? Two essays in this collection offer overlapping definitions for how to formulate transnational feminist critique. More broadly, Nagar and Swarr in this volume argue for attention to three components: 1) logics of globalization and capitalist patriarchies; 2) subjectivities and agency; and 3) self-reflexivity and feminist politics (5). Alexander and

Mohanty also offer an emphasis on three components: 1) location of knowledge production, that is, the university; 2) ethics of cross-cultural work; 3) questions of intersubjectivity, collectivities, and accountability. One must read these working definitions as necessarily open and contingent, rather than as static and prescriptive. We understand the question of what constitutes transnational feminist and queer critique to be critically compromised and embedded within its very site of analysis. Thus the common suggestion that, now that we've problematized the subject, we can return to the more pressing issue of political economy, of "material" conditions, of "real issues," is problematic. In this sense, what we are calling for is not simply a recognition that transnational feminism is heterogeneous and internally diverse. Transnational feminism, like transnational queer critique, should provide a self-critique. It can hold in suspension and in tension a variety of different names and approaches—postcolonial feminism, Third World feminism, women of color feminism, for example—rather than proposing to move beyond and solve "old" problems and the theoretical movements that sought to address them.

While we ponder the possibility of mitigating material and epistemic inequities through collaboration or otherwise, we want to suggest that knowledge production is (always) stealing. The necessity of approaching collaborative work with a continued commitment to reflexivity about one's position, motivations, and aims emerges as a key theme throughout this volume. Self-reflexivity, as we understand it, requires a stated ethics in acknowledging and emphasizing that knowledge production is always based on and shaped by unequal relations of power. In her insightful essay on Native/non-Native collaboration and literary criticism, "When You Admit You Are a Thief, Then You Can be Honourable," Helen Hoy discusses the collaborations between Metis Canadian artist, activist and writer Maria Campbell and white Canadian performer and writer Linda Griffiths, and reflects on her own production of scholarship on Native Canadian literature as a white woman. Hoy suggests that collaboration between Native and non-Native people, that is, those with unequal relations of power, may be best framed as stealing. Admitting one's culpabilities and naming the transaction as stealing allows for honorability.[6] While Hoy proposes that stealing needs to be acknowledged specifically in order to promote "healing," we suggest that this concept of thievery might actually be more useful for working against a simple model of criminality, punishment, and recognizable justice. Similarly, the metaphor of admission need not imply the transparency of interests or responsibility. In our reading here, we pose all knowledge production (and not just the collaborative sort) as predicated upon epistemic violence. We understand this "violence" not in the traditional sense or as something done "to" preexisting subjects and objects, but as a name for the demarcation and delimitation necessary for bringing those subjects and objects into being (thus as something that cannot simply be labeled as "bad" and hence rejected). However, in addition to this, the concept of thievery might allow us to address other issues not encompassed by the recognition of epistemic violence—most importantly, the specific transactional elements involved in particular collaborative projects of knowledge production, and the quite literal economy in which these projects are situated. Critical transnational feminist and queer work might take up the task of theorizing "epistemic violence," "thievery," and other such concepts—attending to their connections and discrepancies—as a means of forwarding responsibility as a persistent question without resolution.

Notes

We want to express our gratitude to Amanda Swarr and Richa Nagar for organizing this collection and the workshop from which it emerged.

1. At times, we refer to both transnational feminism and LGBTQ studies, at other times only to one or the other. In all of our uses, we try to be as specific as possible. Transnational feminism is a more extensive body of literature and, therefore, does dominate our discussion here.

2. Robyn Wiegman suggests that the shift from "women" to "gender" attempts to solve the problem of representation through full inclusion. She argues that the move to "gender studies" seeks to locate a coherent sign that can finally settle the object of feminism.

3. In this regard, the university's general call for collaboration is much broader and includes collaborations with multinational corporations, nation-states, and underrepresented and disenfranchised groups and communities simultaneously, often creating contradictory and tense relationships and knowledges. Transnational feminism attempts to disentangle and distinguish itself from this impossible quandary.

4. In thinking through the question of collaboration, a critical engagement with both meanings of the word may be necessary. The older meaning with its etymology of combined or conjoined labor to produce knowledge (usually scientific, literary, or artistic work) can be traced to the nineteenth century, and is now being extended to include shared labor for other kinds of production including socioeconomic processes and activism via transnational feminism. The newer meaning, arising in the middle of the twentieth century and coming into common use predominantly with the Nazi occupation of France, suggests almost the exact opposite as it references those who work or collude with the enemy, foreign state, or occupier; in this definition, there is a much different understanding of the unequal relations that may engender or necessitate collaborations ("Collaboration," OED online, def. 1 and 2). While the project of collaboration is understood as joint transactions of labor rendering production for mutual benefit, the second meaning seems to

haunt the first in all collaborations about difference; in the second meaning of collaboration, an individual's participation in and collusion with processes that may be against his or her own interests is omnipresent. One might argue that in order to understand collaborations about difference, it is necessary to see the definitions as simultaneous rather than as exclusive. While the first definition appropriately describes transnational feminist collaborations that produce conjoined knowledge, the second definition may reflect how we need to situate the use and meaning of that knowledge within the university itself.

5. See Danielle Bouchard (2006).
6. In this case, honorable implies not an exalted status so much as one that is honest, principled, and not base.

Works Cited

Alexander, M. Jacqui, and Chandra Talpade Mohanty. 2010. "Cartographies of Knowledge and Power: Transnational Feminism as Radical Praxis." Chapter 1, this volume.

Barndt, Deborah. 2010. "Remapping the Americas: A Transnational Engagement with Creative Tensions of Community Arts." Chapter 8, this volume.

Bouchard, Danielle. 2006. "'A Barbarous, Rude or Debased Language': Jargon Democracy." *Contretemps: An Online Journal of Philosophy* 6 (January): 11–24.

"Collaboration." Def. 1 and 2. *The Oxford English Dictionary.* 2nd ed. 1989. 6 December 2007. http://80-dictionary.oed.com.floyd.lib.umn.edu/.

Hoy, Helen. "When You Admit You Are a Thief, Then You Can Be Honourable." *Canadian Literature* 136 (Spring 1993): 24–39.

Nagar, Richa, and Amanda Lock Swarr. 2010. "Theorizing Transnational Feminist Praxis." Introduction, this volume.

Pratt, Geraldine, et al. 2010. "Seeing Beyond the State: Toward Transnational Feminist Organizing." Chapter 3, this volume.

"Praxis." Def. 1. *The Oxford English Dictionary.* 2nd ed. 1989. 29 November 2007. http://80-dictionary.oed.com.floyd.lib.umn.edu/.

Rancière, Jacques. 1999. *Disagreement: Politics and Philosophy.* Trans. Julie Rose. Minneapolis: University of Minnesota Press.

Sawhney, Sabina. 2002. "Strangers in the Classroom." In Robyn Wiegman, ed., *Women's Studies On Its Own.* Durham and London: Duke University Press, 2002. 341–367.

Silvey, Rachel. 2010. "Envisioning Justice: The Politics and Possibilities of Transnational Feminist Film." Chapter 9, this volume.

Spivak, Gayatri Chakravorty. 1988. "Can the Subaltern Speak?" In Cary Nelson and Lawrence Grossberg, eds., *Marxism and the Interpretation of Culture.* Urbana: University of Illinois Press. 271–313.

Spivak, Gayatri Chakravorty. 2003. *Death of a Discipline.* New York: Columbia University Press.

Wiegman, Robyn. 2003. "Feminism's Broken English." In Jonathan Culler and Kevin Lamb, eds., *Just Being Difficult? Academic Writing in the Public Arena.* Stanford: Stanford University Press. 75–94.

Wiegman, Robyn. 2002. "The Progress of Gender: Whither 'Women'?" In Robyn Wiegman, ed., *Women's Studies On Its Own.* Durham and London: Duke University Press. 106–140.

PART II

Dialogical Journeys

‹ 3 ›

Seeing Beyond the State

Toward Transnational Feminist Organizing

GERALDINE PRATT IN COLLABORATION WITH THE PHILIPPINE WOMEN
CENTRE OF BC AND UGNAYAN NG KABATAANG PILIPINO SA
CANADA/THE FILIPINO-CANADIAN YOUTH ALLIANCE

"Collaboration" and "transnationalism" are terms that circulate widely, and probably too easily, within feminist scholarship. Both terms connote betweenness, a sense of exchange, instability, and movement, and rather than being easily circulated, perhaps their value lies in part in making us hesitate, reexamine, and reconsider. Collaborations between activists and academics often arise from some desire for exchange, but this exchange can take many different forms, some of which exaggerate as much as disrupt existing power relations, for instance, when academics imagine that they hold exclusive expertise in research methodology or a superior capacity for theorizing. We take this chapter as an opportunity to examine and hesitate over our research process, which has involved a series of collaborations over the last fifteen years between two Filipino-Canadian activist organizations in Vancouver and a white Canadian university researcher.

Typical of our collaborative academic writing, and reflecting the distribution of a key resource—time—this chapter was written in the first instance by Geraldine Pratt and then passed back and forth between us. Transitions between "I" and "we" reflect this process and the uneven and negotiated process of authorship. Like many collaborations, this chapter involves the busy traffic of collaborators entering and leaving, coming and going. The text also attempts to communicate the chatter of oral communication and more reflective writing. We begin by considering our collaboration, through conversations about the research process and a parallel written text. We resist idealizing one model or cartography of collaboration (that of similarity and close proximity), and suggest that some distances between researcher and activists can be strategically valuable. We describe how our collaborations have differed from project to project and how the terms of collaboration need to be rethought as circumstances change.

My activist collaborators then leave the space of the text and I turn to reflect on some of what I have learned from them. In a now-canonical feminist essay, Donna Haraway (1988) wrote about the need to more fully understand how our social locations and methodologies shape what we can and cannot see. The point of this was to understand the limits of any one way of knowing, so as to create the appetite for and means to forge connections across inevitably partial ways of seeing. Connection can also be a means of understanding the partiality of one's vision. I want to describe some of what I have learned about transnational feminist praxis from my research collaborators, who have long lived and theorized transnationalism in the contexts of their own lives. I have learned from my collaborators not only about the Filipino community's struggle in Canada, but a new perspective on the world, which can be called transnational. This has involved a process of unlearning certain ways of framing the Philippines in relation to Canada, framings that uncomfortably repeat and reproduce some of what we have criticized about Canadian state policy. I have also learned from my collaborators another sense of what academic research can aspire to achieve, which is not just to describe the world, but to seek to change it. One means of doing this is to work within transnational activist networks. There is no single privileged or ideal site within these networks for research and activism, although the risks of epistemological nationalism are considered herein; transnational activism is compatible with doing research in a national space such as Canada.

Collaborating on Research

Taken from a conversation that we staged on May 18, 2006:[1]

GERRY: *What skills have been learned through our research?*

CHARLENE SAYO (Ugnayan ng Kabataang Pilipino sa Canada/Filipino Canadian Youth Alliance): *Well, picking up interviewing skills, understanding even how to read reports, how to write them, how to try and understand them, how to critically analyze. Because that's something that, you know, our community . . . well, I know for myself, for the youth, that's not something that they always have access to. They're so marginalized. You know, they've dropped out of school. Their education is really being affected. Their sense of confidence and development is really robbed of them. The fact that they can have this opportunity to develop themselves, that's huge. Like for me, personally, that's a big, huge benefit.*

CECILIA DIOCSON (Chair, National Alliance of Philippine Women in Canada): But they're also seeing that they're part of this history, part of the reality, the lived experiences. They find that they're part of it. They own it. They have the ownership and so they want to do something to also change their situation. I think that's really very important. So even the interviews. Before [the youth] did not want to do these. But now they're very assertive in going out, and interviewing [other Filipino youth who have experienced separation through the Live-in Caregiver Program (LCP)] and using these interviews in the programs at the center.

CHARLENE: Because they also know that the reports, the stories, they're going to be this historical product. Fifty years from now, people will at least know what has happened to them. And that's important because at least they're then part of this society. I mean they've been so marginalized that they've never felt like they belong here. But knowing that they can have that sense of place . . .

CECILIA: But I think they're really experiencing it also. Like, it's not because we interviewed them, collected their stories, and analyzed them. They're really experiencing it. So, you know, it really helps their own analysis, helps in their realization that "Oh yeah, it's really true, it's really happening." Like systemic racism is really happening. It's not just that the stories were gathered and this is it. But, you know, every day, that critical analysis is really being developed, and through their own experience.

Perhaps the truest thing to say about our collaborations is that each has been different from the others, and that we have kept our distance and come together in different ways at different moments. We first met when Cecilia Diocson of the Philippine Women Centre (PWC) was a community scholar in residence at the Centre for Women's Studies and Gender Relations at the University of British Columbia. This program offered a rare opportunity for community activists to spend time at the university, access resources, and make connections with university researchers (and vice versa). This was a moment of intense scrutiny of the many ways that white supremacy and colonial relations persist within feminist scholarship (e.g., hooks 1990; Mohanty 1991); in the research project that I had already begun on domestic workers in Canada, I was stalled by concerns about appropriating others' narratives for my own professional gain, exploiting research subjects, and reproducing the distinction between expert academic theorist and naïve native informant through my own research practice. I had interviewed nanny agents, government officials, and Canadian employers but found myself immobilized when it came to researching the lives of domestic workers. Collaborating with an activist group working with domestic workers on this issue in a participatory research project seemed one solution to this problem.

One feature that has been constant across all of our projects is the commitment to plan the research collectively and to research issues that organizations at the Kalayaan Centre have judged to be pressing ones for their community at the time. Our first project (described in Pratt 2004) about the significance to conventional academic scholarship of the innovative methodologies was by some measures the most collaborative. After deciding to collaborate in a participatory research project, we met five times for day-long workshops with some fifteen or so domestic workers, many of whom already met regularly at the Philippine Women Centre. We spent our first day together planning the research focus and methodologies. I have written elsewhere (Pratt 2000) about the significance of the innovative methodologies, such as role-playing, suggested by women at the PWC. The next two sessions were spent breaking into three small groups in which women shared stories of their experiences in Tagalog (except for the group in which I participated, which was conducted in a mixture of Tagalog and English). When the tapes were translated and transcribed by the PWC, we met together to read the transcripts line by line, to share and verify what was said and to develop a joint analysis. We met one more day to further develop the analysis. It has always been my job to write a first draft of academic papers and present them to my collaborators for criticism and comments. But we have equal access to the data and they can (and have) used the information gathered through our research to write nonacademic briefs and reports, and we have a history of collaborating on media and press releases. We did our best to clear away a kind of leverage that researchers often hold over community partners insofar as the agreed upon research monies were exchanged before the research began. Domestic workers participated as community researchers: they were not paid for their time.

Subsequent projects have not quite followed this model, for different reasons. In a second project with youth, we planned the research together and I was invited along to a couple of the focus groups, but much of the data was made accessible to me only through transcripts. As Charlene and Cecilia describe in the accompanying conversational text, the youth needed space (and time) to take ownership of the research process and develop trust in our collaboration. The second project with the PWC was less fully collaborative in another sense, and this reflected less a choice or the need to keep a certain distance from a university researcher (as seemed the case for youth) than the changed circumstances of those whose lives we were documenting. For this project, the PWC and I jointly developed the research proposal and budget, and brought the same women from the first study together eight years later to document how they were getting on after fulfilling the requirements of the Canadian federal government's Live-in Caregiver Program (LCP) and settling permanently in Canada (see Pratt in collaboration with the Philippine Women Centre 2005). Although the aim for collective storytelling remained, the effects of deskilling were evident; because so many women were working at multiple jobs on variable work schedules it was difficult to bring everyone together at one time, and individual interviews were arranged in some cases. The idea of engaging participants fully as community researchers over five daylong sessions, to both collect and analyze their own stories, was inconceivable. The women's experiences also had begun to diverge so that the individual interview format was useful because it allowed a more thorough examination of the particularities of individual lives. True, a range of experiences always existed among these women—some had gone first to Singapore, others to Hong Kong; some had left children in the Philippines, others had not; some were registered nurses, some high school teachers. There is the possibility that the complexity detected eight years on reflects the shifting terms of reference and an unwitting (colonial) tendency to view lives in Canadian society as infinitely more complex than those in the Philippines.[2] But in the first study, all participants were registered in the LCP and they shared the common experience of working as live-in domestic workers. They told their stories within a context of organizing to change the conditions of the LCP, and individuals came to recognize the similarities in their circumstances through the telling. A common project—to uphold their rights within the LCP, and to reform or scrap the program—was clear. Eight years on, the tone of many of the women's stories had changed: most women were approaching middle age and, for many, their circumstances had not improved and, in some respects, worsened. A number had resigned themselves to permanent separation from their mothers and extended families, others to never finding a romantic partner (for some because a life of working at multiple, low-paying jobs left little time to socialize). Their immediate problems—though rooted in a common experience of the LCP—seemed more diverse: for instance, some had retrained, but through different courses and to different extents; and the specifics of their employment situations were less immediately comparable.

CHARLENE: *I wanted to share, because of what I said about the white guy [another "expert" researcher she had earlier criticized]. Because I think it's also very much like what Cecilia said: it [our collaboration] has been a long process. And it's been nurtured, and we can see the long-term impacts. When we first did the project about Filipino youth, in particular, it wasn't like you just left and that was it. There was a lot more there that you wanted to explore, which was really important. And so, moving on from that project, we've looked at the issue of family separation and impacts on the youth. So there was that follow-up, or at least continuity. And I think for the youth that were involved in that, they could see that. . . . You know you have to understand that when you're bringing in these youth who don't even want to be here in Canada anymore because there are no opportunities for them. They're criminalized already. There's no trust. You know, they have a hard time trusting people. So when they see that their stories and their experiences are being taken seriously, and that they themselves can also develop from it, then, of course, there's really that sense of ownership and also that sense . . . I guess it's a better relationship knowing that their stories aren't being used to further your career or whatever. But they're really taken seriously. I think the fact that they know that. . . . Well I know for the youth, for some of the younger ones, that when they see that their names, their stories are being published, of course, for them it's like, wow, they're being validated. But they know they can also do it themselves. I think that's a big, huge step. So knowing that there's always that benefit there of education and that process of development.*

In our most recent project, we are interviewing mothers and children, and some fathers, who have been separated for a long time—the median number of years is eight. These are often sad stories, stories of not being recognized by one's own children, or bewilderment about one's mother's sudden departure or feelings of distrust and betrayal. We have collected these stories through interviews with individuals or with mother and children together, using contacts developed by the Kalayaan Centre and the help of a settlement worker. Our goal is to use the stories to draw out a collective, community story. We have brought a number of the interviewed families together on one occasion to build this common understanding, and the center has been using the stories to organize the community around this issue. But because of the change in emotional tone, the more individualistic mode of collecting stories, and the focus on problems settling into Vancouver, the risks of victimization, voyeuristic witnessing of suffering and community stigmatization seem even more pressing for this project relative to earlier ones, and the need for community ownership extremely important.

At issue here is not only the type of stories that are constructed about peoples' lives but the conditions under, and the social relations within and through which they are told. Collecting the stories has to be a community endeavor, and part of community development rather than community exposure. Though this has always been our goal, what we take from our varied experiences across research projects is the understanding that there is not one ideal set of conditions and no single model of collaboration; methods and modes of collaboration depend on the circumstances and the particular needs of the community at that time. In our view it would be unfortunate if feminists idealized one model of collaboration based only on ideals of closeness, proximity, and intimacy.

EMANUAL SAYO (B.C. Committee for Human Rights in the Philippines): *Gerry, a classic example is when we say that Filipino youth have the highest dropout, one of the highest, dropout rates among young people in the Lower Mainland. It's just a statement if it's not backed up by an academic researcher. The credibility is not really that strong within the community. Unless we show them, "Look, Dan Hiebert, Gerry Pratt, these are their findings" and all that stuff. Then even the community is surprised. If we say that [the dropout rate is high] based on our own research alone, it would not have that much of an impact. But now it's being backed up by this community research from the academic. Then that becomes a very powerful tool, and suddenly people start using it, and it just spreads out. It's not just with the youth or with domestic workers. The members of the [broader] community can see that here's the Kalayaan Centre. The credibility of the Kalayaan Centre is also bolstered by the fact that whatever we say at the center is backed up by very strong academic research. And we have succeeded in convincing academics that these are our own terms for doing research if you want to do it with us. And academics are also cooperating; they understand that this is based not only on our personal but collective life experiences as a community.*

We are allies—sometimes coconspirators. But we have never collapsed our roles as academic and activists, and certainly not our identities. In the first instance, this reflects fundamental differences in our life experiences: I am not Filipino, I do not speak Tagalog, and I have not experienced the forced migration and radical deskilling, that is, of being dislodged from my profession as university professor to clean Canadian homes. Our collaboration developed, not from a common identity, but from the common understanding that Canada requires a national childcare policy that does not rest on the exploitation of women from the global South through the LCP. There are also good strategic reasons for maintaining our distance and difference. As Emanual explains in the accompanying oral text, association with an academic can authorize ongoing community research—even within the Filipino community. And because of the perceived neutrality and professionalism, academics sometimes have access to government data or interviewees that are unavailable to community activists. For instance, we have been able to calculate the dropout rates of Filipino youth relative to other youth in Vancouver high schools from a Ministry of Education data set that tracks every youth year by year within the British Columbia school system. Researchers must approach this data through a consulting firm established within the University of British Columbia's Faculty of Education; literally by being buzzed through a locked door and signed in, after making an appointment with one of the two data analysts employed there. Each proposed statistical analysis is closely vetted by the B.C. Ministry of Education and researchers must sign an agreement to obtain ministry approval before publishing or presenting material that draws upon this data.[3] And though it is merely speculation that the proposals of UBC academics and community activists might be evaluated differently, I was told that passage through the evaluation process is eased if the project has been reviewed by the university's ethics review board. Certainly any investigator requires the financial resources to pay for the data analysis, which can only be done by the facility's data analysts.

This raises the thorny issue of inequity of access to material resources, which can reinstate the very hierarchies that collaborators are at pains to disrupt. It should not be surprising that the state assumes and produces a range of "boundary projects" through the allocation of research monies. One boundary that is assumed and reproduced is the distinction between university researcher and community activist. So, for example, though the PWC and I jointly planned and wrote our second research proposal, the funding body would only award the grant to a university researcher, and deposit it to a university account managed both for and by that researcher. So, too, the state maintains a strict division between national and international space, which belies community experiences of transnationalism. When Ugnayan applied for funds from a provincial government agency, Heritage B.C., for their antiracism work in winter 2005, for instance, they were told that they could not be funded if they focused some of their work on understanding the situation in the Philippines. For this, they were told, they must apply for funding from the Canadian International Development Agency (CIDA). This is an instance of boundary maintenance—between national and international space, and domestic and external affairs. Equally, academic researchers bring with their research funds a set of constraints, timelines, and requirements (for instance, in terms of formalized ethical review and the need to produce certain kinds of scholarly research output), which can fit awkwardly with the priorities and schedules of community activists.

But without wishing to sidestep this important issue, there is a danger of reifying power relations and casting community researchers as powerless and dependent, in ways that play out stereotypes of expected distributions of expertise, wealth, and access. It may be that our collaborations over the years have built the center's capacity to generate their own funding from government agencies and that Canada is a distinctive context in this regard, but it certainly is the case that the PWC has had—for many years—considerable success generating its own research monies, through their own research proposals, to do their own community research. To cast the PWC as dependent on my material wealth as a funded university researcher would misrepresent their skills, success, and autonomy. For instance, their latest and largest project, begun in spring 2006, funded by the Department of Canadian Heritage and carried out by the National Alliance of Philippine Women in Canada (NAPWC) over a three-year period, is a comprehensive examination of factors leading to the economic and social marginalization of Filipino communities in Canada, and created a series of forums to strategize toward their communities' fuller participation in Canadian society. It was a long struggle to secure this funding, in part because the government considered this a very large research project for a community group to manage on its own—but the struggle was successful.

CHARLENE: *Because we also know that is also a challenge and struggle [to be both a scholar and activist] especially with youth activism. Because, you know, it's very common for youth to reject school and formal education. Especially since we know that what we're being taught, even at the universities, will not always be the most liberating. Like that's why a lot of youth don't continue.*
CECILIA: *It's about commercializing education.*
CHARLENE: *Exactly. It's not fulfilling. You're not actually learning how to think. You know, there are very few professors who are really able to give that to their students. But then overall, it's that overall sense: "Well, why go to school, if I get a huge loan and can't even get a decent job or whatever? What am I going to get out of this?" But we are also trying to challenge our own members as well. It's not, for one, wrong to pursue school. And second, we also have to be open to collaborating and working with professors who are also very progressive, and are also very open to working with us. One, because we're also not living in a society that takes our community and our research seriously. Second, we want to change our society but we also have to know how to live in it, survive in it. So we also have to be able to, you know, become a little bit more sophisticated, especially if we have to talk about our community, really know how to articulate our experiences. We have to be able to deliver that. I mean, it doesn't mean that we're completely changing our*

principles but we have to wear a lot of hats when we're doing our political work
and activism. So we have to be very comprehensive in our skills. So we do encourage
youth to go to school and to work with professors and academics. In the long term
it's also a capital investment. I mean, we may not make a lot of money out of all of
this but to have, say, a Filipino academic who's also going to address the issues of
the Filipino community, I mean that's big. That could be a big influence one day.

The community organizations' capacity to generate their own research
monies also suggests that the terms of our collaboration will continue to
change, with the possibility that its usefulness—from the perspective of organizations at the Kalayaan Centre—may disappear. We know, for instance, of
four or so Filipino-Canadians currently doing master's and PhD degrees on
their communities in Vancouver, Toronto, and Montreal. Is it still useful to
collaborate with a white, Canadian researcher? Are the terms and forms of
useful collaboration changing? At the weekend consultation in Vancouver in
February 2007, for instance, the first day was spent reporting on the research
that had been done by NAPWC over the previous year as part of their large
national research project. I attended, not as a researcher, but as an interested
member of the public. Sunday was restricted to Filipino-Canadians only—it
was a day of capacity training workshops in which participants gained
experience in policy analysis, formulation of policy recommendations, and
written and oral presentation of policy briefs. I participated in the afternoon
as one of several allies invited to take part in a mock parliamentary hearing.
Each of us was assigned a character (as a municipal, provincial, and federal
government politician or bureaucrat with a specific history and particular
set of priorities), to whom the submissions were made. We were asked to
dress appropriately for our roles, and to perform the task of receiving the
briefs (looking variably stern, bored, official, or sympathetic, depending on
our roles) and then challenging the presenters on the material and positions
that they put forth. This was a serious (and immensely pleasurable, joyful)
exercise in popular education, which exemplified a moment of collaboration through and not despite our differences. It provided a snapshot of the
range of significant collaborations that the Kalayaan have developed over
the years: with university researchers, Grassroots Women, Vancouver's
Bus Riders Union, among others. And it configured my relationship to the
group as ally/activist rather than university researcher. We are also currently
collaborating with theater artists to use our previous research transcripts
to construct a testimonial theater production. This collaboration opens the
possibility of developing different kinds of skills, such as play writing, acting,
and grant writing for theatrical productions. In each of these two cases, the

rationale and the form of collaboration have varied. The only certainty for the future is that our collaborations will continue to change along with the needs and opportunities for community development.

Seeing Like a State

As a way of honoring and underlining the significance of our collaboration, I would like to step away from my collaborators to reflect on what I have learned from them. Certainly I have learned about the struggles of the Filipino community in Canada, but I also learned to theorize these struggles in new terms, and to envision how research can move beyond describing and conceptualizing the world as it is put into circulation within transnational grassroots networks.

My collaboration with the Philippine Women Centre of B.C. has focused on documenting and critiquing the LCP, a temporary work visa program that brings from 3,000–6,000 (mostly) Filipino women to Canada annually to work as live-in servants. Much of our attention has focused on the inadequate state regulation of the program, and the Canadian state discourses and practices that legitimate it. Drawing very loosely on James Scott's (1998) phrase "seeing like a state," we might say that the Canadian state sees the LCP in distinctive ways—for instance, as a solution to carefully defined problems, such as affordable childcare for middle-class Canadians—that make it difficult to leverage an effective critique. After identifying two such ways of seeing, I want to consider how these same frameworks slip into the thinking of allies of Filipino-Canadian activists, including—possibly—our first research collaboration, and then describe a trajectory toward a transnational perspective.

One way of "seeing like a state" in relation to the LCP is to conceive it as a humanitarian response to the horrors of life in the Philippines. The possibility of attaining Canadian citizenship after twenty-four months in the LCP is often seen as an adequate compensation for two years of live-in servitude, and a comparison to economic circumstances in the Philippines self-evidently justifies employment conditions under the LCP that Canadians would not accept for themselves. Sherene Razack has criticized the rhetorical and practical importance of Canada's self-representation as world "peacekeeper" and reflected on its implications for immigration: "It is through such images that . . . when people of the Third World come knocking at our doors, we are able to view them as supplicants asking to be relieved of the disorder of their world and to be admitted to the rational calm of ours" (1998: 91; see also Razack 2004, 2007). Under almost any conditions.

Further, the Canadian government sidelines the welfare of domestic workers and their families within what one might call its own "grid of intelligibility": its overwhelming concern about the availability of affordable childcare for Canadian families, and a jurisdictional fragmentation that makes it difficult to pinpoint responsibility. The jurisdictional fragmentation of the LCP across provincial and federal governmental bodies, for instance, seems to blur and confuse lines of responsibility and accountability.[4] Likewise, though our analysis of the difficulties encountered by families who reunite in Canada after the LCP experience has been met with sympathetic responses, policy makers responsible for the LCP tend to see such problems as the concern of those in charge of settlement issues, in other words, as outside of their jurisdiction. Official statistics are fragmented, and in particular, those collected for the LCP are not integrated with immigration statistics. In Tania Li's words, "experts devising improvement schemes generate only the type and density of data required to constitute a field of intervention and to meet specific objectives" (2005: 388). Separating statistics for temporary work visa programs from those collected on immigration makes it very difficult to document the effects of the LCP on family settlement. When Filipino settlement in Vancouver is abstracted from the LCP experience, there is a risk, at best, of developing very partial analyses, at worst, of pathologizing the Filipino community in Canada for the inadequacy of their integration and economic success.

Even given this critique of state discourse and practice, it is worth reflecting on Tania Li's critique of James Scott's analysis of state modes of seeing. She argues that the binaries that structure Scott's analysis (such as state/society, state space/non-state space, power/resistance) provide "insufficient traction to expose the logic of [state development] schemes or to examine their effects" (2005: 385). She argues that the state is neither as monolithic as Scott presumes nor do politicians and bureaucrats operate in isolation: non-governmental organizations, expert consultants, and scientists are among those who participate in a more general "problematic of improvement" (384). I want to reflect on two ways that I (and other allies of Filipino-Canadian critics of the LCP) may unreflectively participate in "the problematic of improvement" associated with the LCP by unwittingly drawing upon framings of the Philippines and Canada that repeat and reproduce statist ways of knowing. One involves casting the Philippines as a brutal and primitive place from which to flee; the other erases the Philippines altogether.

The tenacity of the first was evident at a conference held in Vancouver in June 2006, focused on the current crises in the Philippines, and designed to invite and gather support from progressive Canadians.[5] After a panel in which the extremity of the current state of political violence in the Philippines was described, a representative from a Canadian organization, Grassroots Women, asked whether this ought to cause Canadian activists to rethink their commitment to scrap Canada's LCP. The question was instructive because it demonstrated how easily Canadians—including progressive Canadians—fall into a framework of liberal humanitarianism, in which the Philippines is cast as monstrous and Canada as a refuge that is preferable under any conditions, including servitude outside of the legal protections of citizenship. This tendency to conceive of the LCP as a type of humanitarian response to the crisis in the Philippines makes it almost impervious to critique, and supports the program on its own transnational itinerary: governments in other countries are currently examining the LCP as a model for their own temporary work visa programs, while within Canada it is now cited as a legitimating prototype for expanding Canada's temporary foreign worker programs (Jimenez 2005).

If humanitarianism is one common posture that feminists from the North take in relation to women from the global South, erasure through a rubric of multiculturalism is another. Gayatri Spivak, for instance, has criticized the tendency to equate globalization with migrancy and diaspora, to ignore rural populations, and to assume "that the entire globe is in a common cultural fix, and its signature is urbanism" (Sharpe and Spivak 2002: 611). Moreover, scholars often cast such urban diasporic communities within the gender-race-class relations of the "receiving" country. Elsewhere Spivak develops this argument through her reading of Jamaica Kincaid's novel *Lucy*, a story of a young woman who leaves Antigua to come to the United States to take up employment as a domestic worker. Spivak criticizes standard U.S. feminist interpretations of the novel for operating within the familiar rubric of race-gender-class. Playing within this "structured ideological field" of well-worn binaries (black/white; poor/rich; periphery/core), Spivak argues, encourages analyses that "remain narcissistic, question-begging" (2000: 335). This is because these analyses return readers to themselves and their own "predicament" of a multicultural society. They treat the migrant as "an effectively historyless object of intellectual and political activism" (2000: 354), thereby reasserting the centrality of the metropolis in the global North and the irrelevance of all places and social relations that lie outside it. But Spivak's point goes beyond this: many overseas migrant workers are themselves middle-class professionals. (For the case of Filipino migrant workers, see Parreñas [2005] and Pratt [2004], although it must be emphasized that many Filipina professionals such as teachers and registered nurses also migrate because of poverty and economic hardship.) If we focus only on their experiences, we miss, in Spivak's view, "the real front of globalization," which she locates in rural areas of the global South (2002: 611).

Locating the "real front" of globalization in one site is hyperbole; the point about erasure of the global South within much feminist scholarship is not. I want to consider how I was operating within this ideological field of erasure-through-multiculturalism when I began the research collaboration with the Philippine Women Centre in 1995, and to describe some of my trajectory toward a transnational analysis.[6] For our first project, as noted earlier, we invited domestic workers, already coming to the center, to join us in recording and analyzing their stories of their experiences under the LCP. Though domestic workers typically began their stories in the Philippines—long before coming to Canada—my memory is that I only started to listen carefully as they described their experiences in Canada. In our early collaborative writing, we described the many ways that Canadian employers violate—and Canadian provincial governments fail to regulate—existing labor laws. We described domestic workers' immense frustration about their deskilling through their time spent completing the LCP requirements. We described the marginalization of Filipino women in Canada in terms of their life in Canada.

Why this lack of curiosity about the Philippines, and blindness to the interconnections between life in Canada and in the Philippines? Similar to the Canadian state, my intellectual jurisdiction seemed to end at the borders of my nation. I offer four explanations for this, one specific to the project, and three of more general relevance for feminist scholarship. First, I understood my focus to be Canadian state policy. Second, and relatedly, penetrating critiques of development discourse (e.g., Cowen and Shenton 1996); of ethnography (e.g., Clifford and Marcus 1986); of a dubious history of complicity between area studies, the discipline of geography, and Cold War politics (Barnes and Farish 2006); and of liberal humanitarianism made a focus on Canada seem more appropriate (and less problematic). And third, this was especially the case because I had not been trained in an area studies tradition. The distinction between particularistic area studies and research in North American and European contexts (often erroneously taken to be less situated and more universal or generalizable) is, of course, precisely one that transnational perspectives attempt to disrupt (Chow 2006), but it remains a powerful organizing schema that I have found difficult to recognize and resist. Fourth, it is now clear to me that I had absorbed what Doreen Massey (2004) has identified as a territorial, locally centered, Russian-doll model of care and responsibility, which she thinks has shaped much ethical thinking in Western contexts: "[f]irst there is 'home,' then perhaps place or locality, then nation, and so on. There is a kind of accepted understanding that we care first about, and have our first responsibilities towards, those nearest in" (8). There is a clear and important geopolitical rationale for a Canadian scholar to concentrate her critique on the LCP rather than, for instance, the Philippine government's Labour Export Policy: it reflects a commitment to investigate exploitation and oppression in a society that prides itself on multiculturalism and social equality rather than displacing attention to other parts of the world. As Rachel Silvey notes there is an important distinction to be made between reflexivity and narcissism.[7] (And it is also for this reason that Spivak's location of the "real front" of globalization in rural areas of the global South seems overdrawn.) But at the same time, an exclusive focus on circumstances in Canada reinscribes the tendency to "constitute our maps of loyalty and affection"—of care and responsibility—within the rhetoric of nation and territory (Massey 2004), and misses the opportunity to develop a more fully transnational agenda

Learning to See (and Act) Transnationally

If I only partially registered the stories told by domestic workers about their lives before coming to Canada, as well as the Philippine Women Centre's strong and well-developed critiques of the IMF, the World Bank, Structural Adjustment Programs, and the Philippine government's Labour Export Policy, I began to listen more closely when working with Ugnayan ng Kabataang Pilipino sa Canada (the Filipino-Canadian Youth Alliance) on the second research project discussed above. This project involved collecting life narratives from Filipino-Canadian youth, most of whom were born and raised in Canada. It is possible that I paid more attention precisely because these youth were born in Canada, and their transnationalism caught me by surprise.

I was struck, for instance, that the play that they wrote, produced, and performed around the time of our research collaboration in 2000 began in the Philippines, with a young woman graduating summa cum laude with a nursing degree. Experiencing difficulties obtaining work in the Philippines, she migrates to Canada under the LCP. Though most of the play took place in her Vancouver apartment after her younger siblings had migrated to join her, it interested me that second-generation youth would choose to narrate their story of racism in Vancouver in the first instance from the vantage point of the LCP. I was struck as well that Ugnayan at that time was dividing its activist energies and resources between antiracism campaigns in Canada and participation in a campaign to oust President Joseph Estrada in the Philippines. When I presented to Ugnayan a first draft of a paper written from our research collaboration, members of the group asked me to "deepen" the analysis by more fully theorizing their lives in Canada within their community's history of forced migration from the Philippines.

It became apparent that, for Ugnayan, transnationalism is a political achievement, and a destination as much as an origin. There are two facets to the transnationalism that Filipino-Canadian youth are striving toward: they are theorizing their situations within a transnational conceptual framework, and they are creating and operating within transnational political networks. As an example of how members of the Filipino-Canadian Youth Alliance explicitly relate their history in Canada to a longer history in the Philippines, the alliance organized its activities to celebrate its tenth anniversary in 2005 under the theme of "Ipagpatuloy: Living the Storm." This referenced the thirty-fifth anniversary of the First Quarter Storm, a three-month period in 1970 of mass mobilization in the Philippines to protest the Marcos regime, and drew a line of continuity between this struggle and their own in Canada. As Charlene Sayo, of the Filipino-Canadian Youth Alliance, explained it:

> In terms of Philippine history, it's the 35th anniversary of the First Quarter Storm. . . . This was at the height of the Marcos era, just around the time that Marcos was about to implement martial law . . . and it's a pivotal point in Philippine history and a lot of Filipino youth really look at that time. That's when youth and students really went out to the streets and it wasn't just rallies. . . . they were protesting and having sits ins . . . in the universities, the students weren't going to school, and a lot of people were being arrested. And so we'd like to integrate that history knowing that this is what we are as a people. Not only is the symbolism strong as youth and students but also this is when a lot of Filipinos were leaving the Philippines to come to Canada. So . . . we also integrate this history and get inspired by it, and integrate it with our own organizing. (Interview, 10 May 2004)

Ugnayan is enfolding and sedimenting its history in Canada within a long and rich genealogy of student struggle in the Philippines. It is constructing Vancouver and the Philippines as a continuous political space insofar as its ten-year anniversary celebration was translated into a key moment in the Philippines' history. Integrating their lives in Canada into a history in the Philippines is important for their sense of identification and belonging, of "knowing that this is what we are as a people." Ugnayan also actively solidifies actual transnational networks by attending international conferences, and sending each year at least one Canadian-born member (and in some years up to three) to the Philippines for an extended period of "integration" into political organizations there.

If second generation youth have the geographical imagination and political commitment to make the connections, how much simpler to envision the transnational lives of domestic workers, who live their lives simultaneously in Canada and the Philippines. As one index of the simultaneity of their transnationalism, in 2003 the PWC staged a political fashion show. They constructed one of the dresses entirely from used overseas telephone cards, gathered from members of SIKLAB, a Filipino migrant workers organization also located at the Kalayaan Centre. It took less than a week to gather the hundreds of cards necessary to construct the dress and matching handbag. This is unremarkable if one considers that roughly 37 percent of those who come through the LCP have left dependents—that is, husbands and/or children—in the Philippines, with whom they are in constant contact (Live-in Caregiver Program Fact Sheet 2005). Recognizing their transnationalism alters the interpretation of their lives in Canada, and unsettles the notion that Canada and the Philippines are discrete national spaces, which can be analyzed separately.

How does a transnational perspective "deepen" our analysis of the LCP and unsettle territorial, Russian-doll models of care and responsibility? Consider the problem of deskilling. Despite the fact that the majority of those registered in the LCP have postsecondary educations, even years after leaving the LCP and securing Canadian citizenship few escape the fate of working as housekeepers and cleaners, or in low-end jobs in the Canadian health care sector. In other words, few regain the occupations for which they were trained in the Philippines. The experience of being in the LCP for a number of years and the impact of state regulations that restrict educational upgrading while registered in the LCP—factors that we emphasized in our early analyses—are clearly important. But it is also true that many Filipinas do not invest heavily in their own "human capital" after leaving the LCP and settling in Canada. If this lack of investment in their own human capital is understood only in terms of their lives in Canada, one might view this as an individual choice for which they must bear responsibility. Situated within their transnational lives, the perspective shifts. The deskilling of women in the LCP is bound up with their ongoing commitments to send remittances to their families in the Philippines and to save to sponsor their families' immigration to Canada. Both sending remittances and saving for their families' immigration leave the women with few financial resources to retrain or upgrade their professional credentials in Canada. Domestic workers recognize the interpretation that Canadians place upon this. In the words of a woman who participated in two of our research projects: "That's really our difference from the whites. They ask, 'How come you're still supporting your family? You have your own life [here in Canada].'" But how should we interpret commitments to send remittances to the Philippines? One interpretation might be to see remittances as yet another sad indication of the destitution of life in the Philippines, or to understand transnational families as the norm for Filipino families (as in, "It's normal for Filipino children to be left with their grandmother or aunt"). But it is important to recognize that the terms of the LCP set by the Canadian federal government—which allow entry of a single worker only (and not her family)—legislate family separation. In other words, it is not just that the situation in the Philippines leads women to come to Canada as domestic workers and to leave their families behind or that this is the norm for Filipino families: the fact that they leave their families in the Philippines is determined by the rules of the LCP. Understanding this deepens an analysis of the extent to which the Canadian state has manufactured Filipino deskilling and marginality in Canada. One could take the analysis of the intertwined histories and futures of Canada and the Philippines even further by considering, for instance, the large presence of Canadian mining interests in the Philippines and their effects of displacing rural communities, which (and this is purely speculative) may fuel the need to immigrate under programs such as the LCP. The point is: the Canadian political economy is intertwined with the Philippines in many different, concrete ways such that our histories and geographies need to be investigated and understood together.[8]

Further, working closely with the PWC has allowed me to see that we are not only researching transnational lives and connections, but our research collaboration is itself a transnational practice that is taken up and reverberates throughout activist networks (even when the research is carried out only in Vancouver). To return to the conference on human rights in the Philippines mentioned earlier, in response to the question about strategy posed by the representative of Grassroots Women, one of the panelists, Maita Santiago, who was at that time secretary-general of Migrante International (international alliance of overseas Filipino workers) based in the Philippines, asserted Migrante's support for the campaign to scrap the LCP, explaining that this is a good example of the importance of research: "it allows us to say that the call to scrap the LCP is the right one." The National Alliance of Philippine Women in Canada (of which the PWC of BC is a member) has also worked closely with six members of the Philippine Congress to introduce Resolution 643 on March 2, 2005, within the Philippine Congress, a resolution "to conduct an investigation, in aid of legislation, into the Live-in Caregiver Program being implemented by the Canadian government." The congressman who introduced the resolution, Crispin Beltran, was arrested illegally and held by the Philippines' national police from February 2006 until June 2007. At the aforementioned conference, Maita Santiago of Migrante International speculated on the links between Resolution 643 and Beltran's arrest, given the importance of remittances from overseas contract workers to the Philippines economy. At the same conference, the chairperson of the Canadian Committee for the Immediate Release of Congressman Beltran traced Congressman Beltran's history in Vancouver, including his keynote address at the opening of SIKLAB in Vancouver in 1995, and his presence at protests surrounding the APEC meetings in Vancouver in 1997. The point, then, is not only that specific actions against the LCP have taken place within a transnational network; actions reverberate throughout the network, can solidify and extend the network in new ways, and become solidified through time. Maita Santiago emphasizes both the importance of research and the role of specific, local campaigns within a transnational field of politics. Situating an analysis of the LCP within a transnational framework opens a network of sites for action and creates opportunities for building solidarities across national borders. Imaginative geographies of belonging and obligation are reconfigured in the process.

Conclusion

Our collaboration—the first participatory research project for each of us—has launched us in new and different directions: for the Kalayaan Centre toward many other research projects, both independently and with other university researchers; for me to retheorize the LCP, and toward a fuller understanding of transnationalism and the possibilities for feminist praxis. We offer no model for collaboration beyond a firm commitment to collectively generate the research focus and methodologies. We have attempted to unsettle expectations about where the problems of collaboration might exist, by questioning the assumption that university researchers always retain control over material resources, or that overcoming differences is the ideal for a close and productive collaborative relationship. Researchers from the global North certainly do have fuller access to research funding, but not exclusively so, at least in the case of a transnational group living and working in Canada, and a distanced academic can have strategic value. Factors that create distance (or friendships and alliances) may not come in expected categories such as race or class or nation.

I have used my own experience as an opportunity to reflect upon the difficulties that feminist scholars from the global North might have envisioning and participating in transnational feminist praxis because of hegemonic ways of seeing the world and academic knowledge production. I brought to our collaboration a body of feminist theory about racial difference in a multicultural society that blinded me to the ways that transnationalism extends and reshapes this theorization. Feminist academics have the responsibility to scrutinize how their geographical imaginations have been shaped by their institutional and national contexts, and the ways that they may (despite their best intentions) see "like the state," whether this be by absorbing and reproducing Russian-doll models of care and responsibility, overgeneralizing the reach of knowledge developed in the global North, erasing the global South, or conceiving places outside the global North through tropes of poverty and underdevelopment. It is difficult to see the assumptions that structure our knowledge (Rose 1997); collaborators situated differently can be helpful guides. Ugnayan's determination to build transnational perspectives and activist lives provided one means for me to see the limits of a multicultural perspective. Organizations at the Kalayaan Centre have challenged me to conceive Canada and the Philippines as interdependent rather than discrete spaces. Grasping these concrete connections resituates the research—away from the helping hand of liberal humanitarianism to an investigation of the ways that this international labor diaspora and the long-term separation of Filipino families are equally structured in Canada and the Philippines.

Witnessing organizations at the Kalayaan Centre circulating our research in transnational feminist networks makes clear two important points: our research is not only about transnationalism—it is a transnational practice; and it is a very small part of a much larger political project. This realization is a fundamental challenge to the individualism of the academy, a system that rewards and celebrates "solo feminism."[9] Working with a community organization is a lesson in working collectively; working with a transnational organization teaches about an even wider world of collaborations. Collaborations with community activists remind feminist academics, not only that there are important things to be done, but that there are important things that they can (and should) be doing through their research practice—which reside far outside their daily struggles in (and the relative comfort of) the academy.

Notes

We would like to thank Kale Bantigue Fajardo, Chris Harker, Rachel Silvey, and Amanda Swarr for comments on an earlier draft of this essay. Thanks so much to Richa and Amanda for inviting us into this rich discussion of feminist transnational collaborations.

1. The conversation took place with Cecilia Diocson (Chair, National Alliance of Philippine Women in Canada), Charlene Sayo (Ugnayan ng Kabataang Pilipino sa Canada/Filipino Canadian Youth Alliance), and Emanual Sayo (B.C. Committee for Human Rights in the Philippines). All of these organizations are housed at the Kalayaan Centre in Vancouver.
2. I thank Rachel Silvey for this point.
3. I received a letter from the ministry two weeks after making an oral presentation without obtaining this approval: "It has come to our attention . . . " I was asked to submit the presentation and to make slight amendments after the presentation had been reviewed.
4. The federal government is responsible for administering the temporary work visa, while the provincial government is responsible for regulating work conditions.
5. The conference, which took place on 21 June 21 2006, was organized under the title: Prospects for Peace, Human Rights and Democracy in the Philippines. For further information, contact bcchrp@kalayaancentre.net.
6. Debts are owed to academic feminists as well, of course, a number of whom have contributed to this volume. For the purposes of this chapter, I am focusing on what I have learned from my research collaborators.
7. Rachel offered this distinction in comments on a draft of this essay, but she explores elsewhere the importance of First World activists investigating exploitation close to home alongside commitments to global justice, specifically in relation to anti-sweatshop activism on her campus (Silvey 2002).
8. This restates the point made in a rich body of scholarship that analyses how colonial relations were coproduced in both the colony and metropole (e.g., Cooper and Stoler 1989; Driver and Gilbert 1998).
9. This is a term that Jennifer Hyndman has used to critique a tendency within the academy to claim ideas as one's own rather than to acknowledge a wider community of feminist scholars.

Works Cited

Barnes, Trevor J., and Matthew Farish. 2006. "Between Regions: Science, Militarism, and American Geography from World War to Cold War." *Annals of the Association of American Geographers* 96(4): 807–826.

Chow, Rey. 2006. *The Age of the World Target: Self-Referentiality in War, Theory, and Comparative Work.* Durham and London: Duke University Press.

Clifford, James, and George E. Marcus. 1986. *Writing Culture: The Poetics and Politics of Ethnography.* Berkeley: University of California Press

Cooper, Frederick, and Ann Laura Stoler. 1989. "Tensions of Empire: Colonial Control and Visions of Rule." *American Ethnologist* 16(4): 609–621.

Cowen, Michael P., and Robert W. Shenton. 1996. *Doctrines of Development.* London and New York: Routledge.

Driver, Felix, and David Gilbert. 1998. "Heart of Empire? Landscape, Space and Performance in Imperial London." *Environment and Planning D: Society and Space* 16: 11–28.

Haraway, Donna. 1988. "Situated Knowledges: The Science Question in Feminism as a Site of Discourse on the Privilege of Partial Perspectives." *Feminist Studies* 14: 575–599.

hooks, bell. 1990. *Yearning: Race, Gender, and Cultural Politics*. Toronto: Between the Lines.

Hyndman, Jennifer. 1995. "Solo Feminism: A Lesson in Space." *Antipode* 27: 197–207.

Jimenez, Marina. 2005. "Canada Opens Door for 700,000." *The Globe and Mail*, 31 October, A1-6.

Li, T. M. 2005. "Beyond 'the State' and Failed Schemes." *American Anthropologist* 107(3): 383–394.

Live-in Caregiver Program Fact Sheet. 2005. Distributed at National Roundtable on the Review of the Live-in Caregiver Program, 13–14 January, n.a., n.p.

Massey, Doreen. 2004. "Geographies of Responsibility." *Geografiska Annaler* B(86): 5–18.

Mohanty, Chandra Talpade. 1991. "Introduction: Cartographies of Struggle: Third World Women and the Politics of Feminism." In Chandra Talpade Mohanty, Ann Russo, and Lourdes Torres, eds., *Third World Women and the Politics of Feminism*. Bloomington and Indianapolis: University of Indiana. 1–47.

Parreñas, Rhacel Salazar. 2005. *Children of Global Migration: Transnational Families and Gendered Woes*. Stanford: Stanford University Press.

Pratt, Geraldine. 2000. "Research Performances." *Environment and Planning D: Society and Space* 18: 639–651.

Pratt, Geraldine. 2004. *Working Feminism*. Philadelphia: Temple University Press.

Pratt, Geraldine, in collaboration with the Philippine Women Centre. 2005. "From Migrant to Immigrant: Domestic Workers Settle in Vancouver, Canada." In Lise Nelson and Joni Seager, eds., *Companion to Feminist Geography*. Malden, MA: Blackwell. 123–137.

Razack, Sherene H. 2004. *Dark Threats and White Knights: The Somalia Affair, Peacekeeping and the New Imperialism* Toronto: University of Toronto Press.

Razack, Sherene H. 1998. *Looking White People in the Eye: Gender, Race, and Culture in Courtrooms and Classrooms*. Toronto: University of Toronto Press.

Razack, Sherene H. 2007. "Stealing the Pain of Others: Reflections on Canadian Humanitarian Responses." *Review of Education, Pedagogy and Cultural Studies* 29: 375–394.

Rose, G. 1997. "Situating Knowledges: Postcoloniality, Reflexivities and Other Tactics." *Progress in Human Geography* 21: 305–320.

Scott, James. 1998. *Seeing Like a State: How Certain Schemes to Improve the Human Condition Have Failed*. New Haven: Yale University Press.

Sharpe, J., and Gayatri Chakravorty Spivak. 2002. "A Conversation with Gayatri Chakravorty Spivak: Politics and the Imagination." *Signs: Journal of Women in Culture and Society* 28: 609–624.

Silvey, Rachel. 2002. "Sweatshops and the Corporatization of the University." *Gender, Place and Culture* 9: 201–207.

Spivak, Gayatri Chakravorty. 2000. "Thinking Cultural Questions in 'Pure' Literary Terms." In Paul Gilroy, Lawrence Grossberg, and Angela McRobbie, eds., *Without Guarantees: In Honour of Stuart Hall*. London and New York: Verso. 335–357.

(4)

Conflicts and Collaborations

Building Trust in Transnational South Africa

SAM BULLINGTON AND AMANDA LOCK SWARR

In contemporary South Africa, progressive coalitional politics are extremely fraught and contentious due to deep divisions and distrust resulting from centuries of colonization and decades of apartheid repression. This chapter explores our navigation of this complicated terrain in our fourteen-year relationship to two social movements (one promoting rights for lesbian and gay South Africans and the other advocating equitable access to AIDS medications for poor people) and their participants. The past two decades have brought dramatic changes in South African history, including the end of apartheid, the passage of the unprecedented sexual orientation clause in South Africa's constitution and a variety of rights to sexual equality won, such as legalized gay marriage, as well as an exponentially worsening AIDS crisis, the denial by former President Mbeki that HIV causes AIDS, and the South African government's resistance to providing antiretroviral medications to stem the devastation. Within our own lives and in the South African communities to which we are allied, organizations folded, relationships broke up, and individuals shifted geographical and class locations, while the dominant frames of poverty and violence have remained consistent threads in our interconnections.

In a dialogic exchange, this chapter considers what it has meant to cultivate these relationships of collaborations over space and time, within an ever-shifting political and material context, marked by ongoing negotiations concerning the meanings of these collaborations. We take "The Place of the Letter: An Epistolary Exchange" (Bammer, Gwin, Katz, and Meese 1998) as our starting point in modeling both the process of collaborating in producing a book chapter and inciting our thinking about how to reframe and rethink ways of writing, building, and sharing ideas collectively. We have collaborated, conducted research, and written together since 1996 and spent months and years together in South Africa in 1997, 1999–2000, 2003, and 2007. Our work together has taken place in multiple locations and communities, including Soweto, Johannesburg, Pretoria, Cape

Town, and Atlantis, South Africa (as well as Minnesota, New York, Missouri, and Washington states). In this capacity, we are deeply invested in and living in multiple communities, predominately communities in conflict, underscored by serious historical divisions and profound mistrust. While we have been attentive to questioning and recreating meanings of transnational academic research, it is frequently our straddling local community boundaries (as well as straddling locations of academic/activist/artist in our home institutions) that prove to be the most stressful and challenging. This chapter highlights the potential for deeply felt shared political and emotional commitments to mediate some of the difficulties of geographical, racial, class, and language discontinuities. We point to successful and unsuccessful ways we've tried to foster trust as the basis of transformative political praxis.

Dear Amanda,

Thank you so much for initiating this dialogue. It is truly a gift to have the opportunity to reflect upon the last decade and my relationship to you and to people in South Africa, as well as the ways that those have always been mutually informing. Our relationships to South African politics, and the kinds of collaborations that were possible, have really changed. I thought I would begin by reflecting on the structure of working in the same place but in different contexts and time periods over the past decade.

During our first visit in 1997 to South Africa to conduct pre-dissertation research, we were primarily involved with self-defined gay and lesbian communities. I was studying lobbying around and the impact of the sexual orientation clause, and you were exploring drag and trying to learn about trans communities that were isolated and hidden. We stayed entirely in Cape Town and spent most of our time in gay-identified spaces—clubs, cafes, bath houses, retail shops—conducting interviews with owners, workers, and patrons. And we quickly realized that "gay and lesbian" meant exactly that. The categories people used to identify themselves and others rarely included "bisexual," "transgender," or "queer," but specifically defined what it meant to be gay or lesbian in the so-called new South Africa.

As part of this trip, we made contact with the gay and lesbian film festival organizers and went to a meeting of the National Coalition for Gay and Lesbian Equality (NCGLE), but the primary gay and lesbian political presence in Cape Town had been the multiracial, politically effective ABIGALE (Association of Bisexuals, Gays, and Lesbians), which in 1997 was in a state of severe decline from which it never recovered. Perhaps due to our status as a couple, our main research collaborators at that time were lesbian couples—a working-class coloured lesbian couple who were founding organizers of ABIGALE, and a middle-class apolitical white lesbian couple who had befriended us and who were going to great lengths to help us with our research—as well as members of the two drag troupes at a community gay bar in downtown Cape Town.

When we returned in 1999 to do our dissertation research, the political landscape had changed considerably. First, many of the activists we had met in Cape Town had moved away from gay and lesbian politics and had formed the Treatment Action Campaign (TAC) to advocate for better access to health care, in particular antiretroviral medications, for people living with HIV. Although we had not prepared to study AIDS politics, we followed the political energy of the time, which led us to become closely involved with TAC, further extending our relationships with activists we had met in 1997 but now in a new context. We also became more closely involved with the NCGLE, in part due to the fact that we amended our research plan to divide our time between Cape Town and Gauteng (Johannesburg, Pretoria, and Soweto), and the National Coalition's main headquarters and influence were in Gauteng.

We began our year and a half of research in Gauteng because of the International Lesbian and Gay Association conference there that we attended (September 1999), and it was during this conference that we connected with most of the people who are our current collaborators and friends. While that included the director of the Gay and Lesbian Organisation of Pretoria (GLOP, now called Out), our biggest surprise was finding a vibrant social network of young lesbians in Soweto and being warmly welcomed by them. This was a collaborative possibility that we never could have dreamed of in Cape Town in 1997 or in our graduate studies at the University of Minnesota. The establishment of connections in Soweto and living there on and off during 1999 and 2000 opened up possibilities for relationships, activism, and collaborations that we continue to cultivate. It was so rare to find white people living in Soweto during that time, I remember that you were once mistaken for an albino and people used to greet us in the streets shaking our hands and shouting about the new South Africa!

By 2003, collaborative opportunities shifted and closed somewhat around gay and lesbian politics. The National Coalition, having established the legal framework it set out to achieve, disbanded and was reconfigured as a small, legally specific NGO called the Equality Project. Meanwhile, the Treatment Action Campaign grew in leaps and bounds, both in size and in prestige, especially after its founder, Zackie Achmat, was nominated for a Nobel

Peace Prize. Their national office became filled with eager undergraduate interns from the most prestigious American universities, all busily working on their individual laptops. While we were lauded as "TAC's first American members," our collaborative involvement with the organization had truly already peaked.

In 2007, new possibilities for collaboration opened up again. While there is some history of transgender organizations in South Africa, these have been mostly in the form of social groups for cross-dressers and are largely defunct. However, between 2003 and 2007, several political and support organizations for transgender individuals have arisen/grown in both Gauteng and Cape Town. They are well organized and politically conscious and, although they are skeptical of American researchers due to the trendiness of transgenderism in the U.S. and the ever-growing presence and irresponsibility of American researchers, we have been well received and trusted—granted legitimacy due to my status as a transsexual and because of our long-standing connection to lesbian and gay communities in South Africa.

It is very exciting to be a part of this new political development in South Africa. And while our previous organizational collaborations have always left me feeling rather ambivalent, mostly due to power differentials and tensions between leadership and grassroots membership (with whom I always felt allied and so I did not feel that comfortable working closely with leadership), the two transgender organizations with whom we recently began working (Gender DynamiX and Budding Roses) do not seem to have any similar tensions. This may be in part due to the reduced racial and class diversity within these organizations. But I feel the potential for a different kind of involvement than we have had with previous social justice movements in South Africa, so I am excited to see what that brings! Already collaborative possibilities are different as two members of Gender DynamiX are coming to Seattle in September [2008] for the international Gender Odyssey conference where my new partner and I will join you and yours.

So, to continue our discussion, I suppose one thing we should establish is what we mean by collaboration, since there are many levels of collaboration happening in our South African research. This is something we have talked about but never put on paper, and I will be interested to hear your current thoughts . . .

Love,

Sam

Dear Sam,

Thank you for sharing your memories of these years and our work together. What many of the pieces in this anthology describe are close collaborations between researchers and organizations. Our research is a little different because, as you describe, we had different kinds of collaborations with several organizations—in fact, organizations dealing with varied issues and often conflicting and competing communities.

On an organizational level, perhaps our closest early involvement was with the domestic violence shelter in a township outside of Cape Town. I know that this collaboration was particularly painful and embarrassing for you. I don't want to betray any confidential details or push you to share things you don't want to share, so you can decide what feels comfortable for you. But, I think the intense conflict that we experienced with the two directors at the time due to their decisions about children in the shelter reminded us of the cultural assumptions that we brought into the situation. What do you remember about this work and what lessons did you learn from it? I know we have talked and written about this, and sharing here might demonstrate the ways that we have learned from our mistakes.

In addition to our collaborations with different organizations that you described, we also engaged in collaborative projects with several individuals. We consistently endeavored to balance our needs as researchers with the personal objectives of those with whom we were working. For instance, the photographs we took both served to document our research as well as affirm lesbian and gay couples, who tended not to have any photographs of themselves together. They also proved useful for drag performers who used our photographs to critique and evaluate their shows. You may or may not remember that the owner of the Brunswick Tavern used our photographs for publicity for his drag shows and one was even published in the *Cape Argus* newspaper ("Glitter Sisters" 1997). I thought this was a form of reciprocity that worked well for us.

Working with individuals, we also entered into two collaborative writing projects, both of which did not have successful outcomes due in part to constraints of time and distance. One of our primary collaborative partners wanted to publish a book about her life but felt discouraged due to her writing skills. So for months and months we met together with a tape recorder, going through her life in extensive detail to later be transcribed and organized into a book project. However, before we could get the material transcribed, we had to return to the U.S. Disruptive circumstances intervened on both sides and the book is disappointingly still in-process seven years later. Similarly, another collaborator was excited to have her life story published in a national South African lesbian magazine, especially as she came out as a butch lesbian in Soweto and subsequently trained to be a *sangoma* (traditional healer) and the magazine featured almost exclusively white middle-class perspectives and concerns. However, soon after we returned to the U.S., before we had a chance to complete the transcribing, the lesbian magazine folded and the story has gone unpublished. Our goal is to continue to reshape such projects and our involvement in South African communities based on the desires of our collaborators. I think that is a big part of how we have built trust in so many different arenas—by working through disappointments and potential conflicts in conversation with our collaborators.

The final collaboration that is essential for us to discuss, and perhaps the most successful, is the one between the two of us. There were immense practical benefits derived from working together. First, we were able to overcome many of the practical barriers we would have faced as individual researchers. Traveling and living together both defrayed costs and increased our sense of safety. Conducting interviews together was logistically easier and surprisingly served to make narrators feel more comfortable than when we interviewed them alone. As you might remember, initially, we both asked questions and took notes. But we found that if one person primarily guided the life history or interview and the other took notes, it was easier to connect with narrators and maintain eye contact.

Our collaborative work also enhanced interviews/life histories and our rapport within communities where we worked. During this collaborative research we were identified publicly as a couple. Much of our research took place in gay clubs and bars, commonly recognized as places to meet sexual/romantic partners, or among people with whom we were asking potentially provocative questions. Being in an established and recognized couple allowed us to approach potential narrators with a request for an interview without it being misconstrued as a romantic advance. While there were times when I was approached romantically, such situations were easily diffused because of our relationship. Our recognition as a couple also made us more visible as lesbians to narrators. Like Kath Weston's scholarship (1991), which you might remember was on our minds when we began this work, our lesbianism, and your transgenderism, allowed for our increased acceptance and legitimacy in gay and lesbian communities. Questions we were asked about our relationship informed us as to the nature of narrators' struggles and their identities.

Our collaboration also enhanced and varied our knowledge of South African contexts and histories. Working collaboratively allowed us to share information, discuss our findings, and come to new understandings together, as well as individually. By collaborating on interviews, life histories, and participant observation we were able to double-check our assumptions and learn about issues not directly related to our respective projects that proved relevant and took us in productive and unexpected directions. For instance, educating myself about nation-building and organizational structures through our collaboration, subjects of your work, highlighted the importance of nationalism and politics to transgendered narrators.

But I hesitate to be too idealistic about our successes because they are always tempered by our failures. I have graduate students who approach me now preparing to do research and who worry about applying their feminist principles to their scholarship. They seem to envision a "perfect" experience. I remind them that research is about making mistakes and that failure is inevitable—but not a bad thing! I think rather than idealism I like embracing failure; this is how we have learned the most.

Earnestly,

Amanda

Dear Amanda,

I am glad that you mentioned what happened in the domestic violence shelter, especially in the context of this reflection about relationships of collaboration. Because, of course, in talking about the transformative potential of deeply felt shared political and emotional commitments, we are taken straight to the importance of emotional involvement. After all, that is what led me/us to abandon my/our research plan and get involved with TAC and with the domestic violence shelter in the first place. I certainly don't think anyone writing in this volume would argue for the kind of psychological distance that many traditional ethnographers advocate, but are there limits to desirable emotional involvement?

I guess I have often thought that academics were too conservative on this point. I am thinking here of someone like Judith Stacey (1991), who seemed to find emotional involvements in a transnational, and hence unequal, context to be rather dangerous to the emotional well-being of those with less power in the situation. Didn't she say something like "the greater the intimacy . . . the greater the danger?" This always seemed to underestimate the agency of those who choose to involve themselves in such long-distance or perhaps temporary relations.

Instead I have been drawn to scholars like Rebecca Campbell (2002)—the book you shared with me about the emotional impact of doing research on rape—who calls on scholars to take a step beyond politically engaged research to "emotionally engaged research." Truthfully, it is this emotional engagement in South Africa that keeps me coming back, not the intellectual explorations that are required of me to maintain my professional status. And I have certainly found that the "ethic of caring" that Campbell talks about was key to how we were able to build trust with our South African collaborators, through different kinds of caring with different kinds of folks at different moments.

However, those experiences in the shelter temper my enthusiastic embracing of heartfelt research and collaborations. While I would say that my ability to empathize was generally my greatest strength in negotiating geographical, racial, class, and language discontinuities, in the shelter, this capacity became destructive and undermined the strong collaborative relationships I was building. Although I was trained as an anthropologist and knew better than to assume what constitutes "appropriate" child-rearing strategies, I became convinced that I was perceiving child abuse by some "universal" standard, and seriously overstepped my bounds in demanding that the shelter act on my perceptions. I became engaged in a power struggle with the managers of the shelter over two young girls, which not only damaged my relationships with the managers (one of whom still will not speak to me), but compromised the autonomy of the organization. It was the only time I felt like the ugly American. Although our relationship with the other manager has continued to grow and long ago moved beyond this incident—she even took us to visit the girls in their new foster home—it serves as a sober reminder to me of the limits of desirable emotional involvement.

Thanks for bringing in the whole spectrum of our experience,

Sam

Dear Sam,

Yes, in so many ways conflict and failure were always present in our South African collaborations. What I am excited about in writing this piece together is using this space to move away from thinking of conflict as inherently problematic, especially as an antidote to popular idealistic views of collaboration. Collaboration is messy! It was messy between the two of us when there was intimacy, equality, and commonality, and it was even more complex in the kinds of collaborations we entered into across time and space in South Africa in a context and history of massive distrust.

Even during our first trip to South Africa together, we heard stories of a filmmaker who had recently come to South Africa for the first time and held a workshop for South African lesbians. They told us how they were filmed during this workshop and learned a little about filmmaking themselves. But they were shocked when they attended a public event and saw that a film had been made using footage from this workshop and that they were featured in it!

We heard again and again of researchers from the United States and Europe who had come to South Africa, interviewed gays and lesbians there, and left within weeks, never to return. Research doesn't occur and is not published in a vacuum, so these so-called informants would later see papers published by "experts" who they knew had only been in South Africa for a few weeks. This kind of exploitative research set an understandably distrustful tone between South African activists and researchers that we consistently and patiently tried to overcome.

But I think that we have learned some of our most valuable lessons and built some of the strongest bonds of trust we have through conflicts. Your detailed memories of these incidents are always so descriptive. Besides the shelter, what specific conflicts can you remember in which we were directly involved?

Sincerely,

Amanda

Dear Amanda,

You are right about conflicts being integral to our research; even our relationship with our primary collaborators, Derese and Trish, began with disastrous misunderstandings! Remember how we met them after a long day of interviews in 1997? We were at the offices of a prominent organization in Cape Town for our final interview of the day. The white woman we were interviewing suddenly decided we needed to hear "the black perspective" and abruptly took us across the hall to see two women she had yelled at earlier to turn down their music. I was so embarrassed as we barged into their apartment, where one of the women was unenthusiastically slumped on the couch watching *Days of Our Lives* and the other was in the kitchen preparing dinner. We were introduced and left there!

These two women were gracious enough to lethargically answer our unplanned questions, despite wanting to watch their soap opera. Although it was obviously a burden, they were trying hard to be hospitable. With a feeling of dread, we gradually realized that the subject of their exchanges in Afrikaans was the extra food they had put on for dinner so that we could stay—except that we already had dinner plans with someone else! When we eventually announced that we had to leave, it was clearly an insult.

This type of communication pattern repeated over the next few weeks. Numerous times when we were visiting with them, Derese would disappear into the bedroom, make a phone call in Afrikaans, and return, announcing, "It is settled then," committing us to social plans without telling us what she was doing. We would invariably have to decline because we already had an interview set up with someone else. On one occasion, upon leaving them, I remarked, "See you later!" I had no way of anticipating that they would interpret my casual American farewell as a literal statement and prepare food for our return. Our miscommunications led to endless ruptures in our relationship, and I found our encounters to be unpredictable and exhausting and began to dread them. Little did I know they would come to be like trusted family members over the following decade.

Those were conflicts that we were part of, but so much of our research and attempts at collaboration were negotiated in the midst of conflict. I think I know what stands out in your mind: the fistfights that we witnessed! Probably the one that you remember most took place at the concert at On Broadway—a cabaret venue in Cape Town—because you nervously ended up in the restroom with both participants, hoping to stay out of the escalating arguments and ending up in the middle of them! I do believe we snuck out the back door that night. But that conflict—a fistfight between an upper-class male to female (MTF) transsexual we knew and another friend of ours dressed in drag—taught us so much about the class connotations involved in gender transgression in Cape Town.

You may remember that the fight started when our acquaintance, Vita, who was sitting at our table, called our friend a "common drag queen." We did not realize at the time that there was a class/race hierarchy between those who performed drag for pay at one of the cabarets (drag artists) and those who dressed in drag in their everyday life (drag queens), which you eventually wrote about (Swarr 2004). While we later might have expected this kind of exchange between, for instance, one of the white performers at On Broadway and one of the black or coloured drag queens from the townships who would hang around at Derese and Trish's place, the fact that it involved Vita, who was a MTF transsexual lesbian, made it especially interesting. While in the U.S. there is a definite hierarchy between transgendered folks who pursue medical intervention and those who are cross-dressers or "just gender queer," in South Africa this was not really a factor since most transsexuals were isolated from gay and lesbian communities.

Of course, the other fistfight was at the International Lesbian and Gay Association (ILGA) conference, after the protest at the plenary session by the black lesbians from the townships. This incident was also extremely illuminating to me because it really pointed to the depth of division and distrust among South African queer communities. There were so many layers of pain involved in that situation. At first it was confusing to me. Why were black lesbians standing up in the plenary session saying that black lesbian voices were not being heard when we were in the process of voting a South African black lesbian to the prestigious position of cochair to the international organization? It is embarrassing now that I didn't get it at the time, but we were not alone in being confused! Most of the delegates in the room looked puzzled, including the moderator—which is why he asked everyone else to leave the room so that the South Africans could "get their house in order."

What followed illuminated the gender and class tensions among the South African delegates. The fistfights actually took place between black lesbians from Soweto and the two male leaders of the National Coalition (one black and one coloured). The women lashed out in the pain and anger of rejection after being dismissed and told that they were "nothing" by the two men. Although part of the explicit mission of the National Coalition was grassroots empowerment, including the development of lesbian leadership, the arrogant attitude of the male leaders revealed more about the actual priorities of the organization. The National Coalition was seen to promote not only gendered interests but class ones, too, focusing, as it did, on such middle-class issues as pensions and immigration rights for foreign same-sex partners. Indeed, the catalyst for the township lesbians speaking out was the alienation they felt from the well-educated professional activist who was about to be elected ILGA cochair. Although she was also a black lesbian, and had grown up in the townships, she had been groomed by the NCGLE, which they felt was tokenistic, during the organization's constitutional lobbying and had accessed all sorts of opportunities as a result (including traveling and meals with Nelson Mandela). The group of lesbians who stood up felt that she no longer represented them.

In South Africa after apartheid, these kinds of class alienations can happen very quickly. Remember when we were invited to that meeting of Sistahs Kopanang, a black lesbian organization in Joburg in the late 1990s? Members spent most of the meeting trying to decide where they were going to hold their upcoming social function. The lesbians who lived in town wanted to hold it in town, but those who had come in from Soweto for the meeting protested due to the time and especially expense of traveling to town. The town lesbians, however, were very uncomfortable with the idea of going to the townships to socialize, citing that they did not feel safe there (despite living there themselves up until quite recently!). These are not entrenched divisions between professionals and working classes but extremely recent distinctions between those who are unemployed and those who found urban jobs—sometimes administrative, but more often fast food or domestic service work. The overlay of class onto geography changes peoples' perspectives and complicates efforts to organize for progressive social change.

Similar tensions are what destroyed ABIGALE in Cape Town as well. ABIGALE had historically been led by coloured members, due to particularities of its founding. However, around the time we entered the scene—1997—several young black gay men led an uprising of sorts to change the composition of the leadership. And there were harsh accusations, including those of financial impropriety, on both sides that led to so much heartache and the demise of one of the most innovative and powerful gay and lesbian organizations in South Africa's history. The kinds of distrust and resentment that we witnessed are a legacy of the differential treatment blacks and coloureds received under apartheid. Although much national (and global) attention is focused on legacies of racial pain and distrust between blacks and whites, the bitterness and suspicion between blacks and coloureds is rarely addressed, with sad results.

With a heavy heart,

Sam

Dear Sam,

The obvious impact of apartheid history is not surprising, but it is distressing. And the resulting tensions played such a big role in our research and efforts at collaboration. For months after the ILGA conference when we would interview people, what happened at ILGA was the primary issue they wanted to talk about. And it was so polarizing—either you supported the National Coalition or you were against it. That made it a tricky terrain for us to navigate. The work of the Coalition was central to your research (and global assessments of the NCGLE were almost exclusively celebratory), and I know that you had hoped to have a closer collaboration with these activists. You thought that investigating the grounded impact of the sexual orientation clause in the constitution would be helpful to their work. However, after the drama at ILGA, we did not want to be too closely identified with the coalition as that would just alienate us from other communities that we cared about, such as the community of lesbians in Soweto with whom we were building trust. It was stressful—especially at events like Pride where the multiple communities that we were working with came together in the same place. I dreaded those events!

There were also two examples of communities in transnational conflict during our research—the Treatment Action Campaign versus the South African government and the U.S. and South African treatment access activists versus conservative patent laws—both over AIDS politics that we were part of on a broader scale. While we were conducting our dissertation research in 2000, two court cases occupied much of our attention. First, TAC took the South African government to the Constitutional Court to force them to provide drugs to prevent mother-to-child transmission of HIV. You might remember that we did research on breastfeeding, nutrition, and voluntary testing and counseling for TAC in preparation for the court case, and TAC was eventually victorious, but only after many angry pickets (that we were also a part of) and disheartening negotiations.

In addition, around the same time a group of thirty-nine pharmaceutical companies came together and brought a court case against the South African government over their national legislation that would allow generic medications to be produced. We had to return to the U.S. before the resolution of this case, but we were able to continue collaborating with TAC long-distance. Upon returning to the U.S., we learned that our home institution, the University of Minnesota, actually held the patent on a very expensive antiretroviral drug marketed by Glaxo-Smith Kline. With another graduate student, Adam Sitze, we founded the Minnesota AIDS Action Coalition to bring local attention to the situation in the global South concerning AIDS treatment access, to highlight the role of the University of Minnesota in the transnational crisis, and to pressure the university to nullify its patent on their drug in low-income countries.

Inspired by a similar situation unfolding at Yale—where student activists were successful in changing not only university attitudes, but pharmaceutical policies—and in close contact with TAC for strategic guidelines, we spoke on campus at meetings, rallies, teach-ins, panel discussions, and in classes. Adam and I orchestrated a campaign that gained international media attention (Adams 2001; *As It Happens* 2001; Borger 2001; Marshall 2001; Zimmerman 2001). You cultivated political allies among other local social justice organizations. And eventually we met with university administrators and achieved some success, though never with as great effect as at Yale.

Although we were thrilled to have a means to continue our collaboration with TAC after returning to the U.S., it was during these times that I felt the distance most strongly. I can remember when the Pharmaceutical Manufacturers Association announced that it was dropping the case against the South African government, due mostly to the public embarrassment they had suffered at the hands of global AIDS activists. We called Derese and Trish, and while we could hear the joy in their voices, and the sound of celebrations in the background, we felt extremely sad to not be able to be there with them. A number of years later, when the Constitutional Court finally ordered the South African government to institute a national roll-out of antiretrovirals, there was no celebratory phone call with Derese and Trish. We did not even find out about the judgment until several days later, as we were so caught up in the demands of our personal lives and academic responsibilities in Minnesota.

The transnational component of our research has had its drawbacks and benefits. We are never fully present in one place because of our commitments and collaborations, but we benefit from being part of something bigger than we are, of being involved in struggles for political, social, and economic justice.

Reflectively,

Amanda

Dear Amanda,

I remember those times of distance with a confluence of emotions—sadness, guilt, anxiety, sometimes anger. They happened even when we were living in South Africa. Remember when we spent several months in Cape Town setting up our apartment and getting established and were away from Gauteng much longer than we had anticipated? When we finally returned, we discovered that one of our closest collaborators had tried to commit suicide and had decided to become a *sangoma*! I felt like we had missed so much—and I felt bad for not being a better friend and support for her. Similarly, when we returned in 2003 to find another friend financially taking care of her family while her sister was dying of AIDS, it broke my heart to have to go back to the U.S. while her sister's life hung in the balance. I can remember calling her from the Johannesburg airport to get the last report before getting on the plane. I think she died just a few days after we returned to the States. My heart always feels divided among multiple locations, but my body can only be in one place at a time.

Because of the distance, I am always amazed that when we return to South Africa, we are always so warmly received. I always have the best intentions about staying in better touch with people when I return to the U.S., but there are so many demands on my time, especially now that I am junior faculty and under the constant pressure of tenure. South Africa can feel so far away sometimes in the face of so many immediate crises competing for my attention, and it is so difficult to maintain the kind of intimacy that I feel with people over the bad connection of my cell phone or letters delayed by weeks or months—and that is when I am able to track people down, which isn't even always possible! So I always expect people to be angry with us for being away for so long. But they just seem amazed and happy (usually weeping!) that we keep returning!

And despite the dramatic changes that usually have taken place in our lives since our last time together, we seem to easily pick up again with one another—perhaps cognizant of the fact that we only have a few weeks together every few years, so we aren't going to waste them! I suppose that is not unlike the rhythm of our relationship as well. Although when we began our collaboration in South Africa in 1997, we were life partners attending graduate school together, by the time we returned in 2003, you had finished your PhD and were moving to New York City for a two-year postdoc at Barnard College. We spent those two years exploring the dynamics of togetherness and separateness, of intimacy and absence, which required the same kinds of skills that we had developed through our collaborations in South Africa. In 2005, you relocated to Seattle for a tenure-track position and just weeks before I headed to Missouri to begin my own faculty position, we finally broke up after an intense decade-long relationship.

After a profound gap of silence, we decided to pick up again with one another and last year that took us back to South Africa. It was this return that made me the most nervous! It had been our longest time away, largely due to all of the personal upheavals. You were bringing along your new partner and I did not know how that would be received among our communities of collaboration, or how it would feel to travel with the two of you. And, in the interim, I had initiated my gender transition and was not only living as a man, but now, due to the influence of my testosterone shots, looked and sounded like one, too! Much of the trust that I had with South African communities resulted from our common identities as lesbians.

However, I think this time we were even more warmly received. Ironically, I was more popular with South African lesbians as a man! Traveling with, but not a part of, a couple gave me a different kind of vantage point on the communities of which we are a part and a refreshing autonomy in my relationships with our collaborators. And I found that some people were disappointed, but not due to our long absence. Instead, many friends expressed sadness that we did not reach out to them after the break up. Although much of my reason for distancing myself from folks I knew in South Africa was because they were so associated with you that it would have been too painful, these comments did prompt me to pause and consider what I mean by friendship and family in South Africa, how those friendships might be different in my mind than my friends in my home environment— due to the impact of distance, of various inequalities, of my professional association with them.

Lots more to think about!

Sam

Dear Sam,

Since you started these reflections, I think I should wrap them up for now. I think one of the most important lessons we have learned from this process is how to build trust and manage conflict. Trust is not something that can be easily explained or can be given freely, so we have worked to earn it with each other and with our collaborators. Sometimes we've succeeded, sometimes we haven't. Most of our successes in gaining trust have been achieved through our openness and vulnerability, as well as our willingness to be part of people's lives.

But sometimes we've failed, and these failures have led to important, if poignant, lessons about ourselves and our positionalities. We have learned that we are both giving and receiving as part of our research—it's never a one-way exchange—and that this balance must be constantly cultivated and negotiated, especially given our location in the global North. We have learned that we can develop trust, but we can't accurately predict what will happen within relationships: our own, those of the people around us, and among political organizations. And we have learned that we will make mistakes. We will hurt people's feelings. We will break trust without even intending to. Sharing these failures with our collaborators directly and not hiding under a guise of ideal research is the best way to explicate and undermine such failures.

I appreciate you and our work together over this past decade. It has not been easy work, but I wouldn't trade it for anything.

Not the end,

Amanda

Works Cited

Adams, Bob. 2001. "One World and One Fight." *HIV Plus Magazine* 4(5): 24–27.

As It Happens, Canadian Public Radio. 2001. Amanda Swarr interviewed by Mary Lou Finlay on Abacavir and activism at the University of Minnesota. April 10.

Bammer, Angelika, Minorse Gwin, Cindi Katz, and Elizabeth Meese. 1998. "The Place of the Letter: An Epistolary Exchange." In Susan Hardy Aiken, Ann Birgham, Sallie A. Marston, and Penny Waterstone, eds., *Making Worlds: Gender, Metaphor, Materiality*. Tucson: University of Arizona Press. 161–202.

Borger, Julian. 2001. "Students Take on Glaxo." *UK Guardian*, April 19.

Campbell, Rebecca. 2002. *Emotionally Involved: The Impact of Researching Rape*. New York: Routledge,.

"Glitter Sisters Open a New Show." 1997. *Cape Argus*, Cape Town, South Africa, Friday, July 18, Tonight Section 1, 4.

Marshall, Eliot. 2001. "Universities, NIH Hear the Price Isn't Right on Essential Drugs." *Science Magazine* 292(5517): 614–615, April 27.

Stacey, Judith. 1991. "Can There Be a Feminist Ethnography?" In Sherna Berger Gluck and Daphne Patai, eds., *Women's Words: The Feminist Practice of Oral History*. New York: Routledge. 111–119.

Swarr, Amanda Lock. 2004. "*Moffies*, Artists, and Queens: Race and the Production of South African Gay Male Drag." *Journal of Homosexuality* 46(3/4): 73–89.

Weston, Kath. 1991. *Families We Choose: Lesbians, Gays, Kinship*. New York: Columbia University Press.

Zimmerman, Rachel. 2001. "Student Protesters Target Universities Profiting From AIDS Research." *Wall Street Journal*. April 12: B1, B4.

⟨ 5 ⟩

Feminist Academic and Activist Praxis in Service of the Transnational

LINDA PEAKE AND KAREN DE SOUZA

Touch paper—a small piece of paper on one end of a firework, which you light in order to start the firework burning: The instructions on the fireworks said, "Light the blue touch paper, and stand well clear."

In this chapter we address the nature of our collaboration as a black activist in the Guyanese women's organization Red Thread, and as a white British academic in a Canadian university who works with Red Thread. In so doing we investigate the dialogic aspects of our political journeys as collaborators and attempt to capture some of the ways in which we bump up against and challenge each other's political and social locations and intellectual and emotional priorities in our "alliance work," We suggest that our dialogues are marked by productive tensions (hopefully reflected throughout the chapter in the account of our journeys together but most specifically in the list of questions we end the chapter with) that have enabled us to identify some of the most pressing political questions about feminist research and activism that largely prevent dialogues from happening between Northern-based academic feminists and Southern-based activist organizations/movements.

Our aim here is to discuss a specific type of transnational feminist practice, that between feminist academics and activists in the global North and South, in relation to the research process itself, and its function as a touch paper serving to ignite and throw into sharp relief a number of issues: political, epistemological, and methodological. In other words, rather than privilege the products of our research, we focus instead on the political and intellectual interventions that are enabled by our collaboration, proving that one can never "stand well clear" of the racialized, classed, gendered, and transnational power relations that saturate the research in which we have engaged.

We first met in Guyana when we were both in our mid-twenties and where our mutual interest in left-wing politics set the stage for a potential friendship and working partnership.[1] It should come as no surprise that, over the twenty years we have known each other, the last fifteen of which we have been working together, the nature of our collaboration has—at times—taken front stage, relegating its products to the background. And although it is a collaboration based on solidarity, love, friendship, and laughter, it has also been characterized, as are many relations, by silences, intense inequalities, difficult discussions about racism/whiteness, and profound differences. All of these issues, as always, are played out through individuals' embodied interactions and lives but they all also speak to manifestations of classed, racialized, gendered, and transnational power relations that resound and circulate on a number of scales beyond that of the embodied individual and of relationships between individuals.

We started out working together very specifically being interested in the research results and the efficient working of the research team we started up together in Red Thread. But we have ended up questioning a much broader set of interests in terms of the power dynamics of the research process itself (albeit at Karen's insistence that these discussions were usually distractions from the daily process of survival in a country whose people she describes as "drowning") and which we think overlaps with a major, and recurring, tension between northern academic feminists' reflexive discussions of power in the research process and their (ironic, often unintentional) estrangement from the political struggles of survival in scenarios where people/communities are, indeed, "drowning." In this chapter we discuss four aspects of the power dynamics of the transnational research processes in which we have engaged: how the research process has been further complicated by the NGOization of development; how we have interrogated the feminist production of knowledge; the links between activism, social change, and research; and addressing dimensions of power raised by the research that also speak to silences within Red Thread. Prior to discussing these issues we give a brief contextualization of Guyana and an overview of the work and mandate of Red Thread.

Red Thread in Guyana

Guyana is a country carved out of transatlantic processes of domination and oppression; it is a product of the interrelated processes of the genocide of Amerindian populations, the genocidal slave trade from Africa, and the importation of the indentured labor of people from India, Portugal, and

China. Dogged by low prices for its exports of bauxite, timber, and sugar, as well as internal corruption, it is currently embroiled in a downward spiral of narco violence, criminal activity, and political/ethnic conflict, all of which are increasingly militarized and overlapping. Health care and education are on the verge of collapse, and there is general agreement that it is the informal sector—the smuggling of people, gold, and cocaine—that dominates the economy. The dominance of political life since Independence in 1966 first by the Afro-Guyanese–supported Peoples National Congress, and since 1992 by the Indo-Guyanese–supported Peoples Progressive Party, has effectively prevented the development of a political culture in which movements (e.g., trade union movement, women's movement, and so on) and organizations that people form and direct, such as the ones they create for practical purposes (e.g., Friendly and Burial Societies), could sustain themselves. It is in this culture that Red Thread has, for the last twenty years, struggled to survive.

From independence in 1966 until the late 1980s Guyana was officially a cooperative socialist republic. As in many countries in the 1980s with a socialist ideology, women's organizations were restricted to religious organizations, trade unions, and wings of political parties. Red Thread emerged in October 1986; it came into existence through the decision of a small, highly educated and politically grounded group of women who had the information, the resources, and the experience necessary for its establishment. Its founders were active members or supporters of the Working People's Alliance (WPA), who had learned from experience that this form of organizing could not specifically focus on the needs of women. Cognizant of the growing impoverishment of women in the 1980s, they disbanded the Women's Section of the WPA and formed the autonomous organization Red Thread, thereby creating the space to raise gender issues that would not be relegated to the back burner of party politics.

Since their establishment Red Thread has had a mercurial existence not only in terms of activities but also in terms of numbers. Currently they form a collective of approximately twenty members, mostly based in Guyana but also including Guyanese and non-Guyanese women in the diaspora. Around this core collective is a set of national, regional, and transnational networks of women associated with Red Thread in one or more of its programs. This small number is a substantial reduction from the 1980s when over two hundred women were involved; the fall in numbers reflects the change in focus from income generation projects to one of activist research and advocacy and community-based interventions. However, these numbers give no indication of the extensiveness and high profile of Red Thread's activities on a regional and global basis. From its inception Red Thread has always engaged in transnational politics, both within and beyond the Caribbean. The organization is currently, for example, a part of the Global Women's Strike, most recently attending the World Social Forum with the Strike in Venezuela in 2006.[2]

Since the early 1990s, starved of funds and working almost entirely on the basis of voluntary labor, Red Thread has scaled down its outreach operations, but the terrain of Red Thread is still one of doing: organizing with local communities, conducting workshops, devising radio skits, performing popular theater, writing and disseminating informational pamphlets, recording life histories, and producing academic and policy reports as well as letters and articles in the press have positioned Red Thread as a significant broker of public opinion.[3] Its members have also been at the forefront of advocating, designing, and producing for popular dissemination legislative information pertaining to the laws of Guyana and women's legal rights. They have conducted educational and training workshops promoting leadership formation and skill transfer; they give advice, help, and immediate support to individual women; and they do advocacy work around issues of poverty, domestic violence and child abuse, the environment, women's work, health care, and literacy. Red Thread has always been a place where women can access social networks, practical help, and analytical skills, providing the opportunity for reflection, analysis, and assessment of what has been taken for granted. All too aware of the fragmented nature of marginalized women's practices, members emphasize that their group strength is an important asset and resource at their disposal. Over the years its politics have moved beyond being articulated by only its middle-class members to include those of its grassroots members, resulting in a more direct reflection of its politics in the work that it does. It has always had intersectionality at its heart and it is still the only women's organization in the country that sets itself the goal of working with women across racialized, classed, and geographical divides.

Arguably, many of these activities have now become part of an NGOized bureaucracy in many parts of the global South, but Red Thread has resisted being defined as an NGO and risk having its agenda skewed by efforts to appease donors rather than the grassroots women with whom it works. Its commitment is to a viable state of development in the country that places poor women and their needs at the center of state policies recognizing that the "care" work in which they engage is the very core of development (see table 5.1, which outlines the aims of Red Thread). Given the polarized and racialized political party structure the country inherited it also attempts to

Table 5.1   The Aims of Red Thread

1. To work for women's unwaged and low-waged, caring work to be revalued and properly remunerated and for equal pay for work of equal value.

2. To work against all forms of violence, especially against women and children, beginning with domestic violence and violence during racial and/or political conflict, and to support victims of such violence.

3. To build solidarity among women across divides and to oppose all forms of discrimination including that on the grounds of sex, race, class, dis/ability, age, sexual identity, and HIV status.

4. Wherever possible, to provide individual women and groups of women with the information, skills, and other support they need to fight against economic, social, and political injustices.

5. To develop, evaluate, and share the lessons of projects addressing key issues including grassroots women's income generation, women's health, and children's literacy.

work across classed and racialized divides that serve to separate women and communities by engaging in acts of citizenship building that create more equitable social relations and communities. Furthermore, its analysis of international relations places it firmly in an antiglobalization framing in relation to the projects of neoliberal capitalist development and modernization.

Productive Tensions and Pressing Questions

It is now fifteen years since we started to work together, establishing the research team in Red Thread, providing us with many occasions to work through the various issues that circulate within our "activism/academia" transnational feminist practice. We turn now to brief synopses of some of the issues that our collaboration has forced us to address. As we stated earlier, exploring the whys and hows of the manner in which we work through these issues is a primary goal of this chapter. These include thinking through how the North and South dimensions of our collaboration relate to each other, understanding how the battles of daily life in the South are being fought out between communities and governments in ways that feminist academia in the North has largely ignored, and working through the ways in which nonexploitative personal and professional relations (on both sides) can be developed.

The NGOization of Development

Since the 1980s, NGOs increasingly have become the vehicles through which funding for development is delivered. Despite the diversity among NGOs and their funders, the extent to which NGOs have become corporatized, acting as arms of the state and playing an active part in the downloading of labor and costs from the state to local communities, is well documented (Farrington and Bebbington 1993). Our concerns with the NGOization of development are twofold.

First, in terms of the increasing utilization of NGOs to carry out development projects, Red Thread, as we stated earlier, is not an NGO. Its history of political engagement and a determination to define its own agenda has enabled Red Thread to resist its incorporation into the NGO sector with all the attendant issues of incorporating activism into an institutional framework that has increasingly come to mimic that of state bureaucracies. But its lack of official status has caused problems with some donors refusing to give monies to Red Thread unless it officially registers for NGO status. Hence, Red Thread suffers from circumscription of funding because of its refusal to make itself accountable to certain donors, not in the sense of drawing up accounts but of being drawn into a process of "moral accountability" (Hilhorst 2003) whereby donors have a role to play in negotiating the meaning and legitimacy of Red Thread's activities.[4] But neither is Red Thread prepared to accept that funding should be the major determinant of what work they do.

Bargaining and negotiating in terms of access to acceptable funding, however, have become increasingly problematic and time consuming, and while this does not necessarily compromise feminist transnational praxis, it has caused us to consider how feminist academic activism can so easily turn into feminist academic colonization. For example, one research project in which we engaged was funded by an international organization that was prepared to accept Red Thread's non-NGO status but which stipulated that the research contract had to label Linda as the "consultant," the so-called expert in charge of the project who was "authorized" to "employ" Red Thread members. There were also further stipulations that a certain (large) percentage of the research monies had to be spent on the consultant's fee. It was impossible to label the northern-based consultant and the southern-based counterpart as equal partners and certainly Red Thread could not be seen as essential to the project's success; the research contract necessitated a hierarchization of the research team in which the North/South and academic/activist divides were further solidified. It was only after much discussion in which Linda agreed to donate her "fee" to Red Thread that we could both feel comfortable enough to accept the research contract. This and other experiences have led to Red Thread no longer agreeing to work with individuals or organizations who offer to pay them a stipend without disclosing the total amount of the grant they have and the proportion that is going to Red Thread compared to the proportion going to consultants, graduate students, coapplicants, and others associated with the research.

A second concern with the increasing corporatization of NGOs is with the attendant practices of establishing targets and measurable outcomes, of making development "sustainable" while at the same time neatly packaging it up into projects that deal, for example, with "women" or other apparently discrete aspects of development for disconnected periods of time without reference to how the organization is supposed to sustain itself outside of funding cycles. The ability to deal with the consequences of this funding model for development—in other words, of dealing with the in-between-ness of projects that does not fit into neatly circumscribed categories—is an issue that we have increasingly had to address by redistributing funds from funded projects to support the basic needs of Red Thread, such as having a building to work from and being able to provide wages for its members "between projects." Yet increasing accountability to donors means being subversive about this, and this is something we both resent, revealing as it does that donors not only influence agendas for development but also impact upon the everyday practices and the meanings that NGOs attach to their organization.

Interrogating Feminist Knowledge Production
in Academia and in Red Thread

Although the NGOization of development goes some way to explaining Red Thread's inability to develop a constant flow of funds into the organization, and hence, of being able to craft a research agenda that addresses the needs of Red Thread, feminist academia has also played a role in this process, and it is to this that we now turn. While Red Thread members had conducted research investigating and publishing life histories of Guyanese women, the Research Team was largely established at Linda's instigation and her need to establish a research agenda as part of a process of securing tenure and promotion. Hence, the timing of research projects has mostly been dictated by funding sources and career trajectories in the North as opposed to Red Thread setting out its own research agenda. In other words, research serves what is external to Red Thread in the sense that it produces analyses that can be used by academics and agencies but not always by Red Thread, whose members can exhaust themselves doing the research and at the end have neither the energy nor the resources to implement transformative practices.

Feminist academics in the North have privileges; even when they are not equally distributed they are likely to be available in greater supply in a country such as Canada relative to those for feminists of all classes in a country such as Guyana. These privileges come from political liberties that include the freedom of speech and freedom from persecution; from economic liberties that include freedom from hunger, homelessness, and poverty; and from social liberties that include access to facilities, education, and training, as well as access to information, and often access to monies. In addition to these privileges, it has also been argued that the increasing institutionalization of feminist academic research in departments of women's studies has resulted in a situation that serves to profit individual women's careers rather than promoting social change. The academic feminist label, for many activist organizations, now has the baggage of careerism, of maintaining the status quo, and of rising to the top rather than aiming for transformation. Certainly, Red Thread's view on Caribbean feminism, while not subscribing to a simple dichotomy between northern feminists (as exploiters) and southern women (as victims), emphasizes its irrelevance, an exclusive club-cum-career path for both northern and, increasingly, southern feminists, increasingly incorporated into the institutionalized world of NGOs as corporate managers or consultants, who often exhibit a lack of consciousness about class privilege and complacency around social change, and who fail to acknowledge their inability to speak for all women.

But this is not to argue that all the benefits of "collaborative research" go to feminist academics and none to Red Thread members. The setting up of the research team was a mutual agreement between us in that participation in the research provided skills development to women in Red Thread that has led to a range of material benefits.[5] So while the results of the many research projects we have conducted have obviously been of interest to Red Thread, it has also been the case that research has continued because it has also provided members with periods of employment such as with United Nations organizations or other international organizations, such as the Department for International Development (DfID), and academics, from the United States, United Kingdom, and Canada, who have wanted to utilize the research skills and contacts of Red Thread.[6] Moreover, throughout the 2000s Red Thread has increasingly engaged in research practices that relate directly to their own desires to know more about situations that will further their community-based work, for example, on women's unpaid reproductive labor and on initiatives to bring women together across racialized divides.

As beneficiaries of research women in Red Thread are not only paid research workers but are also redefining their subjectivities and seeing themselves as knowing subjects—asking questions, setting agendas, and becoming increasingly unwilling to accept that their everyday lives are irrelevant to knowledge production. For example, Red Thread members met with students from the University of Guyana in a joint seminar. It was here that Cora from Red Thread, a working-class black woman with seven children, but with no schooling beyond primary level, questioned the students in a discussion about how family units were defined.[7] The students insisted that only blood members constituted family, albeit living themselves in a society where many variations on the Western-based notion of the nuclear family existed, but Cora continued to insist on defining Karen as a member of her family given the central role she played in her life. On another occasion Cora had a conversation with Linda about how she perceived her as being racist for spending more time with the Indo-Guyanese women in Red Thread than the Afro-Guyanese women. Cora's work in Red Thread over the years had provided her with the confidence and ability to use her own life experiences to give voice to her beliefs and to question the attitudes and practices of others.

However, the creation of a new class of women who can produce their own knowledge and engage in research, and who can be seen as having income generating skills usually reserved for an academic elite, has also created its own problems and is something that Red Thread has struggled with: while Red Thread started off by organizing with grassroots women, there is an ever present danger that without consciousness and questioning of its politics, it will end up creating an elite group of the grassroots instead of promoting an engagement working with women like themselves to promote change for everyone's benefit. The implication for transnational feminist praxis is that we need to think more deeply about how the research process itself is reproducing hierarchies—academic feminists versus activists and elite grassroots women versus other grassroots women—and creating the very same kind of divides that Red Thread is actively trying to work against. Our focus is now on imagining what an alternative set of research priorities might look like, ones, for example, that accept measuring transformative practices, moral accountability, and self-empowerment as the fundamental building blocks of development.

In terms of transnational feminist praxis the current status of academic feminism requires that just as Red Thread has to constantly examine whether its relationship with the communities it works with is based on transformative work rather than Red Thread's survival needs, so academic feminism has to go beyond a solidarity based on convenience; it has to go beyond being more beneficial for the academic than the activist. In other words, while academic feminists conducting research in the global South with women's organizations may have little to give beyond academic knowledge and skill training, it has to be recognized that they are often more likely to benefit professionally from the research conducted in terms of furthering their academic careers, increasing their number of publications, training graduate students, providing a research environment that will lead to the awarding of graduate degrees, and benefiting more financially, while utilizing the knowledge base of grassroots women in order to do so.

Suitable Methods: The Links between Activism,
Social Change, and Research

There are other implications for transnational feminist praxis in reevaluating the links between social change, activism, and research, not least because debates over the nature of feminist knowledge production in the North have come to focus less on the link between praxis, academic knowledge, and activism and more on questions of feminist epistemology, despite Nancy Fraser (1989: 6) so succinctly stating that "you can't get a politics straight out of epistemology." Moreover, academic feminists' concerns with explicating a feminist epistemology have come to define the parameters of debates about the methodological grounding of research, and this has had severe consequences for the methods that have been deemed suitable for feminist research, in brief, qualitative techniques are good whereas quantitative techniques are bad. Notwithstanding the obvious, and many, problematic assumptions these divides assume, we emphasize here they are divides that pertain to northern academic constructions of knowledge production and they have little purchase for feminist activists in the global South.

It is increasingly being recognized however within the northern academy that feminist debates about the unsuitability of quantitative methods for feminist purposes are less about these techniques of inquiry being incompatible with feminist research but more about attempts by academic feminists to "professionalize" feminism by claiming its own distinctive approach to knowledge production, one that was least likely to mimic the objectivist, value-neutral epistemological positions adopted in mainstream scientific approaches. As Oakley states:

> Feminism needed a research method, a distinct methodology, in order to occupy a distinctive place in the academy and acquire social status and moral legitimacy. Opposition to "traditional" research methods as much as innovation of alternative ones provided an organizing platform for feminist scholarship. This opposition, and the whole contention of positivism and realism as inherently anti-feminist, was reinforced when postmodernism entered the feminist critique in the 1980s. As Wolf (1996: 60) has commented, it is probably no accident the "often inaccessible, abstract and hypertheoretical language" of postmodernism gained ascendancy at the same time as women increased their representation within academia. (Oakley 1998: 716)

Hence, much feminist research in the global North, even in many social science disciplines, is virtually synonymous with qualitative techniques. We suggest that there needs to be much greater flexibility over questions of suitable feminist methods. Over time, alongside the understanding that all data are representations, we have increasingly come to interrogate the methods that Red Thread has utilized, questioning the equation of feminist practice with qualitative approaches and reclaiming the value of quantitative research by feminist activists. We think this is important because while there is a divide between those who do quantitative research and those who do not, there is a larger divide between those who do not and those who *cannot*, because they lack the training in even the most basic of statistical analyses. Northern academic feminists run the risk of producing new generations of feminist academics who are unable to use quantitative methods in a non-positivist way. Resistance to using quantitative methods creates another divide then between North and South; a desire by northern feminist academics working in the global South to refrain from using quantitative methods is taken largely in ignorance of the situation of grassroots women's organizations in the South for whom research funding is often tied to the production of quantified data.

Much of the research training in Red Thread has been about becoming aware of the ways in which women can become "data literate" in that they can understand what data sources are available, how data come to be collected, and how they are translated into statistics, statistics that often purport to portray aspects of their own social lives, as well as the deficiencies of such data.[8] As one woman in Red Thread stated: "Many decisions about our lives are taken from figures and we don't know where these figures come from and we should be able to control this." Engaging in these research exercises has also allowed us to discuss such questions as why only certain data are collected and why the data are organized into particular categories. Not only do these questions expose the political nature of the process of production of social statistics about women; they also reveal assumptions about the valuing of women.[9] Our aim has also been to prove to funding agencies that women who often had no schooling beyond primary level could work together to produce reliable and valid data; indeed it is their very positionality that has allowed women in Red Thread to collect exceptionally high-quality research data.

Dealing with Silences: Engaging with Sexuality

While it has been easy to have conversations around such apparently neutral issues as appropriate methods it has been much harder to address other issues for which the political space not only across the country but also within Red Thread has been nonexistent. Guyana is commonly regarded as a homophobic country in which the only acceptable sexuality is heterosexuality. Recent attempts to introduce a new clause into the Constitution on nondiscrimination on the grounds of sexual orientation provoked such public hostility that the president has refused to endorse it. Research we conducted in the late 1990s (Peake and Trotz 1999) showed that lesbians and gay men are despised for engaging in sex for reasons unassociated with procreation; their failure to reproduce is not only considered to be a biological betrayal but also a social betrayal in their failure to contribute to the reproduction of the nation and their "race." In such a deeply religious and culturally intolerant country gays and lesbians are seen as "unnatural"; in our research they are generally described as being wicked, depraved, corrupt, impure, immoral, polluted, filthy, and profligate. Viewed as sexual deviates, gays and lesbians are socially shunned and ostracized. Such is the opprobrium attached to homosexuality that there are no gay or lesbian couples living openly in the country. There are no clubs, bars, cafes, restaurants, or other sociable public spaces where gays or lesbians would be tolerated. It follows that there is no social or political space for gay men, lesbians, or trans folk in Guyana. Given their low to practically nonexistent public profile neither had Red Thread—until 2006—taken any public position on issues of sexuality.[10]

Coming from North America, where nondominant sexualities are often celebrated or at least tolerated, into a society where there is no room for discussion of the discrimination faced by those who are not heterosexual has been a struggle between the two of us, with Linda advocating that it should be an issue that is raised within Red Thread and Karen not being convinced that it was an issue (until recently) that had the capacity to generate discussion and hence social action. Linda's assumptions, ones that are often made by northern-based academic feminists, about how the silences around issues of sexuality should be erased, has obvious implications when engaging in transnational feminist praxis in that the political spaces that northern feminist academics may find themselves within simply do not exist in some places in the South (and vice versa). We have recently reached an agreement to conduct research on youth and sexualities in Guyana, to investigate the extent to which the narrow range of acceptable sexualities hinders participation in development processes.

Conclusion

In this chapter we have grounded our discussion of transnational feminist praxis in the specific context of Guyana and within the evolution of Red Thread. We have also suggested that feminist conversations in northern academia (as progressive as they may seem) may not be relevant to many southern groups. We turn to one comment that Karen made when we were discussing this chapter because we feel it encapsulates many of the issues and contradictions to which transnational feminist praxis gives rise:

> You know I am coming to this meeting [the workshop in Minneapolis where these chapters were first discussed] but I should really be in Guyana dealing with crises. . . . I could turn into one of these people, one of these meeting people, but all these meetings take me away from my work. Whether it's the academy or the funders' meetings . . . it has happened to a lot of people in the Caribbean. They end up only representing but not doing any local work. . . . These transnational conversations are of much more use for the North; there is no direct benefit to the South as there could be for folks in the North, like academic publications and so on. In terms of the service of the transnational much more could be done to put groups like Red Thread in touch with other southern groups, like Sangtin for example. Given the racial context in Guyana we could learn so much from women activists in India and Africa, and indigenous groups in Latin America. You

know, feminist academics have access to all worlds but they are not putting those worlds in touch with each other. Red Thread exists to contribute to transformative politics. Its concern is to look at how to change things and we don't get the kind of help we need from feminist academics on this . . . because they also need transforming [laughter].

What this quotation highlights is the belief that the notion of transnational feminist praxis is a conflicting one; as much as it provokes promise it also provokes suspicion in that it is seen to perpetuate many processes of inequality. We agree that there is a need for research practices to be consciously studied in terms of dialogues that admit conflicts, silences, and differences—indeed transnational feminist praxis demands this—but this is never easy. The timelines and the agendas that operate in feminist academic circles, particularly in the North, often have little purchase in places in the South where the political spaces needed to open up dialogues simply do not exist or are not considered to be important to the context in which women's organizations operate.

While we believe it is important that northern feminist academics engage in discussions about transnational feminist praxis, this needs to be in tandem with the recognition that it is often at an enormous—political and perhaps feminist—distance from organizations such as Red Thread. Indeed, the extent to which this recognition is on the table both in the South and the North may well determine the failure or success of any transnational collaboration. What counts as "academic practice" needs to be interrogated and expanded to address this question of southern activists serving as representatives of struggles but not becoming direct beneficiaries of conversations that take place in northern academic spaces about transnational feminisms and praxis.[11] This central contradiction between transnational feminist praxis being accommodated in the neoliberal research university demands a radical transformation of northern academic feminist spaces. We argue that northern-based academic feminists cannot be engaged in transformative politics in the South, unless they are simultaneously committed to challenging academic structures, norms, and practices in their own institutions. A central task of radical transnational feminist praxis, then, is to hold academic feminists responsible for this and demand accountability from them along these lines.

Our conversations have led us to agree that one of the primary purposes of our collaborative research has been to question the nature of personal and professional relationships, and we have reached a consensus that we have to think more carefully about the research we do in terms of using it to construct more democratic practices of engagement and knowledge production between ourselves, between the members of Red Thread, between Red Thread and the communities with which it engages, as well as between feminist academics in the global North and feminist activists in the global South. Thus, we end by suggesting some practical questions that northern feminist academics who want to engage in transnational feminist praxis can address with their southern partners:[12]

- What do women in the South gain from transnational feminist exchanges? More relevant, what do they stand to lose?
- How can southern grassroots women's organizations resist the privileging of their members in relation to the grassroots community-based women they work with?
- How do the privileges of northern feminist academics create distance?
- How much of themselves are northern-based feminist academics willing to put on the line, given that they work in institutions that reward obedience and the status quo and in which connecting action and research is not often a widely encouraged cultural practice of academic production?
- How can feminist academics challenge the academic structures, norms, and practices in which they work to make them inclusive of women in the global south?
- To what extent is the increasing lack of engagement in praxis by feminist academics damaging relations with women's grassroots groups?
- How to account for the emotional labor, on all sides, that becomes invested in this process?
- What about self-reflexivity? Is it only a quest for self-validation? Is the emotional and political labor involved in its interrogation a diversion from the "real work" of daily processes of survival?

Notes

We want to give special thanks to the following who gave such generous comments on previous drafts: Andaiye, Deborah Barndt, and Richa Nagar.
   1. Linda first visited Guyana in 1981, and over the next few years she taught at the University of Guyana in the Geography Department and in Women's Studies as well as conducting research. Through her involvement with the British Labour Party she ended up meeting some of the women in the Working People's Alliance (WPA) political party, including Karen. Karen, along with a small number of women almost all of whom were in the WPA, decided in 1986 to

start up an independent women's organization, which they named Red Thread. She has played a central role in the organization ever since, ensuring its survival. In 1992 Linda started working collaboratively with Red Thread, establishing a research team working together on a wide range of issues.

2. The Global Women's Strike started in 1999, when women in Ireland decided to welcome the new millennium with a national general strike. They asked the International Wages for Housework Campaign to support their call, who then called on women all over the world to make the strike global on 8 March 2000. Since 2000 the strike has brought together women, including grassroots organizations, in over sixty countries.

3. Given the increasing level of poverty throughout the 1980s the initial needs that Red Thread recognized were economic ones. Red Thread chose embroidery, a skill that many women possessed even if only in a rudimentary form, as an organizing tool. But their work went far beyond establishing simple projects to generate income. It was a move to develop women's groups, in a number of coastal villages, with a focus on consciousness raising and valuing women's work. Within a few years Red Thread had established embroidery groups in a number of communities, with a small retail outlet in Georgetown for their sales. In the late 1980s they proceeded to diversify their income generating projects. Recognizing the short supply and exorbitantly high prices of school exercise books, they embarked on a pilot exercise book project, moving on to community production and sale of low-cost primary education textbooks, which led to the acquisition, in 1990, of a printing press. Throughout the 1990s the press and a desktop publishing house provided a steady source of income for Red Thread. Operating on a commercial basis, they also publish educational and cultural material on a nonprofit basis. Increasingly throughout the 1990s Red Thread's attention was less on income generation and more on efforts to change social consciousness through community education. Bringing together, on a daily basis, both Indo- and Afro-Guyanese women from communities outside Georgetown, they formed an education team. The team, which has received in-house training as well as training from the Jamaican Sistren Theatre Collective, has conducted hundreds of community workshops performing skits based on issues such as women's work, child abuse, family survival, community development, women's legal rights, sexual harassment, and violence against women. They also produced a series of videos for television on child abuse and domestic violence. Along with a group of women lawyers and other concerned women, Red Thread supported the setting up of a counseling service for battered women, Help and Shelter, transforming an issue defined as private into one having a public and political status. Women in Red Thread have also participated in a national campaign against violence against women and in 1993 produced a popular radio series on domestic violence from which they developed the script for a play called *Everybody's Business*. One result has been a flood of enquiries from individual women whom they have helped to file petitions in court over sexual harassment, rape, and domestic violence. Red Thread's recognition that women's struggles have to be linked to those of other marginalized groups and concerns around social justice has also led to their involvement with Amerindian groups and environmental issues.

4. So often at the mercy of their funders and their ability to pull their support, NGOs have had their own agendas usurped in order to further the political agendas of funders, even to the extent of being used to undermine and overthrow democratically elected governments, such as the ousting of the Aristide government in Haiti by U.S.-backed forces (Pina 2007). In the context of Guyana the power of funders is evident in their ability to determine the agendas that NGOs are able to address (see also chapter 6 in this volume by the Sangtin Writers). For example, funding for raising awareness about HIV in Guyana is plentiful, but it is also tied to the ideological stances of funders who emphasize and try to sell abstinence at the expense of condom provision and sex education.

5. Employers include the University of Guyana, the Inter-American Development Bank (IDB), the International Organization for Migration (IOM), International Development Research Centre (IDRC), UNIFEM, UNICEF, DfID, Dr. Neisha Haniff, Dr. Mark Pelling (Kings College, London), and Dr. Vera Chouinard (McMaster University).

6. Research has focused on the following issues: structural adjustment, the construction of gendered and racialized identities, and the increasing globalization of social imaginaries (Peake and Trotz 1999; Trotz and Peake 2000, 2001); women's role in development processes, particularly in relation to processes of urban planning and housing provision (Peake 1987 and 1996); poverty (Peake 1998); sex work (Red Thread 1999); women's reproductive health (Peake on behalf of Red Thread 2000); domestic violence (Peake on behalf of Red Thread 2000); trafficking (Marcus et al. 2004); as well as on Red Thread itself (Andaiye 2000; Peake 1993, 1996; Trotz 2007).

7. We have Cora's permission to discuss these examples.

8. For example, during our training sessions we studied the latest census and the Living Standard Measurement Survey (LSMS) as well as the Household Income and Expenditure Survey (HIES), the latter two of which are extremely important for planners and policy makers in Guyana given the lack of confidence in the reliability and accuracy of the censuses. We also studied reports produced by various international agencies and critiqued them on the basis of the women in Red Thread's understanding of everyday life in Guyana.

9. Time-use studies have also been conducted in communities by Red Thread so that they have been able to document both the paid and unpaid work women do in the family and community, revealing both the gendering and the value of the domestic production process.

10. The only organization dealing directly with issues of sexuality is SASOD. This is a Lesbian, Gay, Bisexual, and Transgender (LGBT) human rights, nonprofit NGO, which started in 2003 as a university-student pressure group (then called Students Against Sexual Orientation Discrimination). Also supported by non-students, it is lobbying for the passage of an amendment to ban discrimination on the grounds of sexual orientation in the Guyana Constitution. Although the amendment has still not passed, this diverse group of concerned citizens, community leaders, and activists blossomed. This voluntary, informal network of individuals then decided to change "Students" to "Society" to reflect the small but growing community of support for LGBT citizens in Guyana.

11. Although many southern activists would also argue that those who do get a chance to become representatives of specific struggles in the North often return with benefits that set them apart from others who are not seen as "qualified" to acquire that status.

12. These questions arise from our own conversations as well as a perusal of various literatures and Blomley (1994) in particular.

Works Cited

Andaiye. 2000. "The Red Thread Story: Resisting the Narrow Interests of a Broader Political Struggle." In Suzanne Francis Brown, ed., *Spitting in the Wind: Lessons in Empowerment from the Caribbean*. Kingston: Ian Randle Publishers. 53–98.

Blomley, Nick K. 1994. "Editorial: Activism and the Academy." *Environment and Planning D: Society and Space* 12: 383–385.

Farrington, John W., and Anthony Bebbington, with Kate Wellard and David L. Lewis. 1993. *Reluctant Partners? Non-Governmental Organisations: The State and Sustainable Agricultural Development*. London: Routledge.

Fraser, Nancy. 1989. *Unruly Practices: Power, Discourse and Gender in Contemporary Social Theory*. Minneapolis: University of Minnesota Press.

Hilhorst, Dorothea, ed. 2003. *The Real World of NGOs: Discourses, Diversity and Development*. London: Zed Books.

Marcus, Nicola, Halima Khan, Andaiye, Karen de Souza, & Linda Peake of Red Thread, Guyana, with the assistance of Cora Belle, Jocelyn Bacchus, Wintress White, Vanessa Ross, and Margaret Inniss, Red Thread. 2004. *"You talking 'bout everyday story": An Exploratory Study on Trafficking in Persons in Guyana*. Georgetown, Guyana: International Office on Migration. 80 pages.

Oakley, Ann. 1998. "Gender, Methodology and People's Ways of Knowing: Some Problems with Feminism and the Paradigm Debate in Social Science." *Sociology* 32(4): 707–731.

Peake, Linda. 1993. "The Development and Role of Women's Political Organisations in Guyana." In J. Momsen, ed., *Women and Change in the Caribbean*. London: Macmillan.109–131. Reprinted in V. Shepherd, ed. 2009. *Engendering Caribbean History: Cross-Cultural Perspectives (A Reader)*. Jamaica: Ian Randle Publishers.

Peake, Linda. 1996. "From Social Bases to Subjectivities: The Case of Red Thread in Guyana." In David V. L. Bell, Roger Keil, and Gerda R. Wekerle, eds., *Global Cities—Local Places: Issues in Urban Sustainability*. Toronto: Black Rose Books. 147–154.

Peake, Linda. 1997. "From Co-Operative Socialism to a Social Housing Policy? Declines and Revivals in Housing Policy in Guyana." In R. Potter and D. Conway, eds., *Self-Help Housing, the Poor and the State in the Caribbean*. Kingston, Jamaica: University of the West Indies Press. 171–194.

Peake, Linda. 1998. "Living in Poverty in Linden, Guyana in the 1990s: Bauxite, the 'Development of Poverty' and Household Coping Mechanisms." In D. McGregor, ed., *Resource Sustainability and Caribbean Development*. Kingston, Jamaica: University of the West Indies Press. 171–194.

Peake, Linda. (on behalf of Red Thread Women's Development Programme). 2000. *Women Researching Women: Methodology Report and Research Projects on the Study of Domestic Violence and Women's Reproductive Health in Guyana*. Georgetown, Guyana: Inter-American Development Bank. 300 pages.

Peake, Linda, and D. Alissa Trotz. 1999. *Gender, Place and Ethnicity: Women and Identities in Guyana.* London: Routledge.

Pina, Kevin. 2007. "Haiti and America Latina." *Race and Class* (special issue on Caribbean trajectories: 200 years on) 49(2): 100–108.

Red Thread. 1999. "'Givin' lil bit for lil bit': Women and Sex Work in Guyana." In K. Kempadoo, ed., *Sun, Sex and Gold: Tourism and Sex Work in the Caribbean.* Boulder, CO: Rowman & Littlefield. 263–290.

Trotz, D. Alissa. 2007. "The Politics of Hope in Guyana." *Race and Class* (special issue on Caribbean trajectories: 200 years on) 49 (2): 71–79.

Trotz, D. Alissa. 2004. "Between Despair and Hope: Women and Violence in Contemporary Guyana." *Small Axe* 15(March): 1–20.

Trotz, D. Alissa, and Linda Peake. 2001. "Work, Family and Organising: An Overview of the Contemporary Economic, Social and Political Roles of Women in Guyana." *(Caribbean Journal of) Social and Economic Studies* 50(2): 67–102.

Trotz, D. Alissa, and Linda Peake. 2000. "Work, Family and Organising: An Overview of the Emergence of the Economic, Social and Political Roles of Women in British Guiana." *(Caribbean Journal of) Social and Economic Studies* 49 (4): 189–222.

Wolf, Diane L., ed. *Feminist Dilemmas in Fieldwork.* Boulder, CO: Westview Press, 1996.

(6)
Still Playing with Fire

Intersectionality, Activism, and NGOized Feminism

SANGTIN WRITERS[1]

(Reena, Richa Nagar, Richa Singh, and Surbala)

बरसों से ठहरे पानी में ऊपर से एक नन्हा सा कंकड़ भी टपका दिया जाये तो हलचल-सी मच जाती है। कुछ देर तक तरंगें उठती हैं और फिर पानी दोबारा स्थिर हो जाता है अगला विघ्न पड़ने तक। एक तरह से यदि हम संगतिन के सदस्यों द्वारा सीतापुर में किये पिछले दशक के काम को देखें तो कुछ ऐसी ही तस्वीर नज़र आयेगी। जब-जब किसी नये मुद्दे को उठाया गया चाहे वह महिलाओं के ख़िलाफ़ हो रही हिंसा हो, चाहे वह नहर की सफ़ाई हो, या फिर नहर में पानी लाने का मसला हो –– हर बार घरों से लेकर प्रशासन तक अलग-अलग क़िस्म के मतभेद, मुठभेड़ें और तनाव हुए, और फिर सारे शोर और खलबलियाँ शान्त हो गईं और कार्यकत्ताओं के जतन और जनता के सहयोग से हुए बदलाव सामान्य जीवन का हिस्सा बन गये।

लेकिन इसी क्रम पर हम ज़रा दूसरी निगाह डालें तो एक भिन्न पहलू उभर कर आता है। किसी भी बदलाव का सामाजिक व राजनैतिक तन्त्र में समाहित हो जाना इतना कठिन नहीं होता अगर उस समाज में उभरी हुई ताक़तों और आम जनता के बीच जमे आर्थिक समीकरण पर कोई आँच न आये। किन्तु यदि किसी बदलाव से इस समीकरण में दरारें पड़ने लगती हैं तो बदलाव की वह प्रक्रिया सामाजिक तन्त्र में घुलने के बजाय एक निरन्तर जारी रहने वाली लड़ाई में तब्दील हो जाती है।

जिन चिन्तन-प्रक्रियाओं, विवादों, और चुनौतियों के बीच से गुज़रते हुए संगतिन का सफ़र 2004 से अब तक आगे बढ़ा है उसने हमें एक सच्चाई भली-भांति सिखला दी है –– कि महिला मुद्दों की परिभाषा केवल महिलाओं के जिस्मों और जज़्बातों पर होने वाली हिंसा तक सीमित नहीं रह सकती। न ही वो बाक़ी समाज से महिलाओं को काटकर उनको दिये जाने वाले संसाधनों और अवसरों में समेटी जा सकती है। अगर हमें अपने गांवों में हाशिये पर ढकेले हुये लोगों के लिए सही मायनों में एक लम्बे दौर तक टिकने वाला सामाजिक, आर्थिक और राजनैतिक बदलाव लाना है तो परिवर्तन की धाराओं में समस्त ग्रामीण समुदायों का जुड़ना अत्यन्त आवश्यक है। इसके लिए हमें अपनी सोच और काम में औरतों से जुड़ी ग़ैरबराबरियों और हिंसाओं को बराबर उन ढाँचों से जोड़ते रहना होगा जो समाज में पैठी तमाम अन्य हिंसाओं और असमानताओं का पोषण करते हैं।

हमारा सफ़र

—From *Hamara Safar*, Sangtin Kisaan Mazdoor Sangathan's community newspaper, 1: 2 (2006): 1

Ripples and Waves

If a pebble is dropped into still water, it produces turbulence. Ripple after ripple passes through the water, but after a few moments, everything becomes calm again. If we look at the political work done over the last decade by those who now constitute the membership of Sangtin Kisaan Mazdoor Sangathan (Sangtin Peasants and Workers Organization, hereafter SKMS), a similar picture emerges. Whenever we raised a new issue—be it violence against women, or the cleaning of irrigation channels, or of bringing waters to a dry canal—there were many conflicts, encounters, and tensions in spaces ranging from homes to government offices and then all the noises and storms calmed down, and the transformations brought about with the efforts of community-based activists and the people became a part of everyday life.

However, if we change our lenses and refocus on the same events, we could state things differently. It is not so difficult for the social and political machinery to absorb a transformation if it does not disturb the economic equations that exist between those in power and the ordinary people. But if any sociopolitical change poses a radical challenge to these equations, the processes of change, rather than getting interwoven with the social fabric, acquire the form of an endless struggle.

The thought processes, controversies, and challenges through which Sangtin's journey has progressed since 2004 have taught us one truth quite clearly—that the definition of women's issues cannot be limited to the violence that is inflicted upon women's bodies and emotions. Nor can it be confined to the resources and opportunities that target women while cutting them off from the rest of their society. If we are truly interested in bringing about sustainable, long-term sociopolitical and economic change in the lives of those who have been pushed to the margins, it is essential for all the members of our rural communities—women and men; children, young, and old; *sawarn* and *dalit*; peasants, sweepers, workers, and shopkeepers—to constitute the waves of change. And this will not happen unless inequalities and violence associated with women are analytically and strategically linked in our vision and political labor with the structures that nourish all other forms of violence and inequalities in our society—including the violence of caste and class oppression and communal untouchability. In other words, the experience of collective reflective politics "revealed" to the evolving organization that, in order to bring about long-term changes in power relations, Sangtin had to be taken out of the ghetto of "women's problems" and its political struggles had to articulate with wider struggles.

Worlds, Fields, and Tales

Writing simultaneously *for* audiences in two starkly different worlds is not easy. Writing simultaneously *from* those starkly different worlds for audiences that reside in different worlds is even more challenging. Yet, in the collaborative praxis that we have embraced as members of SKMS, we confront this challenge repeatedly—with its joys and frustrations, strengths and limitations. The labor of activism, for us, is tightly interwoven with the labor of producing knowledge about processes of social change and struggles for social justice. It is only in and through the moments of critical reflection when we grapple with the meanings and effects of our own political actions that we strategize about the next steps in our journey. Our shared agenda as members of SKMS grounds us locally in our political vision, but that vision cannot materialize without an accompanying agenda of intervening in the institutional practices associated with knowledge production across multiple borders. To sustain our ongoing reflections, self-critical analysis, and strategy making, then, we must continuously come together to have dialogues—and to write—across borders.

This commitment, although specific to the contours of our own alliance and struggle, can nevertheless, be seen as one of the many possible practices that Sheppard (2006: 1) asks us to imagine: practices of engagement and knowledge production that "challenge the dangers of neoliberalization in our institutions, to radically diversify our geography of knowledge production, and to get out more (out of both the ivory tower and the global north)." As we write about our dialogues in SKMS, then, we have two audiences in mind. One sits primarily in the villages of Sitapur, participates in our rallies and struggles, and reads and writes for our newspaper, *Hamara Safar.* The other resides primarily in the classes and seminar rooms of Anglophone universities and colleges, whose members sometimes become volunteers in movements such as SKMS, and at other times, they become experts producing knowledge about struggles such as ours. Because our analyses, frameworks, and visions emerge as a result of our engagements with both of these audiences, we also feel that our critical reflections might have something useful to contribute to conversations about struggles of peasants and workers and movement building in each of these sites.

The concrete practices that are emerging in movement building and alliance work of SKMS can be seen as contributing to this radical diversification of geography of knowledge production (Sheppard 2006) in two interrelated ways. The first involves actively resisting the separation between three kinds of fields: the fields that are worked by the hands of the peasants and laborers who are part of the struggle; the fields of non-governmental organizations (NGOs) that seek to empower the women or the poor in economically marginalized places; and the academic fields that produce articles, books, and critical discourses about such processes. The second aspect of this radical diversification—which enables the first resistance to happen—involves a conscious engagement with the politics of language. That is, it involves producing practices that allow us to diversify the conceptual and "real" languages in which knowledges get produced, evaluated, and recognized as critical and significant (Nagar 2008). This approach overlaps with the vision that E. Patrick Johnson (2005) articulates for addressing the omissions of white-centered queer theory. For him, queer theory must be "quared"; that is, it must address the concerns and needs of gay, lesbian, bisexual, and transgendered people across issues of race, gender, and class as well as other identities and subject positions so that theory can do its work not simply in academic spaces, but also in our communities, churches, and homes (2005: 149). For Johnson, such an interventionist disciplinary project calls "for a conjoining of academic praxis with political praxis" (128) so that it can be:

> specific and intentional in the dissemination and praxis of quare theory, committed to communicating and translating its political potentiality. Indeed, quare theory is bi-directional: it theorizes from bottom to top and top to bottom. This dialogical/dialectical relationship between theory and practice, the lettered and unlettered, ivory tower and front porch, is crucial to a joint and sustained critique of hegemonic systems of oppression.

While we support Johnson's intentions, we find it important to challenge the premise of theory and practice, ivory tower and porch, the lettered and the unlettered as opposite poles that need to be brought together. Instead, we see these as interwoven and mutually constitutive spheres that shape practices of knowledge production in and through community-based struggles. The reflections we present here can, therefore, be seen as part of SKMS's continued efforts to resist the compartmentalization of theory from practice, the lettered from the unlettered, and the academic from the activist, and to actively participate in the coproduction of dialogical/dialectical relationships among the *fields* inhabited by members of SKMS, NGOs, and academic scholars.

SKMS is a growing movement of poor farmers and manual laborers in the Sitapur District of the Indian state of Uttar Pradesh. The movement is highly critical of the state-supported neoliberal program of rural development and poor women's empowerment, and SKMS mobilizes and agitates with people of sixty villages of Mishrikh and Pisawan Blocks[2] in Sitapur District to push the governmental machinery to become more accountable to the people in whose name it has launched schemes that guarantee minimum employment and the right to information to the rural poor.

As the movement evolves and gains strength, we seek to document the stories of our successes and failures with the members of SKMS, while subjecting our actions and political processes to constant critical scrutiny by the SKMS members, supporters, and critics. The stories we tell here are based primarily on dialogues that unfolded among four members of SKMS in the context of producing the first four issues of SKMS's community newspaper, *Hamara Safar*, in 2006–2007. We narrate two intertwined tales. The first tale focuses on the political transformation of Sangtin, an organization that was conceptualized in 1998 as an NGO for rural women's empowerment based on the mainstream donor-based model of social change. However, a three-year-long process of critical reflection and writing by nine women on the politics of caste, class, religion, and gender in the context of rural development and women's empowerment programs—as well as on the global politics of knowledge production—paved the way for the emergence of SKMS, an organization that today consists of approximately five thousand poor farmers, manual workers, and their families, over 90 percent of whom are *dalit* (formerly called "untouchable") and, to a lesser extent, members of Sunni Muslim communities. SKMS believes that definitions and processes of empowerment must evolve from rural people's struggles and active participation instead of emerging from donor institutions, NGO headquarters, university-based experts or think tanks and then being diffused among the rural people. The second story focuses on hurdles in the path of SKMS as it remains grounded in feminist principles, but refuses to work exclusively with women. Together, the two intertwined stories map the archaeology of the shift from Sangtin to SKMS, and all of the larger questions pertaining to "women's issues," "feminist politics," and "transnational collaborations" that are thrown up in the course of this shift.

Beginnings

Let us first situate these organizations in the state of Uttar Pradesh and the district of Sitapur. Uttar Pradesh is the most populous state of India, highly influential in the country's political life. As a mainly agricultural state ranking low in conventional measures of economic and human development, Uttar Pradesh has been the target of numerous "development" initiatives, many of which are funded by the state or central government and operated by non-governmental organizations (NGOs). NGOs run the gamut from sectoral initiatives in water or agriculture to programs for education or women's empowerment.

Sitapur district is located about ninety kilometers away from Lucknow, the capital of Uttar Pradesh. According to the 2001 census, approximately 3.6 million of Uttar Pradesh's 166 million people lived in the Sitapur District. A third of the total population of this district is *dalit*, another 17 percent of the population is Muslim, and the electoral politics are dominated by the Samajwadi Party and Bahujan Samaj Party (both are seen as favoring minority communities and lower castes, but that is not always the case). However, since 1992, the district has also witnessed a heavy influence of Bhartiya Janata Party, the extremist Hindu nationalist party. This *Hindutva*-inflected district is well known for heinous acts of violence against women. A recent study on district-level deprivation officially classifies Sitapur as one of the "69 most backward districts" of India.[3] The close proximity to the state capital not only affects the electoral and communal politics in Sitapur, but it also makes this district an attractive backyard for various experiments in development schemes. Until the rise of SKMS, Sitapur had largely remained untouched by periodic waves of socialist, workers', or peasants' movements; activism against state-aided communalism; or even the influence of the women's movement in the 1970s and 1980s.[4] The mid-1990s saw the appearance of donor-funded women's NGOs in the district. For the stories that we tell here, the arrival in 1996 of Nari Samata Yojana or NSY (a pseudonym we use for a large government-run organization in various states of India) marked a new beginning in the lives of the people in Sitapur.

A program for the empowerment of rural women from marginalized sections, NSY-Sitapur was funded by the World Bank and implemented through the Human Resources and Development Ministry of the Government of India. As a state-level program, NSY follows the principle of geographical decentralization. Headquartered at the state level, NSY works through district-level offices so that rural activists working at the village level can create spaces for women to define their own priorities as well as how they want to mobilize and address the problems that seem most urgent to them. Until 2004, NSY had a policy to encourage its village-level workers to register their own organization under another name so that the work of women's empowerment could continue after the time-bound funded program of NSY withdrew from the particular district. It was under this policy that nine village-level mobilizers and the district coordinator of the Sitapur branch of NSY-Uttar Pradesh registered an organization called

Sangtin in 1999.[5] In Awadhi, the main language spoken in rural Sitapur, the term *sangtin* denotes solidarity, community, and intimacy among women. At the time of its founding, the idea was that Sangtin would step in to follow NSY's model of women's empowerment after NSY-Sitapur "rolled back" from the area around 2005. Here is where our first story begins.

From NGOized Activism to a People's Movement: Sangtin Becomes Sangtin Kisaan Mazdoor Sangathan

The story of how Sangtin became SKMS starts with an unplanned meeting in Lucknow in March 2002 between Richa Singh, a founding member of Sangtin and the district coordinator of NSY-Sitapur at that time, and Richa Nagar, a teacher and Hindustani creative writer, based in Minnesota and Uttar Pradesh, who had been studying processes of NGOization in women's organizations in India. The two Richas started exchanging notes on the class and caste politics of women's NGOs in India and in Uttar Pradesh; on the structures of reciprocity and accountability that were present or absent in the existing relationships between experts who produced knowledge about the poor, on the one hand, and those who were subjects of that knowledge, on the other; and on the question of what would happen in Sitapur after NSY rolled back from the district.

These initial conversations triggered a series of dialogues whereby eight founding members of Sangtin—seven of whom held different positions in NSY-Sitapur, and one (Surbala) of whom was a former employee of NSY-Sitapur—built an alliance with Richa Nagar, with an aim to generate collective reflections, writing, and analysis on four sets of issues (Sangtin Writers 2006): First, how do the politics of gender intertwine with casteism, communal untouchability, classism, and with the systematic marginalization of specific rural places, communities, and languages? Second, how do these processes shape rural women's experiences of hunger, deprivation, sexuality, motherhood, and activism? These two sets of explorations were undergirded by a broader focus on the ways in which NGO structures as well as knowledges produced in both NGOs and academia that seek to end poor women's oppressions often end up feeding the same hierarchies that produce those oppressions (Peake and de Souza, chapter 5 in this volume). Last, but not least, the collective committed itself to reflect on the specific processes of "NGOization"—a term that involves an implicit or explicit critique that NGOs and their ties with the state are significantly reshaping—even replacing—community-based activism (Faust and Nagar 2008).

The articulation of these reflections evolved into a book in Hindustani called *Sangtin Yatra* (Anupamlata et al. 2004), so that it could become a basis for dialogues in the "vernacular" among village- and district-level activists and communities struggling with these issues. *Sangtin Yatra* led to a vibrant public debate as well as a backlash by the leadership of NSY-Uttar Pradesh, where seven of the nine authors were (and six are still) employed. From this controversy arose newspaper articles, reviews, editorials, a petition, Richa Singh's resignation from NSY, as well as the English version of *Sangtin Yatra*, entitled *Playing with Fire*. Each of these products was inserted in a series of dialogues with readers, intellectuals, activists, solidarity groups, and people's movements—from the villages of Mishrikh and Pisawan development blocks in the Sitapur District to the villages of Uttaranchal and Rajasthan, and from the cities of New Delhi and Pune to Minneapolis and San Francisco.

Translating Critique into Practice

The process of creating *Sangtin Yatra* and the events after its publication caused Sangtin to interrogate and critique the dominant model of poor rural women's empowerment, where "poor rural women" was often seen as a predefined category in need of emancipation by paid NGO staff, who were accountable to their supervisors and donors. It also became abundantly clear to the activists that women's issues could not be limited to the physical and emotional violence that is inflicted on female bodies. Nor could they be limited to demands that seek to secure resources and opportunities for marginalized women in complete isolation from the rest of their society. The emerging consensus was that if we sought to work for sociopolitical transformation of our villages in favor of the most oppressed, it was critical for us to articulate our feminist activism in relation to village communities as a whole.

The making of the book *Sangtin Yatra* presented us with rich opportunities to internalize such an intersectional approach where gendered difference could only be understood in relation to other axes of sociopolitical differences. For example, we learned to grapple with the manner in which untouchability makes the pangs of hunger felt by a *dalit* girl quite distinct from those suffered by a *brahmin* girl. Similarly, we learned to question the rhetoric of NGOs who claim to give equal opportunities to all their women workers. For a poor *dalit* or Muslim woman who claims her voice, education, and employment amid years of insults and segregation, the emergence as a "successful organizational worker" acquires a radically different meaning than it does for a *sawarn* (non-*dalit*) Hindu woman who has always felt entitled to proudly live in her society, irrespective of her class.

As Sangtin embraced this intersectional approach and radical community pedagogy, it came to oppose the narrow gynocentrism of many NGOs working among the rural women, and decided to organize both women and men. It also decided to place intellectual empowerment of the poorest rural peoples at the center of its efforts to "empower" such communities—socially, economically, and politically. Given the nature of alliance that produced *Sangtin Yatra*, such a vision of empowerment necessarily involved struggling against the dualisms of North/South; elite/vernacular languages; academia/activism; and theory/practice. Furthermore, it necessitated interrogating the local, national, and global hierarchies that help sustain lopsided structures of accountability in the production, dissemination, and consumption of knowledges about the most marginalized communities and places. Accordingly, we sought to interweave grassroots organizing, critical self-reflexivity, and collective writing to build dialogues with rural communities, social movements, solidarity networks, academics, and public intellectuals.

We also acutely recognized that Sangtin was headed on an exciting political journey, but one which involved significant economic and personal risks for those who were going to devote most of their time building the movement without any fixed salaries or payments. For each author of *Sangtin Yatra*, these dangers meant making critical decisions about the kind of feminist activism she was in a position to embrace in her own life, as well as about her livelihood, career, and commitments in and outside of the NGO sector.[6]

Learning from Mazdoor Kisaan Shakti Sangathan

These developments in Sangtin's journey coincided with the passing of two acts by the government of India that some see as "revolutionary" in a structurally adjusted and economically mutilated rural India: the people's Right to Information Act (RTI) of 2005 and the National Rural Employment Guarantee Act (NREGA) of 2005 (Ghosh 2006). Sangtin's campaign to ensure the implementation of these two acts in Mishrikh and Pisawan became inseparable from its commitment to reclaim feminism and empowerment on the terms of rural communities. *Sangtin Yatra* also reconstituted the pedagogical labor that was involved in each phase of the journey. For instance, Richa Nagar's job was not simply to help with the writing of the reflections and analyses emerging in the collective. She also became increasingly devoted to first researching and then teaching her coauthors about people's organizations and movements that were not propelled by donor-driven NGO-based models of social transformation. A discussion of the book *Sangtin Yatra* served as a useful entry point for beginning political dialogues with such organizations.

One such organization was Mazdoor Kisaan Shakti Sangathan (MKSS) in Devdoongri, Rajasthan. In August 2005, six members of Sangtin (including the four authors of this chapter) spent several days with members of MKSS in Devdoongri. We learned how MKSS raised the issues of right to information and right to employment and minimum wage among the rural communities and how, through their mobilization, it transformed itself into a formidable people's movement in several districts of Rajasthan. Upon returning from MKSS, Sangtin organized a series of meetings in Mishrikh where women and men identified that the most immediate source of their disempowerment was their lack of access to the waters of a major irrigation canal called Sharada Nahar that ran across large areas of Mishrikh and Pisawan. While the first five kilometers of this seventeen-kilometer-long canal contained water, the caste and electoral politics of this area had prevented the rest of the irrigation channel from getting any water, depriving about forty thousand poor farmers and their families (mostly *dalit* and Muslim) from sixty villages from access to irrigation for over a decade and a half. Sangtin decided to agitate with the people of Mishrikh and Pisawan to ensure a fair access to irrigation waters for all.

Reclaiming NGOized Fields

Once a well-wisher chided Richa Singh: "In 1996, you were working in the villages of Mishrikh. In 2006, you are still in Mishrikh! . . . other people in the NGO world . . . have leaped across places and done so well for themselves. How long will you remain stuck in Mishrikh?"

The well-wisher's comment reminded Richa Singh of another incident. On 22 May 2006, a large crowd had *gheraoed* (encircled) the Block District Office in the Pisawan Block of Sitapur to protest the government's failure to deliver the job cards that were guaranteed to the rural poor under NREGA, and a woman tore through the crowds and reached out for Richa. Holding Richa's face with her hands, the woman said in Awadhi, "Ari mor son chirayia, aitte din kahan rahyo?" (O my golden bird, where were you hiding all this time?). Surbala, who was watching this, commented: "People wish to become many important things these days. But rarely does anyone who comes to work in a village from the outside get a chance to become someone's *son chirayia!"*

Richa Singh's acquaintance had tried to convince her that she had stagnated in her life and career. But we doubt whether the acquaintance's scale of "self-progress" could ever be calibrated to measure the joy and contentment that Richa lived in the moment when she became that woman's *son chirayia!*

In August 2004, the controversy over *Sangtin Yatra* had led Richa to resign in protest from her position as a district project co-coordinator of NSY-Sitapur, and the Minnesota chapter of the Association for India's Development (AID) awarded her a fellowship to continue Sangtin's work in Sitapur. At that time, AID questioned whether it was appropriate or wise for Sangtin to work in the same villages that constituted the *field* of NSY-Sitapur, and we found ourselves agonizing over whether we should avoid working in villages that were the focus of NSY's women's empowerment schemes. But really, what does it mean when NGOs or movements begin to determine for a village which issues it should mobilize around and which people it should work with? Whose village? Whose issues? Whose empowerment? And who is authorized to claim credit for that empowerment? Sangtin became critical of the ways in which NGOs often divide up the countryside into areas of operation without involving the people they seek to empower. If the definitions of empowerment were to emerge from the struggles of the poorest women and men of Mishrikh and Pisawan, the villages in which we would do our political work must also emerge from how those struggles spread and constituted themselves.

Renaming Ourselves:
From Sangtin to Sangtin Kisaan Mazdoor Sangathan

The months of August through December 2005 were heady as we plunged ourselves into the labor of building a people's movement. Village-level committees were formed in more than thirty villages, and these committees collaborated with Sangtin to organize rallies, marches, and demonstrations to sign letters, applications, and petitions to the district's Irrigation Department. Our alliance succeeded in bringing water to the next five kilometers of the canal on 25 December 2005.

The campaign to release canal waters for the small farmers went hand in hand with the struggle to procure employment and minimum wages (under NREGA) for manual laborers who were hired to clean the canal. The Irrigation Department had illegally hired labor contractors to do this work, but with Sangtin's intervention, the villagers who participated in the campaign also came to constitute the legally hired workforce for cleaning the canal. Over one-third of these cleaners were *dalit* women who embraced this work for the first time in Sitapur, a critical development that triggered new battles along gender and caste lines in many villages, causing tensions in many poor households as well. Another critical involvement was that of male peasants whose subsistence needs could not be met fully by agriculture and who had to work as manual laborers for a good part of the year. The water campaign thus blended with another campaign that sought to secure rural people's rights to guaranteed employment under NREGA.

A symbolic turning point in our movement was the moment when Shammu, a young Muslim man, insisted on signing a petition to the subdistrict magistrate not as a member of his village's committee, but as a *sangtin*. "I am also a *sangtin* and I will sign as one," he declared. Shammu's words forced us to recognize that Sangtin's name needed to expand in a way that adequately welcomed and represented the new members of our movement. Thus began a series of discussions that culminated in the renaming of Sangtin as Sangtin Kisaan Mazdoor Sangathan.

These two moving moments, when a woman in the demonstration called Richa Singh her *son chirayia* (golden bird) and when Shammu declared himself to be a *sangtin*, vividly capture the contradictions that are at the heart of Sangtin's shift away from the dominant NGOized definitions of women's empowerment. Significantly, these two moments are enabled by Sangtin's shift from a self-declared women's organization to an alliance of poor, mostly *dalit*, farmers and workers who are both women and men. With this shift SKMS makes three political moves: First, it refuses the ghettoization of poor women's issues. Second, it makes women, their labor, and their rights and entitlements visible as both farmers and workers. And third, it establishes itself on the turbulent terrain of development politics as a movement that organizes women and men. Not surprisingly, such a shift met with resistance, often in the form of new masculinist attitudes and practices of caste and class.

So what kinds of contradictions emerge in the context of feminist activism that organizes poor men and women—not just in relation to outside funders or other NGOs, but also in the districts and villages where SKMS works? The second story we tell here examines the archaeology of our emerging movement from these lenses.

Pushing Feminist Activism into Purdah?
Challenges to SKMS's Vision of Movement Building

As SKMS becomes a strong alliance of poor farmers and workers that insists on grounding its understandings of both empowerment and feminism in its immediate struggles, it encounters hurdles from the directions of both donors and NGOs that are far removed from its local context as well as from powerful vested interests—and members of family and community— who have deep roots in Sitapur. To appreciate these hurdles, we must place the donors and NGOs in active mutually constitutive relationships with the national and local state, the private market institutions, the local administrative machinery, rural development establishments, and the patriarchal households with which NGOs voluntarily or forcibly collaborate.

When SKMS embraces male and female farmers and workers as part of its *feminist* activism, and sees the politics of sexual and bodily violence as thoroughly intertwined with the battles to claim irrigation waters, employment, minimum wages, and right to information, SKMS's credentials as a "feminist movement" tend to become suspect in the eyes of donor organizations that wish to sponsor poor women's empowerment in the global South. The irony is that the suspicion that is cast upon us by the rural development administration of Sitapur is also expressed in a similar language. When several of the key SKMS activists had been employed in NSY, their work on "women's issues"—especially on violence against women—was lauded throughout Sitapur by the governmental machinery. But SKMS's later growth began to alarm the beneficiaries of the existing sociopolitical system. The same people who were once praised by government officials were now repeatedly warned by the political mafia in the area, "Go and save your women from violence and leave the delicacies of rural development to us."

In May 2006, Reena revisited MKSS with ten new members of SKMS to participate in the latest round of marches and discussions on rural people's right to information, employment, and minimum wages. As soon as the group returned to Sitapur with a new confidence to forge ahead with the campaign, SKMS began to emerge as a thorn in the side of *pradhans* (heads of *gram sabhas* or *gram panchayats,* the village administrative units), block development officers (BDOs), and holders of ration quotas (*kotedars*). Even as the elected representatives at the national level pass new acts in the name of the poor, new mechanisms are invented by government officials at all scales to loot the food and grains that are allotted to the poor through ration cards and programs such as *kaam ke badle anaaj yojana* (grain in exchange of labor). Sangtin's organizing not only encouraged poor women and men to question these long-standing practices of profiteering and corruption, it also began to interrupt the dominant caste-based equations that had been in place for decades.

Our past activism in NSY on violence against women had not threatened these vested interests, and they had also left us alone. However, as water appeared in one segment of the irrigation canal, as government warehouses were forced to distribute the wheat to the workers, as women stepped into the work of cleaning the canal and digging of ponds, and as prehired labor contracting men from upper castes lost their profits, the membership of SKMS was convinced that it could fight the microeconomics of corruption, misinformation, and stolen rights that are intricately intertwined with rural "development" schemes.

In SKMS's campaigns to implement people's right to information, poor *dalit* women and men began to understand—and take steps to disseminate, refine, and act upon their new understandings—how wheat from government warehouses that was entered on official registers as payment for labor would then disappear into the pockets of BDOs, *pradhans*, and quota holders. They now produce political analyses of gendered, classed, and caste-based contradictions that happen in the everyday politics of implementing legislation such as NREGA. They are producing political analysis of gendered, classed, and caste-based contradictions that happen in the everyday politics of implementing NREGA. They scathingly critique the very premises of the state's developmentalist agenda, including NREGA, while insisting on becoming the lawful "beneficiaries" of all that NREGA offers. However, as the membership becomes more confident about its own critical analysis and collective strategies, the resistance from the rural development administration continues to stiffen. To take one example from July 2006, the block development officer of Mishrikh publicly declared that he was eager to give work to anyone who asked for it. But when *dalit* women of Khanpur Village in Mishrikh Tehsil came forward to demand work under NREGA, the *pradhan* discontinued the work of digging the ponds rather than comply with the law that reserves 33 percent of all jobs for women. The rhetoric used to discontinue the work was that women could not handle the hard work of digging the ponds. The reality, however, was that the *pradhan* and other rich farmers who employed the *dalit* women as agricultural laborers on their farms at excessively low daily wages (Rs. 30 to Rs. 40 per day) did not want to lose the women's labor and hire a new labor force at the minimum wage, which at that time was 58 rupees per day (Hindustan Times Correspondent 2006).[7]

The *pradhan*'s discontinuation of the work in response to the demand for work by *dalit* women from Khanpur was also meant to challenge SKMS. Under the Right to Information Act, SKMS issued a written request to the district and block administration of Mishrikh and Pisawan to reveal to us the official record of how much work was done under *kaam ke badle anaaj yojana*, the scheme that sought to compensate the workers for their labor in the form of food grains. When our letter reached the government offices, we started feeling pressure from various quarters to withdraw our demand. "How much money do you need to keep quiet?" we were asked. Reena was threatened that she would be "fixed" if she did not withdraw her request, and her husband was instructed to keep Reena under strict control: Couldn't he stop his wife from roaming around with a bag on her shoulders? Didn't she have any children to look after at home?

The block *pramukh* in Surbala's village who was from her own caste created both caste and familial pressure and sent his warning through Surbala's sister: "Stop your sister or we will have to send Chamariyas and Pasiniyas[8] to beat the crap out of her." Surbala's husband and brother-in-law immediately began their efforts to instill some sense into her head: "Whoever has dared to raise his or her head in this manner has always been crushed. Why do you insist on destroying our family?"

The gendered politics of labor and power in the familial establishment also developed along similar lines. At the time when the canal was being cleaned, poor *dalit* women appeared in large numbers to seek employment without any efforts by SKMS to convince them. But when each household was guaranteed minimum wage under NREGA, husbands and brothers, who were eager to claim this opportunity, tried to stop the women from claiming their right to employment. The argument that men repeatedly made was that jobs such as brick work and digging of ponds that are allocated under NREGA were not socially sanctioned in our villages as "women's work." Similarly, when the struggle over canal waters involved confrontations with the district administration, not a single family stopped its women from coming forward for this risky work. But as soon as ration cards, BPL cards, Antyodaya cards,[9] and job cards appeared in the picture, men—in the households and in the development offices—began to argue that they alone should count as the head of a family, and therefore, as the legitimate claimants of subsidized food quotas.

The Journey Continues . . .

महिला मुद्दों पर काम करने वाली अन्तर्राष्ट्रीय संस्थाओं पर अगर हम ग़ौर करें तो अक्सर पायेंगे कि एक तरफ़ तो ऐसी अस्मिताओं और संघर्षों को सम्मानजनक जगह दिये जाने की कोशिशें हो रही हैं जिन्हें मर्द या औरत नाम के लिंग में बाँधा नहीं जा सकता। दूसरी ओर वही संगठन महिला मुद्दों को या तो लिंग, यौनिकता व आत्मीय रिश्तों के दायरों में संकुचित कर देते हैं, या फिर उन्हें पँचायतों व ग्रामीण बैंकों जैसी संस्थाओं के ज़रिये होने वाले परम्परागत सशक्तीकरण की सीमाओं में बाँध देते हैं।

ध्रुवी राजनीति से ज़रा अलग हटकर अपने ही सीतापुर ज़िले का नज़ारा लें तो पाते हैं कि सरकारी प्रशासन और जन-प्रतिनिधियों से लेकर परिवार-जन तक संगतिनों के काम को कसे हुए दायरों में समेटकर ज़नानख़ाने में ठेल देना चाहते हैं — ताकि हमारा शोर केवल गुड़िया के पीटे जाने व औरतों के कटने, मरने या जलाये जाने पर ही सुनाई दे।

महिला मुद्दों की परिभाषा जब औरत नाम के एक ख़ास लिंग से, एक ख़ास तरह के जिस्म से, और पहले से ही निर्धारित मुद्दों की सूची में समेट दी जाती है तो वह ऊपर से थोपी हुई व्यवस्था या व्यवसाय का रूप लेने लगती है। आज जब जगह-जगह छोटे-छोटे समुदायों के सशक्तीकरण का नारा लगाया जा रहा है तब तो हर नन्हें-से-नन्हें समूह को भी अपना नारीवाद और अपने मुद्दे स्वयं निर्धारित करने का न्यौता दिया जाना चाहिये। लेकिन महिला मुद्दों का अगर ऐसा विकेन्द्रीकरण हो जाये तो फिर वैश्विक बाज़ार के रक्षकों और उनके बूते पर पलने वाले मुनाफ़ाख़ोरों का भला क्या होगा? ऐसे माहौल में संगतिन पूरे दम से अपना आन्दोलन आगे बढ़ाने के लिए यही मानकर चल रही है कि हमारा आगे का सफ़र निश्चित ही कठिन और चुनौतीपूर्ण रहेगा। यात्रा जारी है।

हमारा सफ़र

—From *Hamara Safar*, Sangtin Kisaan Mazdoor Sangathan's
community newspaper, 1: 2 (2006): 2

NGOs have increasingly been called to help manage the problems produced by neoliberal policies and to pacify those who have been hardest hit by such policies. Small movements—made up of people whose livelihoods are the most threatened—often find it hard to exist without engaging with donor agencies or professionalized NGOs in some form or another. The challenge before such movements is to find support for their political work while also maintaining their accountability and transparency before the people they work with (Faust and Nagar 2008).

Within this general scenario of NGO- and donor-driven organizing, the category "woman" poses a special problem. If we focus on international organizations working "on" or "for" women's rights, we often detect a contradictory pattern: On the one hand, the success of identity-based movements has created a political environment where some liberal organizations make a genuine effort to support the struggles of sexual minorities and LGBTQ organizations that argue for a fluid conceptualization of "woman" and "man." On the other hand, the same organizations often betray a tunnel vision that artificially separates issues of sexuality and intimacy from questions of livelihood, resource access, and displacement. As a result, issues of both women and LGBTQ communities continue to get ghettoized in the larger politics of development and globalization, and our sexual bodies and beings are peeled apart from our economic bodies and beings.

Several steps removed from this global politics, our own district of Sitapur is marked by similar tendencies. Whether it is bureaucrats in the District Development Office, the elected representatives of the *panchayats*, or husbands, brothers, and mothers-in-law in our own homes, everywhere those in power want to squeeze the work of SKMS into tightly secluded spaces that are reserved "for women only." These people expect to hear our rage and screams when *gudiya*[10] is beaten or when women's bodies are cut or burned alive, but they consider our political work grossly inappropriate when we demand a social audit of the money allotted to the district to create employment for the rural poor, when we protest the policies that force peasants to commit suicide, or when we refuse to separate the murders of women in our community from the larger political economy of displacement and dispossession in our villages.

When women's issues are collapsed into a predesignated gender and a pre-marked body, and "feminist activism" is gathered and piled into a predetermined list of issues, and when a complex political and cultural economy at local and global scales becomes associated with such a classification, feminism becomes an institutionalized structure, a bureaucracy, and a commerce that feeds the status quo. A compartmentalization of poverty and violence along the lines of gender helps sustain the existing caste- and class-based structures of privilege and deprivation. Today, when the slogan of empowerment for small collectives has become clichéd, it should be possible for every movement to define its own feminism. But such decentralized feminism cannot happily coexist with the interests and requirements of our pro-globalization governments and economies, and the sociopolitical hierarchies that sustain them.

SKMS's victories since October 2005 indicate that resistance to NGOization and to the compartmentalization of women's issues continue fiercely in many small organizations even as such resistance invites the wrath of local government representatives, threats of personal violence, and escalated conflicts with spouses and family who wish to circumscribe and seclude our activism. These threats and conflicts that stretch from the spaces of the block development offices to our courtyards and beds are deeply interwoven with the politics of vote banks; of vested interests that oppose legally sanctioned distribution of employment and compensation of manual labor; and of the manner in which interwoven patriarchies—from national-, state-, district-, and block-level government offices to village *panchayats* and intimate spousal relationships—benefit from keeping "women's issues" separated from "men's." For SKMS to continue its faith in its own movement, then, it is necessary that we recognize the strong possibility that our journey might advance only amid economic hardships and political threats, largely in isolation from those institutions that sponsor activism in the name of "oppressed women only."

In the end, we would like to return to the argument about the need for dialogical practices that are committed to linking academic praxis with political praxis. In providing an illustration of such praxis SKMS's work suggests that the quality of any intellectual project cannot be evaluated solely on the basis of the soundness of a research design or its successful implementation. Similarly, the success of any community-based effort cannot be evaluated primarily on the basis of some predetermined measures of "empowerment" that are met (or not) within a given time frame. If we truly believe that the political and the intellectual are mutually constitutive, then the durability and the value of a collective community-based struggle—or a journey, as we like to conceptualize it in SKMS—must also be assessed on the basis of whether all the members of an alliance can participate fully in the processes of making, revising, and deploying the coproduced knowledge, and in developing rigorous structures of accountability that allow people from all fields—the farms, the disciplines, and the villages of "intervention"—to evaluate the relevance of that knowledge in their own lives and journeys.

Notes

We thank Chandra Talpade Mohanty, David Faust, Sharad Chari, Linda Peake, Rose Brewer, and the members of the Transnational Feminist Praxis collective for their incisive comments on earlier versions of this chapter, and their challenging and nourishing engagement with the ongoing journey of SKMS. An earlier version of this essay appeared in *Critical Asian Studies* 41(3) in 2009..

1. The organization Sangtin was registered in 1999. In 2005, this organization was renamed by its membership as the Sangtin Kisaan Mazdoor Sangathan (Sangtin Peasants and Workers Organization). "Sangtin Writers" (in English) and "Sangtin Samooh" (in Hindi) are names we use for different combinations

of members of Sangtin Kisaan Mazdoor Sangathan who come together from time to time to write our reflections and analyses. As in the case of *Sangtin Yatra* and *Playing with Fire*, some authors in the collective choose to use their last names while others reject them either because they are taking a stand against using last names that reveal caste affiliations or because they do not want their families to feel "outed" by their own stories and critiques.

2. Tehsils and blocks are administrative subdivisions of a district.

3. Debroy and Bhandari 2003. The identification of these "most backward" districts is based on estimated poverty ratios, percentage of households going hungry, infant mortality rates, levels of immunization, literacy rates, and enrollment ratios for 2001. Women's social status is reflected in Sitapur's low sex ratio, which has increased in the last decade from 833 to 862 females per thousand males.

4. For historical overviews and critical analyses of women's movements in colonial and postcolonial India, see Kumar 1993; Sen 2002; and John 2002.

5. Two of Sangtin's founding members, Surbala and Richa Singh, are coauthors of this chapter.

6. Three of the nine authors of *Sangtin Yatra* have continued to work closely with Sangtin's new members and campaigns. The remaining six authors who have continued their jobs in NSY have been promoted and three have moved out of Sitapur. While these transitions have been difficult for SKMS, we have found the metaphor of a train ride extremely helpful in making sense of these changes: If the vision of feminist politics that we articulated in *Sangtin Yatra/Playing with Fire* is only realizable through a long journey, then the cotravelers on that journey can be imagined as being on an extended train ride. Some travelers will accompany SKMS through some stops and then leave the train, others will get on board with an intention of staying till the end, and there will be still others who will come and go and return to the train as they can. But each traveler who climbs on the train will remain critical in shaping the course of SKMS's journey irrespective of the length for which she or he stays on board.

7. One U.S. dollar was equal to approximately 44 rupees at the time of this struggle. The minimum wage in 2009 increased to Rs. 100 per day.

8. *Chamariya* and *pasiniya* are derogatory terms used in this context by an upper-caste man for women from Raidas and Paasi castes, two *dalit* communities that constitute a visible force in SKMS.

9. In March 2006, the central government of India notified thirteen new parameters for defining the Below Poverty Line (BPL) category of people in the country. Doing away with the earlier definitions based on food calories or annual earnings, the government's revised definition of BPL was based on landholding, type of dwelling, clothing, food security, hygiene, capacity for buying commodities, literacy, minimum wages earned by the household, means of livelihood, education of children, debt, migration, and priority for assistance (Special Correspondent 2006). BPL families are entitled to special subsidies. The Antyodaya Anna Yojana is an additional food subsidy for the poorest of BPL families.

10. The reference here is to the monsoon festival of Gudiya that is observed in many parts of Uttar Pradesh, including Sitapur District. During this festival, girls and young women make rag dolls and bring them to a public place,

where their brothers thrash the dolls with a whip. For the founding members of Sangtin (now SKMS) the transformation of rituals and symbolic violence associated with this festival constituted the first major activist struggle, one that brought considerable recognition by government authorities within Sitapur as well as in feminist circles outside Sitapur.

Works Cited

Anupamlata et al. 2004. *Sangtin Yatra: Saat Zindgiyon Mein Lipta Nari Vimarsh*. Sitapur: Sangtin.

Debroy, Bibek, and Laveesh Bhandari, eds. 2003. *District-Level Deprivation in the New Millennium*. New Delhi: Konark Publishers Pvt. Ltd.

De Souza, Karen, and Linda Peake. 2010. "Feminist Academic and Activist Praxis in Service of the Transnational," chapter 5 in this volume.

Faust, David, and Richa Nagar. 2008. "Nongovernmental Organizations (NGOs)." In William A. Darity, ed., *International Encyclopedia of the Social Sciences, 2nd Edition*. Farmington Hills: Macmillan Reference USA/Thomson Gale. 520–521.

Ghosh, Jayati, 2006. "Making the Employment Guarantee Work." http://www.macroscan.com/cur/may06/cur200506Employment_Guarantee.htm (Accessed 12 August 2006).

Hamara Safar. 2006. Editorial, "Paribhasha Mahila Muddon Ki" [The Definition of Women's Issues]. *Hamara Safar* 1(2): 1–2.

Hindustan Times Correspondent. 2006. "Women Deprived of Employment Under NREGS." *Hindustan Times*, July 12, Lucknow.

John, Mary E. 2002. "Feminism, Poverty and Globalization: An Indian View." *Inter-Asia Cultural Studies* 3(3): 351–367.

Johnson, E. Patrick. 2005. "'Quare' Studies, or (Almost) Everything I Know about Queer Studies I Learned from My Grandmother." In E. Patrick Johnson and Mae G. Henderson, eds., *Black Queer Studies: A Critical Anthology*. Durham: Duke University Press.124–157.

Kumar, Radha. 1993. *The History of Doing: An Illustrated Account of Movements for Women's Rights and Feminism in India, 1800–1990*. New Delhi: Kali for Women.

Nagar, Richa. 2008. "Languages of Collaboration." In Karen Falconer Al Hindi and Pamela Moss, eds., *Feminisms, Geographies, Knowledges*. Lanham, MD: Rowman & Littlefield.120–129.

Sangtin Writers (and Richa Nagar) 2006. *Playing with Fire: Feminist Thought and Activism Through Seven Lives in India*. New Delhi: Zubaan (and Minneapolis: University of Minnesota Press).

Sen, Samita. 2002. "Towards a Feminist Politics? The Indian Women's Movement in Historical Perspective." In Karin Kapadia, ed., *The Violence of Development: The Politics of Identity, Gender and Social Inequalities in India*. New Delhi: Kali for Women. 459–524.

Sheppard, Eric. 2006. Quandaries of Critical Geography. Plenary Lecture. IGU Regional Conference, Brisbane, Australia.

Special Correspondent. 2006. "New Parameters for Defining BPL Category." *The Hindu: Online Edition of India's National Newspaper*, 22 March, http://www.hindu.com/2006/03/22/stories/2006032216750100.htm (Accessed 17 August 2008).

PART III

Representations and Reclamations

〈 7 〉

So Much to Remind Us We Are Dancing on Other People's Blood

Moving toward Artistic Excellence, Moving from Silence to Speech, Moving in Water, with Ananya Dance Theatre

OMISE'EKE NATASHA TINSLEY, ANANYA CHATTERJEA, HUI NIU WILCOX, AND SHANNON GIBNEY

I

undercurrent, undercurrent, wave, up, stretch, out: arms move like this, and feet are toes and ball and sole and heel against the floor solid to the bone and then it isn't. pour one, two, three, four until water covers in quick rivulets and feet splash, leave curves of toes and movement that dissolve again. on the west bank of the mississippi, where slave women jumped ship to land in the love of their own kind, ten brown women are dancing together and i'm one of them. at rehearsal we've been dancing through eleven twelve one two o'clock and first my muscles thawed clumsily and now they've dissolved, warm lava ropes under skin and i'm not thinking half moon leg bend to come up arms undercurrent undercurrent wave.

listen, i'm not sure you heard. on the west bank of the mississippi river, where slave women jumped ship to land in the love of their own kind, ten brown women are dancing together and the name of the piece is duurbaar, unstoppable; duurbaar, a meditation on water and women and how both keep going and create ways to the horizon when you think none is possible. ten brown women dancing, don't just look, listen: odissi footwork jumps and plants and raises so you land strong and every cell of skin kisses earth and connects with her to make sound, because why should brown women land quietly when our own feet can be drums? in april i saw these women perform and when they turned their bodies into music i knew i wanted to do this. and, here i am. here i am, training and my body doesn't know this movement, struggles like legs walking through water before they lift and swim, my brown body

*is small and angular and wants to curve perfectly like a creek over rocks or the gold
of an earring against a neck. so i come back, and back and back to rehearsals, glaze
eyed almost trying, and one day i learn the whole of a dance with the company and
i realize: they are brown women and i will be water with them. duurbaar, water as
women's way of moving through the world and water as the world's way of moving
through women.*

*the first act is cremation at the river, water as the cycle of departure and loss; the
second act is tsunami and womb, bursting ocean as the violent eruption of energy
and life; the third act is water bearers and the shouldered fullness of pots once
empty, the work of carrying dreams and healing. yes, the work. this is the act i'm
learning as we move on stage all hips and push with brass water pots and let them
splash in small amounts until finally, backs to the audience and torsos curved like
crescent moons, we pour the water over our head one two three four five six seven:
exquisite, ananya says, as it overflows and we become all liquid and the light honeys
us even though we can't see it. we dance, then, in the spilled water and she's right,
it's beautiful, all the legs through the wet like play and love making shapes new each
time. so filled on the west bank of the river the vessel overflows but that isn't the
end: because to dance in cascaded water is work, moving legs so we glide without
slipping, trying to find footing in a new element without losing the beat.*

*women! ananya shouts. women! move more! torsos! remember this is not a ritual
but we must make it ritualized, making meaning out of the everyday work of
women's lives. your body is a surface, don't be afraid to let water and hands run
over it. women! brown women, landed.*

II

When I landed in New York from Kolkata, India, in 1989, I came with expectations, unfounded in any reality, that I would find myself in the midst of artists from different aesthetics and cultures, who would be enthusiastic about working together to find resonances and create "something new." Nothing of that sort happened and I soon realized that despite the much-publicized rhetoric of "multiculturalism" intercultural projects usually involved white and other; and artists of color, and artists from Asia and Africa, were meant in fact to be ghettoized in particular ways. They were, and are, meant not to communicate, or build solidarities across racial and cultural lines, which make sense, if the power structures are going to stay intact. In a context of limited resources, as is the case with art-making, the alignment of "minorities" along a hierarchy of oppressions and a designated pecking order spell disaster.

Figure 7.1   Act III from *Duurbaar*, when, after burning thirst, water finally enters and fills the space. Stefania Strowder (*standing*), on the floor, back row, (*left to right*) Ananya Chatterjea, Ruchika Singhal, front row (*left to right*), Hui Niu Wilcox, Chitra Vairavan. Photo courtesy of Ananya Dance Theatre.

Ananya Dance Theatre was conceived as a company of progressive (not just liberal) women artists of color from the Third World specifically to combat one of the most dangerous results of a pervasive lack of conversations among communities of color, without which creating a cooperative, mutually respectful society is ultimately impossible. Community-building workshops we have conducted repeatedly reveal the deep need to create more spaces where difficult dialogues among communities of color could happen, such that histories of alienation and hostility toward each other could be faced and the process of building new communities could begin. For me, the shared labor of the dance, sweating together as we search for a shared articulation of dream, beauty, what we hold in our lives, is part of that process of building an artistic community, an active citizenry for dance. This has meant that the forms I work with—the only ones I know well, Odissi, yoga, chhau—need to be deconstructed and reconstructed in keeping with the shared narratives that are created by the women together, in intersection with their diverse cultural and political histories, their shared histories of struggle and resistance, and their shared articulation of dream.

The choreography articulates a form that, while still clearly recognizable in a South Asian aesthetic, still resituates itself as it settles in different bodies, and is specifically deconstructed and hybridized to tell this complex, diasporic, story.

III

minneapolis, minnesota, the great white north, city of water and land of ten thousand lakes: in winter this city is all water, yes, frozen into snow and ice rushing the streets so you're walking through another kind of ocean and, if mermaid-identified like me, you have to be able to see it flowing still. i relocated here in 2005 to take my first job as an assistant professor, my research excavating and exploring a century of poems, novels, songs, and dances by caribbean women who love women. late in my first winter with march forcing its way to april i sat by dark windows and lit computers, reading and writing about someone swimming through my texts—a femme called a manman dlo. manman dlo: the creole mother of waters, a mermaid come from west africa on slave ships who now lives in lakes and rivers in trinidad, martinique, grenada, guadeloupe, domenica. manman dlo: the power of women's knowledge, spiriting girls and young women under water to tell them secrets that change their lives when they come back; the power of fluid gender and sexuality, body changing underwater so s/he can either penetrate lovers or be penetrated by them as s/he chooses. but this winter i was reading about her in another way too, as a character reinvented to intervene in something more concrete, more contemporary. in trinidad, another (is)land of water surrounded by sea and crisscrossed by rivers, beaches have been captured enclosed for tourists and oil and so many women now live beach-, fresh-, and running-waterless in cities where, bucketed, they go every day to draw water from one dripping standpipe a few blocks away—on this (is)land so hot water never could freeze literally it's frozen in another way, too far away or too choked with pollution to flow into inhabitants. manman dlo is power for these women, too, who organized an environmental movement to demand access to clean water and took the angry mermaid as the group's namesake and inspiration because, never forget this, being mermaid-identified has its practical purposes too. manman dlo became a name for a group of brown women demanding water for other brown women, teaching each other how to access it and that they had a right to.

as i was reading this here in minneapolis (minne, dakotah for *water* and polis, greek for *city*) march did push its way into april, rain opened its way so all the snow ran into the mississippi and its siblings, and one night when this was happening in an umbrella-bending way i went to see ananya dance theatre perform. shannon invited me and explained that this was a woman of color dance troupe based in deconstructed/reconstructed classical indian dance but, really, i didn't know what that meant or what to expect. the show i saw that night was about women's dreams and how they change the world, and dancing with bamboo poles this troupe of multicolored women showed how with rhythm and flow instead of rigidness, with all cinnamon bark feminine suppleness, you can move around things that otherwise could cage you and there, in the theater dark, i cry when i see them move like melted rivers around barriers. afterward in question and answer a thin-skinned paunchy man asked, ananya, why don't you choreograph for men? and i wanted to shout *what part of this piece or this world didn't you pay attention to?* because i'd seen it clearly. this woman of color dance company in the improbable city of minneapolis was another current of manman dlo's work, another way of women calling on the natural resources of their bodies and imaginations—sometimes that's the technology you have—to take old forms and reconstruct them for new purposes, women demanding resources for other brown women and teaching each other how to access them, that they had a right to. with two weeks and shannon's intervention i was rehearsing with the company, stumbling through steps that seemed to be walking over me but every bit as determined as winter had been cold.

when i came we were creating *duurbaar*, a piece where dancers were working with water. now, to write *working with water* might be redundant. because to say *water* to women in so many parts of the world—parts of eastern europe, west africa, northern south america, south asia—is to say *work*. to say *water* is to say get up before the household, put a bucket on your head, fill it so heavy you can't carry it back any other way, know you're open to assault on your way there and back, know once you're back what heavies the bucket will be exhausted in washing and cooking you'll do day after day. this you can read about in the united nations report on women and water, which spells out:

In most cultures . . . women have accumulated an impressive store of environmental wisdom, being the ones to find water, to educate children in hygiene matters and to understand the impact of poor sanitation on health. At the same time, women and girls are often are obliged to walk many hours every day fetching water, while men are rarely expected to perform such tasks. A 2002 UNICEF study of rural households in 23 Sub-Saharan

> African countries found that a quarter of them spent 30 minutes to an hour
> each day collecting and carrying water, and 19% spent an hour or more.
> With closer water comes greater self-esteem, less harassment of women and
> better school attendance by girls—three things spontaneously mentioned
> by people in Ethiopia, Ghana, Tanzania and India.[1]

and ananya dance theatre was unlike any group of dancers i'd ever been with because before, during, and after the choreographing of these pieces we were discussing this, sharing knowledge of brown women's material relationships to water in the global south that connected to our global north. (if we forgot this connection the mississippi was there to remind us.) and we were carrying water, too. by the end of the third act the stage was drenched in it and we poured it all in ourselves and, beautiful as it looked, it was not easy. all that water was heavy, cold, noisy, messy, it took several buckets on every dancer's part—too little and dancers slipped moving between the wet and the dry, too much and it threatened the lights and the audience, dry spots had to be smoothed over as if it were part of the dance and dams had to be engineered to keep the water on stage. people shouted, complained, praised, laughed, cried, refused to speak, drew diagrams as part of this process. it would have been one thing to build on water as a metaphor for femininity, to splash a little across our costumes; it was quite another to immerse ourselves in the materiality of it and it was hard. but this piece was an act of solidarity with other women who work with water and a statement of the need to imagine transforming this work, and *so to be water with the women of ananya dance theatre was never ever easy.* and it was never supposed to be.

IV

Ten years after I left everything behind in China, I found a new home, where my body explores its limits and my spirit roams free. It is my hope that my daughters will dance, dream, and journey with me and other brown women, to a horizon where our beauty and power defy all questions, doubts, and accusations.

V

I began learning dance as a child, often through what I call the "desire of generations"—I never met my grandmother but was told she loved to see dance.

Figure 7.2   Act II from *Duurbaar*, the womb section, where the women rebirth themselves. Across (*left to right*): Shannon Gibney, Gina Kundan, Serena Thompson, Beverly Cottman, Pramila Vasudevan, Ruchika Singhal. Photo courtesy of Ananya Dance Theatre.

VI

I was a new mother, still nursing a nine-month-old baby. My mobility had been severely confined by motherhood. Not with Ananya Dance Theatre. Claire has since grown up with Ananya Dance Theatre, attending numerous rehearsals, mouthing everybody's water bottles, tugging on other brown women's legs thinking they were mine, mimicking the footwork and even the choreography.

In November 2004, in the midst of rehearsing for *Bandh*, I found myself pregnant. I dreaded breaking the news to Ananya: "Will she kick me out of the company?" I was aware of the problem a pregnant body poses for many dance aesthetics. Ananya looked at me with her famously intense eyes: "Are you going to be OK? Will you be able to handle, having two kids and all that? Just do what you can." I was touched by her concern about my well-being. And I couldn't believe that she didn't make a huge deal out of my "bad news." Imagine my surprise when she created a solo part for my pregnant body, and when she had the costume designer highlight my bulging belly with costume and makeup. I performed *Bandh* when I was nearly eight months pregnant, and I had never felt more powerful in my entire life. I was big, heavy, and grounded. The baby moved more than usual during the shows—she must have felt all that excitement as well. When I did the "frantic search" dance during the performance, in the wings, Gina (another dancer) saw the baby's movement traced out on my bare belly. It was a magical moment, one that affirmed life, and the power of women's bodies.

Despite all the half-nervous joking about the possibility of water-breaking and labor on stage (I was getting really big), the baby decided she would wait a few more weeks. But we did labor on stage—women's labor was one of the themes we explored in creating that performance.

Our collective labor continued, until the water did break on stage, during *Duurbaar* in 2006. In a section we call "Womb," we inch on the ground, heads tucked close, torsos and limbs contracted, hands clasped. In these fetal positions, deep memories from within our bodies surface: pain and violence, ambiguity, contradictions, the birthing of our children, and even, the actual birthing of ourselves. For our bodies store the memories of our mothers and grandmothers, too. Now our backs are on the ground, legs bent and wide open. As if we were on a hospital bed. But wait, we lift our heads and gaze out into the audience, while tracing the curves of our bodies with our own hands. Yes, we are looking back, knowing that in the darkness out there hide gazes that are curious, disgusted, or moved. Never relenting our gaze, we rise up and confront the world with full awareness of our own sexuality and its worldly and spiritual consequences. After the prolonged labor on the ground, the moment of rising exhilarates. We now take up the vertical space, spine tall, legs extended and spread, feet firmly planted—strong, invincible wall of brown women. Slowly, with intention and deliberation, we carve the space with our charged arms, and turn our heads to the direction of Ananya, emerging from the collective womb to gather with her young daughter Srija. Instead of looking at them, we gaze far beyond them into the infinite. We are the feminine divine, aware of our lives' vulnerability and tenderness, but emanating our collective power that has to be reckoned with.

It was with this power and knowledge that I welcomed Lynn into this world. Not surprisingly, Lynn is entirely in tune with the space of ADT, having known it since the beginning of her existence in the womb. She would fall asleep in the stroller right in the middle of our resounding footwork. Now she toddles around the beautiful, powerful ADT women during rehearsals, sometimes immersed in the joy of exploring the space, sometimes demanding to be seen and heard. I can't help but wonder: What memories do our children's small, growing bodies hold and create? What dances will they do when these memories scream to be told? I know they will dance, because they are dancing now.

VII

My mother recounted many stories of her watching dance performances as a child, mesmerized by the magical beauty of it all. However, due to (a) the destructive policies of the colonial regime, and (b) the dubious politics of a postcolonial reconstruction era, where women's sexuality and national identity were inextricably entangled with the work of revival, and other factors of access and financial ability, my mother and my grandmother were not able to follow anything of their interest in dance. However, by the time I was five, my mother had researched all possibilities and enrolled in dance classes with great enthusiasm. It is really her desire that drove me in the beginning—the getting-up at 6 am to get to the early Sunday morning classes, the classes right after school on weekday evenings, so I would quickly eat a snack and change into dance clothes in the back seat as she drove me to dance class—and I complained often. But in the end she had the last laugh, because dance became a bigger passion for me than anything else, and I have come to believe in its potential to articulate ideas and beliefs and to move people more than she had ever thought possible at that time.

Initially spellbound by the beauty, philosophical richness, and rigor of the classical forms, I gradually came to question some of the bases of these forms as I grew older. As a young woman, connected with the women's organizations that were protesting against domestic violence, state-sponsored assault on women's bodies, and other similar issues through street theater, I developed a strong dis/ease about the classicism that seemed to live in the dance studio, disconnected, totally, with the issues that I, and others around me, were struggling with on a daily basis. Throughout my adolescent and college years, I felt that the heady beauty and richness of the classicism that I could embody and could shape my body with great ease, despite the prickly questions about gender, sexuality, and beauty that raced through my blood and threatened to break through my skin, ultimately entrapped me in a mute body. Through the years, the many instances in which I saw women's bodies being subjected to the several kinds of violence—emotional and epistemic, domestic and state-sponsored—put me at odds with the smooth harmony of the dance I was learning. For me, these signaled to me an aporia, a rupture that would never heal.

VIII

There have been several moments in my life when I saw my own body for the first time.

IX

And differently from much classical repertoire, where there is a romantic and harmonious notion of heterosexual love, I have found it imperative to interrogate the overt silences and plumb the depths of a violence that destroys many women's lives and undermines the celebration of the love and passion of Radha and Krishna and other mythological characters shared, and that we danced about as part of our classical repertoire. These questions were rooted in experiential reality, in what I saw and heard growing up in Kolkata, India, and what I continue to see and hear, with escalating force, around me here in the United States. Ultimately, I moved away from the performance of these classical forms to re-embody them in ways that could resonate with contemporary life experience, and to choreograph pieces about issues that move me or change my life in different ways.

X

One was the first day of junior high school, when I entered my homeroom, and a group of black kids huddled in the middle of the room snickered at me, and made loud and disparaging comments about my hair, clothing, and way of talking. Instead of confronting them, like I had done to most kids in my life up to that point, I held back for some reason, and shrank into myself. I wanted to be *unseen*. As it was, my body had a valence, a charge that I felt I couldn't control—a relation to all the other bodies in the room that I didn't want. The thought crossed my mind: *I have a black body*, as I gathered my elbows in my palms and hunched my shoulders. What I couldn't say then but could articulate with every emotional fiber of my being was that my body belonged, not to myself, but to a particular history—a history of economic, political, and social oppression based on American conceptions of "race"—that the black kids in my class knew this, and that they were prepared to teach me, if not the history itself, then its present ramifications, one way or another.

Another seminal moment in which my body became anew—or, should I say, situated within a sociohistorical context, connected with other brown

Figure 7.3   Act II from *Duurbaar*, desire and connection. (*In the foreground*) Chitra Vairavan and Ananya Chatterjea. (*In the background*) Pramila Vasudevan. Photo courtesy of Ananya Dance Theatre.

bodies that had undergone the same or similar epistemological violence as my own—was when I moved to the Twin Cities, in 2002. I was twenty-seven at the time, and knew exactly three people in the entire metro area. By then, I had quite a developed sense of my identity as a middle-class mixed black woman, and the ways in which race, gender, class, and other alterities both limited and opened up possibilities for movement and self-determination. I saw how many white liberals responded to my presence in their personal and professional circles as the "good" black person, and I also saw how some black women were uncomfortable with my light skin and tight curls, and how some black men were equally uncomfortable with my age, abilities, and strident outspokenness. I had decided by that time to claim both the "mixed" and the "black" parts of myself, to resist the easy binaries that some blacks and whites seemed to want to put me in. I began to adopt at that time, and still do, the identity of the "mixed black" woman—that is, one who identifies as black politically, but who is adept in both white and black social circles. It had taken me quite a while to get to this point in the complex interstices of my identity—especially since the everyday negotiations it entailed could be quite sticky and also exhausting. Being in my late twenties, I was also feeling particularly grounded at this point, and did not foresee any large shifts in my self-concept in the immediate future. Imagine my surprise then, meeting a host of other people of color, who were, as I was, adopted and raised by white people, and who called themselves "transracial adoptees." This was the first time I had ever heard the phrase, and its attendant question both terrified and thrilled me: "Am I a transracial adoptee?"

All of my life up to that point, I had thought of myself as an aberration of sorts, a person who exists on the fringes of multiple communities and therefore makes her home "on the borderlands," as Gloria Anzaldua has written. Indeed, I had become quite comfortable being uncomfortable, and was pleased with the price of social homelessness: an ability to shape-shift, fit in, and negotiate my way through multiple communities, languages, and meaning systems. I had no idea that I was not special in this regard, that most transracial adoptees learn this skill in order to survive, and hopefully, in their later years, thrive.

Hearing the experiences of these new friends, I realized suddenly that I was an archetype. At a very basic level, I was a body that had responded to what was being enacted upon it by striving for, constantly reaching for the choice that would yield me the most freedom, the most unrestricted movement, in each case. These friends of mine, who were predominantly Korean American, had made similar choices. I began to see a line, something tangible, that was connecting my life, my body, and my struggle to find, articulate, and embrace a liberatory politic, to each of them. Although we were vastly different people (some of them had children, partners, houses), there was a throughway, a rope to swing me over an abyss I had not even known I was on the edge of. I finally had words to describe what had happened to me, what was happening to me. And they weren't random words either—they were the same words my friends used to describe what happened to them. It would not be hyperbolic to say that getting this narrative down—this narrative of resistance, of critique, and of the complexities of familial love—changed every part of my life, and made me see the vastness of history in my own body. This body was black, but it was also (perhaps more importantly, in this particular moment of Empire?) brown.

Enter Ananya Dance Theatre. Soon after I began calling myself a transracial adoptee, I received an email message, calling for women of color in the Twin Cities to audition for a new dance work that would be based in South Asian movement forms. The call stated that participants need not be trained as dancers, but should definitely have some kind of commitment to social justice. As a girl, I had taken ballet lessons for years, but in the end, I felt more comfortable kicking a ball across a field than pirouetting across a floor, so I gave ballet up for soccer when I was eleven and never looked back. Having no familiarity with South Asian dance, I doubted that I would make it past the first audition, but I thought that there was no harm in checking it out anyway.

When I arrived at the dance studio in spring 2003, I saw a crowd of African American, South Asian, and East Asian women at the door. I had seen a few people at various functions around town, but I basically didn't know anyone. The project's leader, Ananya Chatterjea (also a contributor to this volume), gathered all of us in a circle and began to tell us about her vision—why she had asked us to come, and what she hoped we could build. The more she talked, the more I felt my energy rise and connect with the other women in the room, and the more I hoped that I would make the cut and be able to participate in this budding community. "As women of color, we are so often kept from each other," Ananya said. "Living in this racist culture, we are dealing with whiteness so much of the time that we never have the chance to really deal with *each other*. And patriarchy plays the same role. This project will try to bust that wall, by giving us a space to engage each other through the medium of movement—specifically, movement based in South Asian art forms." I looked at the Chinese American woman to my right and the African American woman to my left. From where I had started, as a mixed girl adopted into a white family, it was a long road to where I sat now, Shannon Gibney, a mixed black transracially adopted woman. It had taken me years to see that my upper lip jutted out at the same angle as this woman beside me, that that was because we both had black ancestors, and that these distinct features of ours, as different as they were from others, had their own kind of beauty. But, listening to Ananya speak, I saw that when I thought of myself in relation to others, it was always a white other, a male other, or a non-adopted other. Seldom did I consider what my relationship was to South Asian, Latino, Native, or East Asian people, *in and of itself*. Sure, I interacted with many different kinds of people from many different backgrounds in my daily life, but how much did I actually know about their collective histories—in this country, or internationally? As we continued talking about the specific aesthetics that the project would utilize, I realized that I knew next to nothing about South Asian arts and political activism. Of course I was familiar with Gandhi, and I knew a little bit about the Indian independence movement, but I had no idea, for instance, that Indian women were on the forefront of women's movements around the world. I had no idea that the Indian state of Bengal, where Ananya is from, has a long and illustrious history as a communist state—one in which the arts are generally viewed as an integral part of social change, not separate from it, as is the common view here. The longer I danced in the group (yes, I actually *did* make the cut), the more uncomfortable I became with the fact that whole histories—many of them histories of colonization, of languageless experience, and of resistance—were foreign to me. It was like the moment in my last year of graduate school when one of my professors gave me Frantz Fanon's *Black Skin, White Masks*. After devouring the book in two days, one thought pounded my cranium so hard that I wanted to break something in the hopes that it would relieve the pressure: "How have I never read this before? Who has been keeping this from me?" As a curious and voracious reader, it was hard to swallow that Fanon would not have stumbled across my path until I was twenty-six. It was equally difficult to accept that I had just stumbled upon the incredible groundedness I felt standing in *chauka*, the basic step in the Odissi repertoire we were learning. Women had been dancing this form for centuries, women who did not look exactly like me, but who were marked by their color and sex in ways that were very similar to me, women who had engaged in building community and resisting their own oppression as I was. Where were their stories? Was the only place I could find them in my own body, as I struggled to grasp the movement, to see the beauty, sensuality, and sexuality in the feminine energy that Odissi is rooted in? Was I, a black woman in the United States, completely responsible for the fact that I had never engaged this knowledge before? Was it simply a question of personal agency (that hallmark of Western thought), or were there more structural impediments to consider?

The more I questioned, looked deeper, questioned, and looked even deeper, the more I came to believe that it was, indeed, the structural walls of racism, sexism, classism, nationalism, homophobia, and other social malaises that kept me from the knowledge I needed to free myself. That was what had kept me from black people in the beginning, that was what had kept me from transracial adoptees in the middle, and that was what kept me from deep engagement with other women of color, most recently. My problem was, is, not specific. In fact, it is the problem of people everywhere: How can I free myself if I don't understand what I must be free of? How can I tell my story if I have no language to tell it? Who will hear my story if no one understands my language?

Figure 7.4   Act II from *Duurbaar*, memory/flow, where the serpentine walk of one group of women with empty water pots intersected with a trio dancing to breathe in the flow of memories and a soloist working through historical memory. (*From far left to right*) emerging slowly from the background (serpentine walk): Kaysone Syonesa, Stefania Strowder, Omise'eke Tinsley, Shannon Gibney. (*Left foreground*) soloist Beverly Cottman. (*Far left to right*) flow trio: Gina Kundan, Hui Niu Wilcox, Kayva Yang. Photo courtesy of Ananya Dance Theatre.

XI

For those of us who want to continue to break the silence that we often impose on ourselves, there is a complex set of negotiations to work through. There is a continuous difficulty in creating art that arises out of critical commentary on problems internal to the "community" (understood, no doubt, in a rather essentialist way) and simultaneously combating racist generalizations, whereby particular situations of criminal or abhorrent behavior can be used to stigmatize and demonize a whole people.

On the other hand, there is also the need to battle the community's charge of "washing dirty laundry in public," of acting only to enhance the embarrassments and discomfitures of living in a racist society. This is the kind of pressure that often pushes artists of color into silencing themselves about issues that then continue to haunt and plague their lives. Indeed, to navigate one's way sensitively in between biased responses in creating artwork on such issues is a challenging task.

XII

Bodies . . . a potent site of struggle.

XIII

we were literally working with water; we, northern-living brown women were figuratively working with fluidity. this is a woman of color dance troupe, and central to its vision are artistic excellence, political awareness and community, and creating these across lines of race, ethnicity, and sexuality to perform meaningfully postcolonially. if i brought my stumbling ankles back day after day it was because this pan-brown fluidity was not only inspiring but necessary, absolutely necessary to being whole and present here in this place northern europeans violently robbed first from the dakotah, then the ojibwe, and that they imagine as "their" own land (not water). to hear women talking about their family in india in china, about cherokee ancestors and mixed-race stereotypes, about where to get your hair braided and where to buy lychee, was to be grounded, to be where you make sense. it was to have space to say something that you really need to say and can only say in many voices, enough to speak like the overflowing gorgon you know you are.

but to work with this figurative fluidity is also hard. what does our work of bridging colors, religions, races, sexualities mean? what does it mean to imagine being "minorities" together? hui grew up in china, where as a han chinese she was not a minority; stefania was born in jamaica, where she wasn't either; i also grew up thinking of myself as a majority, since i went to a high school ninety percent african american and thought when people spoke of blacks as being minorities they meant they had a minority of power. more than one woman in the troupe grew up in overwhelmingly white communities, and clearly minorities, didn't identify as *women of color*: who would they identify with, after all, and why go to pains to divide themselves when they were so clearly divided? the term that qualifies us for this company—women of color—means very different things to its members, and allowing for these divergent meanings is politically indispensable and sometimes personally painful. what womanness means, too, is not the same for all. when i first joined someone joked to me to be careful, adt members are always getting pregnant: and while that knocked the wind out of me yes, i got then and there heterosexuality and potential reproductiveness can be tacitly assumed by fellow dancers to be part of the womanness we share.

While i always have identified as *of color* i sometimes identify as woman and sometimes as queer femme, and maintain the importance of holding that difference.

figurative fluidity is hard, and i know this as materially as i know the heaviness of a bucket of water. i started tracing a parallel between women organizing around water in the caribbean and women dancing around water here and i did this knowing, always, the difficult stories of my friend and inspiration thomas glave, one of the founders of the jamaican forum of lesbians, all-sexuals, and gays (jflag). thomas is mermaid-identified too, he looks in the caribbean sea and sees it inhabited by a special queer brown dreamer: a "child—let us know him/her as 'S/he'—possessed of a slender penis of startlingly delicate green, the truest color of the sea that s/he had always loved—that sea which licked and foamed out and back, out and in again, all about the shores of that place; s/he also possessed a pair of luminous blue breasts the tone of the purest skies that, on the gentlest days, nuzzled their broad, soft chins against the sea."[2] still looking in the sea so strategizing on the basis of all being children of the same waters, thomas urged jflag activists to participate in solidarity in the actions of jamaican women's groups—only to find, when the time came to reciprocate, women's groups didn't want to associate with sodomites. and this isn't even just a problem of homophobia (that, yes, blaring as a conch shell) but of organizing. because some brown women there are sodomites, you know this, but strategically every group has to have its limits—i understand after all why the paunchy white male questioner shouldn't dance with us—and where, how often, and how hard will feminists of color draw theirs? always, always, when there's a little water it makes it easier to fall when you step on the dry spots.

but the solution to this unevenness can't be eliminating fluidity, can't be throwing over attempts to organize in multicolored, multigendered ways in favor of organizing (yet again, the eighties returning like bush) around a single identity. much as i and my co-dancers might long for a dry, smooth stage some days, as if that were possible with all our sweat. no. the solution can only be no solution, can only be maintaining tension between what rushes us together and what flows us apart, returning endlessly to negotiate this balancing act and then renegotiate it and renegotiate it again. as rinaldo walcott, another queer caribbean theorist, puts it: "What is demanded is a rethinking of community that might allow for different ways of cohering into some form of recognizable political entity. Put another way, we must confront singularities without the willed effort to make them cohere into oneness; we must struggle to make a community of singularities."³ singularities that roil and clash and teem with life like the spaces where currents meet: because jumping in here you know it will hurt and you know it will be hard but it will be movement, this, putting pressure on water means movement.

XIV

We cannot afford to give up hope. Is that specific to the experience of marginalization? Possibly. Hope is what pushes us to resist and fight against forces so much bigger than us. If we rationalized hope, it is about survival, it generates energy and passion. All our projects are about hope ultimately. . . . What enables us to dance? To dance, really? There is so much to remind us we are dancing on other people's blood. It takes work to be able to create that beauty as a healing force and to enjoy creating it. Building that community and ensemble is about finding a way to let hope materialize into energy.

Epilogue

What does it mean to collaborate in physical and visceral ways, not sharing space in terms of discrete chapters of a book, but dancing on a floor drenched with all of our sweat, articulating shared rhythms, if with different accents? Our writing of this has followed that model/experience of working together in movement and performing, interwoven thoughts and ideas, moving together even as our feet rise and fall individually.

Collaboration is no romance though, a contested and contesting journey, especially as we try to work out particular kinds of South-South alliances, to forge strategies that can sustain a space that is at once radical and safe. We mean to indicate a geopolitical scope of alliances, built across global communities of color, keeping in mind the divergent and shared positionalities of these groups. As many women have left the company as have come in, struggling to balance work, family, and dance. In addition, the demands of integrating a developing political consciousness, interpersonal relationships (particularly with those whom you have been structurally pitted against for centuries . . . sometimes more), and an intensive rehearsal regimen are not to be overlooked. These are the internal difficulties, internal to the working group, and to the creative process. And yet, how else to work? How else to function without replicating models generated by and regenerating in turn, hierarchical relations of power? Working collaboratively through intersecting lines of antiracist, antisexist, antihomophobic strategizing seemed to be the only way to work to dissipate the hegemonic placement of intellectual activity and talk about the bodily production of knowledge. And to think about danced images that work through live encounters and movement metaphors to suggest multiple possible articulations.

Then there are the external challenges, which concern having to battle antiquated ideas in the reception of such artwork, and finding the funds and human resources to carry on. For instance, in recent performances in New York City, apparently the citadel of innovative/experimental performance, we struggled with the critical reception of our work, in a context where audiences simply did not understand the value of intersecting racial and social justice with art-making. The leading critic in the *New York Times* complained about the "suffering" in the piece, and about the lack of "finger-work" that supposedly marks the finest of Indian dance. How to keep pointing out that, while our work is based in Indian movement forms, we are in fact not doing Indian dance? How to suggest the power of performance as a mode of organizing communities? So much of what those on the outside would term "subtler" concerns are actually central to everything we do, which is why they often do not even see it. And as for funding, we are constantly trying to fit ourselves into the "artistic excellence" and "social justice" binary, which as we've explained earlier, is antithetical to our very mission. So many artistic organizations and individual artists are struggling in the current funding environment, but we feel especially vulnerable, given the social, political, and aesthetic location of our work.

In light of all this, working on this chapter has been incredibly rewarding for us, because it has given us the opportunity of reflecting on a process that we are only beginning to understand now. There are few models for this work, and the difficulties, the sense of isolation and defeat have often overwhelmed us. Here, we share primarily the residue of that struggle, and of that intense labor.

Notes

1. "Women and Water," United Nations Division for the Advancement of Women and Girls (February 2005).
2. Thomas Glave, *Words to Our Now* (Minneapolis: University of Minnesota Press, 2005), 43.
3. Rinaldo Walcott, "Outside in Black Studies: Reading from a Queer Place in the Diaspora," in E. Patrick Johnson and Mae G. Henderson, eds., *Black Queer Studies: A Critical Anthology* (Durham, NC: Duke University Press, 2005), 93.

(8)

Remapping the Americas

A Transnational Engagement
with Creative Tensions of Community Arts

DEBORAH BARNDT

How can transnational feminist praxis inform social struggles not necessarily focused explicitly on women's issues nor limited to woman participants? What tensions and challenges does it share with transnational education, activism, and art? The conversation with other contributors to this book has created a space for me and fellow collaborators in the VIVA! project to probe the deeper historical and epistemological underpinnings of both our subject—community arts and popular education in the Americas—and our methodology—participatory action research and arts-based research methods.[1] Both our content and process connect to central issues of transnational feminist praxis such as an intersectional analysis of power in cross-border collaborations, an honoring of multiple ways of knowing and embodied practices, and a dynamic relationship between collective reflection and political action.

A Border-Crossing Project

The VIVA! project[2] involves eight partners, NGOs, and progressive pockets of universities in Panama, Nicaragua, Mexico, the United States, and Canada. The NGO partners in Central America—the Mexican Institute for Community Development and the Panamanian Social Education and Action Centre—are the key popular education centers in their respective countries, with more than four decades of engagement in local, regional, and transnational social movements.[3] My collaboration with them began in the early 1980s, when we all were part of an internationalist contingent in the historic popular education experiment within the Sandinista Revolution in Nicaragua. A hemispheric cross-fertilization of popular education practices began during that fertile period, sparking the establishment of the

Doris Marshall Institute for Education and Action in Toronto in 1985 and, in 1997, its successor, the Catalyst Centre, one of the northern NGO partners in the VIVA! project, which also includes Jumblies Theatre.

The university partnerships are built both on institutional links (Toronto-based York University, my base, offered a master's degree for faculty of Universidad Regional Autónoma de la Costa Caribeña Nicargüense (URACCAN), a new community-oriented university central to the autonomous movement on the Atlantic Coast of Nicaragua) and on personal contacts: a muralist working with the Zapatistas and based at the Universidad Autónoma Metropolitana (UAM) in Mexico City, a teacher of activist

VIVA! Project Partners

Figure 8.1   VIVA! project partner organizations and community arts projects.

art at UCLA's School of Art and Architecture, an instructor of community arts at York University in Canada. It should be understood, too, that my home, Faculty of Environmental Studies (FES), also at York University, where the project is based, offers a crack within the hegemonic practices of academic knowledge production by allowing (if not encouraging) interdisciplinary, community-based, praxis-oriented participatory research utilizing alternative ways of knowing, including arts-based inquiry.[4]

Our common ground? A commitment to social justice, a history of practice in and theorizing about Freirean-based popular education, a belief in the power of community-based art-making to tap deep cultural histories, to engage peoples' hearts and minds through transformative processes, and to build more democratic and human community organizations and social movements.[5]

In 2003, six of us developed a proposal for collaborative research articulating an emerging framework of creative tensions of community arts and popular education in social movements. After securing a three-year grant from the Canadian Social Science and Humanities Research Council (SSHRC) in 2004, we met in Toronto to craft two major objectives of the project: 1) A local objective (a case study by partners in their own context[6]): Using participatory action research, to recover, promote, and create diverse cultural and artistic practices integrated into processes of popular education and community organization; and 2) A transnational objective (to be achieved through our interchange): Through gatherings, workshops, videos, and books, to organize exchanges of practices and theories, promoting a critical and self-critical perspective and strengthening multicultural and transnational solidarity.

In what ways does this initiative enter into a dialogue on transnational feminist praxis? While my previous work on women workers in the NAFTA food chain was more explicitly feminist in content, the VIVA! project is more explicitly feminist in process.[7] It has been primarily informed by certain feminist epistemological questions and methodological practices:

- Adopting an intersecting analysis of power;
- Honoring local and historically contingent practices but within a context of globalizing processes;
- Focusing on situated knowledges and collaborative knowledge production;
- Promoting self-reflexivity about the internal power dynamics of the project;

- Using arts-based research methods to examine arts-based educational practices that challenge body/mind and reason/emotion dichotomies;
- Developing an ecological and feminist analysis of interconnectedness toward a more holistic popular education;
- Countering top-down imposition of structures and processes, remaining open to emergent and unexpected questions and insights;
- Advocating praxis both in a theory/practice dialectic of research and in a commitment to political action emerging from the community arts and popular education processes.

Still, this brief description of the project begs a broader contextualization and a deeper probing of intent.

Zooming Out: VIVA! in Context

The geopolitical frame is the Americas, and the historical reach goes back to the naming of this hemisphere after an Italian mapmaker who never set foot on the so-called New World. This statue of Christopher Columbus (figure 8.2) offers one representation of the colonial history and the postcolonial theoretical framework of the VIVA! project. On the one hand, we can critically assess it as public art by a European sculptor commissioned in 1867 to erect a monument to the "conquest" in Lima, Peru (though it could be anywhere in the hemisphere or Spain, for that matter), immortalizing the white male European "discoverer" who brought "civilization"—epitomized by opulent clothing, a cross, and an upward gaze—to the "savages/heathens," here a naked Indian maiden. The military struggle involved in the subjugation is erased from this rendition, only hinted at by her arrow tossed to the side. Whenever I use the photo as a catalyst to generate discussion about hegemony in classes or workshops, people inevitably see their own lives within the persistent (carved in stone?) and intersecting power relations: sexism, heterosexism, classism, militarism, religious evangelization, racism.[8] Both its content and its form say something about Eurocentric ways of knowing and artistic expression. Yet, as Ania Loomba (2005: 91) reminds us, there is a danger in reproducing the binary opposites represented in the figures of the colonizer and colonized, even as we attempt to expose how they have functioned historically to construct the European self and the other.

As the VIVA! project has evolved, it has become clearer that we are engaged in a process of decolonization: of education, of research, of art, and of community. Examining any one of these practices/constructs inevitably implicates the others; that is, in attempting to decolonize them, we are reclaiming their inseparability. The Spanish invaders used the Arawak word *areitos* to describe "a collective act involving singing, dancing, celebration, and worship that claimed aesthetic as well as sociopolitical and religious legitimacy," reflecting that the cultural expressions of the Indigenous communities "exceed the compartmentalization, either by genre, by participant-actors, or by intended effect . . . that ground Western cultural thought" (Taylor 2003: 15).

Figure 8.2   Statue of Christopher Columbus and Indigenous woman in Lima, Peru.

The Haida in British Columbia have no word for art, yet their elaborate masks and powerful totem poles were exquisite handiworks that passed on ancestral knowledge in the context of community ceremonies. Santa Clara Pueblo educator Gregory Cajete (1994: 145) sees "the process of art making and the realization of the visioning process as part of the (tribal) educative process."9 Concomitant with the ravaging of the natural resources of the Americas, the colonizers ravaged the cultural and epistemological landscape of the First Nations. A major weapon was Enlightenment philosophy (in its very name a racist project), based on Greek dichotomies and Cartesian dualisms that separated body/mind, nature/culture, human/nonhuman, male/female, emotion/reason.

Our minds are still colonized by Eurocentric ways of thinking, though there are various intellectual and political challenges of the dualisms. The VIVA! project (ontologically) critiques the materialistic and mechanistic worldview driving global imperialism, (epistemologically) identifies with postcolonial notions of knowledge and power, and (methodologically) adopts a feminist poststructural stance that honors the subjective, emotional, aesthetic, and natural (Strega 2005: 203). We ally with feminists, Indigenous scholars, critical race theorists, and environmentalists in countering notions of knowledge as static, positivist, and commodified, and in arguing for an epistemology of multiple perspectives, an understanding of power/knowledge as historically contingent, and an emphasis on the processes rather than the products of research, education, and art.

We have adopted participatory action research (PAR) and a related Central American practice of *sistematización* as methods for exploring community arts projects in each of the eight contexts, all of which engage Indigenous and/or diasporic populations. While PAR is problematic in its origins, which often trap it within a Western development paradigm so that it perpetuates colonial relations (see McKenzie 2002; Kapoor 2002), its intent is congruent with our commitment to promote critical and collective self-reflection within popular education and community arts processes aimed at stimulating collective action for social change. Participatory research in fact originated within popular education networks, and is understood to be integral to the three-pronged process of research, education, and action associated with Freirean-shaped popular education (see Kane 2001; Nunez 1994; Barndt 1991).

Feminists such as Colleen Reid (2004) and Patricia Maguire (1987) have interrogated PAR with a feminist lens, integrating gender concerns into the process, in terms of the composition of the team, the issues investigated, and the emerging analysis. A gender analysis of the VIVA! project's transnational exchange itself was brought into the December 2006 meeting of the team in Chiapas, Mexico; we noted, for example, that the major organizing for our annual gatherings was carried out by women participants, even in cases where the hosts were male collaborators. Two local projects, in particular, were queried around gender dynamics: a northern project that was dominated by white women artists and a southern project that appeared to exclude women from decision-making.

While PAR offered a common language and practice for all VIVA! collaborators, our southern partners adopted a related practice of *sistematización*, developed in Central America, and more suited to situations where outside facilitators are not involved; this process engages participants in a program or project in a focused reflection on some aspect of their shared experience for the purpose of understanding it more deeply, potentially impacting on their subsequent actions (Antillón 2002). A VIVA! intern working with our Panamanian partner was asked to facilitate a process of *sistematización* with the Kuna children's art project participants, and grappled with the contradictions of taking on such a role as an outsider to the context, project, and process (see Reinsborough 2006).

While some would see our poststructural stance (promoting self-reflexivity and questioning any imposed political agenda) as incongruent with the project's transformative impulses (based on critical social theory and an underlying political commitment to social justice), we choose to live with this tension by embracing the local histories as sources of critical reflection and deepening agency while simultaneously analyzing them in relation to a global political economic analysis. This insistence on integrating the local and global, the capacity to question and to act, resonates with other coauthors and feminist theorists.[10]

Framework of Creative Tensions

In conceiving the VIVA! project in 2003, we collaboratively elaborated our own theoretical framework of "creative tensions of community arts and popular education," naming five tensions that we have observed in this work: process/product, aesthetics/ethics, cultural reclamation/cultural reinvention, spiritual/political, and body/earth. We see these tensions not as dichotomous, but rather as dialectical in the Gramscian sense, and not to be resolved (as in hierarchical tensions where one wins over the other) but rather to be acknowledged and engaged creatively.

Process/Product

In contrast with the banking education Paulo Freire so eloquently challenged, and the elitist, individualized, and commodified art promoted by
Enlightenment thought and its extension, corporate globalization, popular
education and community art both foreground the processes of collective
knowledge production and art-making. This does not deny the importance
of an end product, which may then generate other processes when shared
in a broader community. This process orientation resonates with feminist
pedagogy (Luke and Gore 1992) as well as feminist art movements, such as
performance and public art emerging out of second-wave feminism in the
1970s.[11]

The process/product tension is a creative one being explored in several
VIVA! projects. Toronto's Catalyst Centre trained young artists in the Telling
Our Stories project to facilitate community art-making with "at-risk" youth,
breaking out of the dominant mode of their individual productions to lead
processes that help young people develop self-confidence, break silences, and
build community. Nonetheless, a culminating event in Toronto's Lula Lounge
provided the impetus to finish some products—and perform them—from
break dancing to spoken word.[12] The performances, or products, were also
important to the process of publicly affirming the youth and their forms of
self-expression.

Aesthetics/Ethics

"Art and politics don't mix, they (westerners) always say." Postcolonial
theorist Robert Young mocks this notion of aesthetics based on a dualistic
and patriarchal mentality, and suggests our choice is either "to collude
with the aestheticized structure that enforces apartness, or to contest it,
by turning theatre into a site of resistance, for example" (2003: 58). In the
diasporic contexts of most VIVA! projects, diverse cultural aesthetics collide,
and, ethical issues inevitably emerge, related to social justice goals and an
emphasis on collective process.

One poignant example is the Pintar Obediciendo (Painting by Listening)
project, the community-based mural production approach developed by
Mexican muralist Checo Valdez. Whether working with street youth in
Mexico City or with Zapatista autonomous communities in Chiapas to create
murals celebrating their own histories, Valdez refuses to impose any of his
own ideas or aesthetic values. His position is that Indigenous groups have

too long been represented by outside artists, and that given the opportunity, their own aesthetic will emerge. This is one end of the spectrum of positions that artists take in their myriad forms of collaborating on community-based productions. Toronto-based Jumblies Theatre, in contrast, insists that their community process is led by art-making, not politics, and professional artists contribute even as they nurture the creativity of community residents. As animators, the artists must also engage divergent cultural aesthetics in multi-cultural neighborhoods, a dynamic reflected in the next tension.

Cultural Reclamation/Cultural Reinvention

As community arts is often identified with marginalized groups and communities, processes of participatory research and collective art-making involve what Central American popular educators call *recuperación historica-cultural* or cultural reclamation. Tuhiwai Smith (1999) suggests that "coming to know the past" is central to a critical pedagogy of decolonization, especially for communities whose ways of knowing have been driven underground or destroyed by institutions such as the residential schools in Canada. For Indigenous communities like the Kuna Yala in Panama, art is a tool in this process of historical and cultural reclamation; the Kuna Children's Art Project in the late 1990s used storytelling, drawing, mask-making, theater, song, and dance to recover Kuna cultural values and to promote ecological awareness.

But such recovery projects do not unearth static notions or practices; cultures and their representations are constantly being recreated. Chicana artist Amalia Mesa-Bains and colleagues at La Galería de la Raza in San Francisco, for example, reinvented the Mexican tradition of family altars, reframing them as public forms of "memory-making and history-making" while fusing them with Day of the Dead celebrations (hooks and Mesa-Bains 2006: 119). In the case of the Kuna in Panama, the children who participated in the art project are now adolescents living in Panama City, where they are reinventing themselves in a new context and creating new forms of self-expression built on and moving beyond traditional practices. The postcolonial notion of hybridity is useful here, as it "involves processes of interaction that create new social spaces to which new meanings are given" (Young 2003: 79).

Spiritual/Political

The powerful voices of a growing number of feminist diasporic and Indigenous scholars and activists have challenged the spiritual/political dichotomy in the thought and practice of activists, ideologues, and even orthodox feminists, lamenting that in Western materialist culture, as co-contributor M. Jacqui Alexander deplores, "the secular has been divested of the sacred and the spiritual of the political."[13] Again, we must excavate the roots of this schism. Tuhiwai Smith (1999: 174) sees Indigenous concepts of spirituality, which Christianity tried to destroy, as critical sites of resistance, "one of the few parts of ourselves which the West cannot decipher, cannot understand, and cannot control . . . yet."

Ecofeminist perspectives, though Western in origin, have also challenged the spiritual/political dichotomy, as well as nature/culture and mind/body dualisms. In Latin America, one strand of ecofeminism has emerged out of liberation theology, regrounding the spirit in the body—of both humans and the earth—while critiquing the patriarchal and anthropocentric framings by mainly male liberation theologians (Rees 2006). Most VIVA! projects resonate more with a socialist ecofeminism than a cultural ecofeminism, eschewing the notion that women are biologically closer to nature, and focusing rather on the intersections of capitalism, sexism, racism, and environmental degradation.

Community arts can provide spaces for the recognition and contribution of various spiritualities; the ritual dimensions of community art-making processes themselves are often imbued with spiritual meaning. VIVA! project collaborators have both created rituals and explored them in our annual gatherings; the first meeting in Toronto in late October 2004 culminated in a cultural evening, Beyond Halloween: Celebrating Life and Death, allowing us to share stories from Anishnawbe and Kuna, Mexican and European traditions that honor the dead, and reveal, in fact, very distinct worldviews of the processes of living and dying. Our storytelling was followed the next evening by a community event in Toronto, Night of Dread, which has appropriated the Day of the Dead to involve a downtown neighborhood in parading their fears (ranging from SARS to George Bush) with large puppets and masks, then burning them in a ritualistic bonfire.

Body/Earth

Contrasting notions of life and death actually reveal another deep Western dualism, the separation of human and nonhuman nature, body and earth (rooted in classical Greek philosophy). The Mohawk people in Ontario describe their world as All Our Relations, and thank all elements, plants, and animals as well as human kin in their prayers. Mohawk writer Beth Brant emphasizes this equality quite simply: "We do not worship nature.

We are part of it" (qtd. in King 2003: 144). Indigenous peoples, of course, are not homogenous nor do they escape the influence of Western dualisms or fusions of Western and non-Western frames.[14]

Central American popular educators have developed the concept of *integralidad*, or holism, to emphasize a pedagogical practice that embraces embodied and analytical knowing, theory and practice, and affirms the interconnectedness of all living entities. Our Panamanian hosts of the second project meeting in August 2005 deliberately located our five-day gathering in an ecological center in the midst of the jungle, where we could be daily reminded through the sounds, smells, heat, and humidity that we are part of a vibrant biocentric community. At the Chiapas meeting in December 2006, an opening ritual honored the four elements—air, water, earth, and fire—and our relationship with them as sources of both material and cultural survival. Such a holistic vision has also been central to the worldviews of deep ecologists and ecofeminists.

Zooming In: Three Cross-Cutting Tensions

The tensions introduced here have served as starting points for collective analysis of local projects, where VIVA! partners have also identified their own different specific tensions. Our annual transnational conversations have named other salient tensions that cut across projects. Six of the North American collaborators (all women),[15] in preparation for a conference on arts-based research in Vancouver in 2006, identified tensions we saw operating both within and across projects in our transnational collaborative exchange. These included: 1) the dominance of white women in community arts, raising issues of gender, race, and class; 2) the tension between our conscious honoring of embodied knowing/practice in community arts and our incessant use of new (disembodied) technologies to document and discuss this practice, and 3) the insider/outsider dynamics present both in local and transnational collaborations.

White Women and Community Arts

Self-reflexivity, subjectivity, and power are central concerns of a feminist poststructural methodology, yet, while we are challenging hegemonic power relations in the content and process of the VIVA! project, we also reproduce them in ways that we must constantly confront. Certain inherent structural contradictions in the project are easy to identify: it was initiated in the North, by me, a white female university researcher, seasoned popular educator and community artist, who secured the funding from a Canadian academic research body and who administers the grant. Shaped by my middle-class NGO past and contacts in the South, the project also reflects an alternative stream of progressive research, education, and art, one that is dominated by women. Ironically, the people I first contacted in the southern NGOs were women, but partner organizations sent only men to the first meeting. The gender balance has now shifted, with core partners including four North American women, four men and two women from Latin America.[16]

Certain structural inequalities are reinforced by the project funder, SSHRC: while the national funding body increasingly employs a rhetoric promoting international, collaborative, and university-community partnerships, the criteria of eligible expenses privilege the principal researcher (Canadian), northern graduate student research assistants, and travel to conferences and meetings. We have tried to be flexible in budget allocations, with a goal of decentralizing and disseminating the funds;[17] nonetheless, there are moments when "privilege slaps us in the face,"[18] and we must reconsider the impact of every decision, aiming for a strategic use of privilege.

During our transnational meeting in Panama in 2005, there was a "sticky moment"[19] during a discussion of the work of a Canadian community theater project, where most of the community artists are white women, while most of the participants from the community in question are people of "color." Diane Roberts, the sole woman of "color" in the Canadian delegation, jokingly tagged this dynamic in the project as "the white ladies syndrome." Most Latin American partners resisted a discussion of racism in their work, revealing, on the one hand, different social constructions of race and gender.[20] The Canadian white women, on the other hand, adopted the term to highlight what we saw as a key issue to be addressed in the VIVA! project, a domination by white women not only in community arts in the North, but in our project as well. In appropriating the term, however, we also misinterpreted its original intent, and reproduced the very dynamic we were using it to critique, placing ourselves (again) in the center of the conversation.[21]

Official practices of community arts have been built around colonial art forms, so public discussions often exclude people and practices that don't fit the dominant cultural mode, even though women artists of "color" have led the struggle within arts councils to address such exclusions. We have to ask not only how we reproduce ourselves in such projects but also how the very terms of reference limit participation. While VIVA! partners identify with a more politicized practice, the terms we use and the organizational forms we adopt often exclude activist artists and artists of "color." These artists may also reject the growing institutionalization of community arts, challenge the rigid disciplinary boundaries of the arts altogether, practice a more integrated cultural expression, and/or choose to work mainly within their own specific communities.

White women, too, have likely benefited from the increasing attention to the community arts field by government bodies and funders in North America. Some of this propensity comes from white women's historical roles in charitable social work activities with so-called underprivileged populations; a more contemporary version of this phenomenon in community arts has generated considerable debate among artists who eschew a social work connotation of their work. White women often have greater social capital and strategic connections that contribute to their dominance in the field, and so maintain a role of gatekeeper, all the while facilitating processes with communities not their own.[22] These are contradictions that need to be named and addressed, not only to address institutionalized racism, but also to curb the perpetuation of Eurocentric organizational and artistic practices.

Tensions reflecting gender, race, class, and generational differences are alive in most of the local projects as well, many of which explicitly engage diasporic populations. Jumblies Theatre's project uses the metaphor of the Bridge of One Hair to highlight the challenge of building connections (as fragile as one hair) between early Irish settlers and recent Caribbean and Somalian immigrants in social housing high-rises in a downtown Toronto neighborhood. The tensions of conflicting cultural aesthetics were revealed, for example, in a multicultural performance in 2006: a black Caribbean youth group felt upstaged by a professional Somalian opera singer, while she struggled to follow sheet music composed by the Canadian composer/conductor. Jumblies artists/animators also identified the Somalian women's sewing skills, which inspired another art project of making tea cozies and papier-mâché teapots, a symbol that cut across the various communities involved in the project. A vestige of British colonialism in both Africa and the Caribbean, tea has become the drink that symbolically unifies the new and old settlers in the neighborhood. The multimedia performance both parodies the colonial symbol while also using the tea drinking ritual as a vehicle for connecting across differences.

Embodied Knowing/Technological Mediation
in Transnational Projects

Most of the community arts projects we are exploring are based in performance traditions: the song/dance/theater practices recovered by Kuna children in Panama, the centrality of dance and hip-hop to UCLA's ArtsBridge program as well as to Toronto's Telling Our Stories projects, the multidisciplinary community plays by Jumblies Theatre in Toronto's multicultural neighborhoods, the drumming and spoken word components of Guadalajara's Tianguis Cultural, and the researching of body memory to create performance pieces in the Personal Legacy Project in Canada.

This latter project perhaps most deeply challenges Eurocentric dualisms and privileges embodied knowing. Drawing on non-Western theatrical practices centering on Central and West African movement, dance, ritual, and performance traditions and the roots of her Caribbean legacy, Diane Roberts is working with two women representing distinct diasporas to probe their ancestral history, both through archival research as well as through exercises that tap the multigenerational stories that, she would say, "we have collected within our bodies." The context for this work is the colonized body, and the process "encourages people to go deep into their own personal legacies through a complete embodied process in order to experience, share and begin to dialogue in a deeper and more real way what it means to be a part of an intercultural experience" (Roberts 2008). This approach ruptures Western constructs of the individual and of the body as separate, it challenges our linear notions of time, as the women recover memories tapping a collective unconscious in their bodies and integrate characters from past centuries into their own contemporary performance representations.

Performance theorist Diana Taylor would identify this form of research as part of the *repertoire*, our store of embodied knowing and expression, which was negated, demonized, repressed, and even outlawed by America's colonizers. The centuries-old privileging of written texts over embodied ways of knowing still dominates contemporary academic practice, including our spoken and written communication with each other in conferences and books like this one. As Taylor admits, "It is difficult to think about embodied practice within the epistemic systems developed in Western thought, where writing has become the guarantor of existence itself" (2003: xix).

Taylor uses the metaphor of the *archive* to frame text-based learning, which "separates the source of knowledge from the knower," while the *repertoire* "requires presence: people participate in the production and reproduction of knowledge by 'being there'" (2003: 19–20). While resisting a dichotomizing of these two ways of knowing (which are often complimentary or integrated), Taylor nonetheless problematizes the equation of writing with memory/knowledge and suggests that embodied practices might "invite a remapping of the Americas," offering another perspective on transnational contact—both historical and contemporary. And the embodied practices themselves may offer a greater integration of thought and feeling, challenging the Cartesian split and reflecting what Central American popular educators have tagged *sentipensando*, or thinking/feeling (Nuñez 1998).

Local and international popular theater practitioners participating in the second meeting of the VIVA! partners in Achiote, Panama, in August 2005, helped shift our communication and collective analysis into the embodied realm. Opening rituals, chanting, and dancing, creating sculptures with our bodies to represent the tensions we wanted to probe—all countered and complemented our tendency to limit our dialogue to linear word-based conversation. It also gave us a break from the intense work of bilingual exchanges, always mediated by earphones and translators.[23] We would move outside the ecological center and actually inhale the fragrances of the jungle we were nestled in, hear its howling monkeys and cacophony of tropical birds. We could viscerally challenge the separations embedded in Eurocentric thinking and language, revealed poignantly by Margarita Antonio, our Nicaraguan partner, who taught us a Miskitu word, *taya*, which simultaneously means skin, bark, and family.

However, another layer of activity was superimposed on both our verbal and nonverbal exchanges. Our tiny, stark meeting room in the midst of the humid jungle was filled with the tools that mediated our conversations: four simultaneous translation transmitters, twenty-five receivers and charging cases, an LCD projector for viewing the video-letters that introduced each project, video recorders and a playback, digital still cameras, and mini-disc audio recorders, cords to step carefully over, a noisy fan both competing with our voices and mitigating the heat (nicely reflecting the contradictory nature of all our tools). We were set to capture every utterance and movement, to freeze images and store conversations for future review, digestion, analysis, and dissemination.

This hyper-documentation translated into hours and months of work by two graduate student research assistants, who had to learn new software for downloading sound and video, for transcribing and translating, for designing and desktop publishing a photo-filled report, or *Memoria*, as our Latin American partners call it. And then there were our commitments to keep in "touch" with each other across the vast distances between our annual meetings. We experimented with webcam conversations using Breeze (but that required everyone to have high-speed Internet), and Skype teleconferences (but then the power went out in Nicaragua). These technologies at least offered aural connections and a more intimate sense of each other than we got through email, but we spent as much time working out the technical glitches as we did talking substantively. Then there is the now requisite website, totally bilingual (thus requiring a regular translator), creating spaces for internal conversation, a genealogy of relevant terms, as well as stories, image galleries, and articles, our own and others, for more public consumption.[24] We are faced here with another challenge: a generational divide; some older technophobic partners feel awkward if not resistant to the tools and their use, while younger collaborators move easily from one form of technological connection to another. The North/South divide is evident as well, in terms of differential access, quantity, quality, and use of electronic equipment.

How does our adoption of every new technological device sit in juxtaposition to our passionate commitment to embodied knowing and practice? Are we distancing ourselves even further from the practices and people that we prioritize? Are we destined to be cyborg researchers? The technological mediation of the VIVA! project might, in fact, build on Donna Haraway's classic notion of the cyborg not only as a hybrid of machine and organism but also as a metaphor for transgressing boundaries, "not afraid of permanently partial identities and contradictory standpoints."[25] There are definitely contradictions we must confront daily in our transnational exchange: financial, material, technical disparities and limitations, even as we also depend on these new information and media technologies for communication and dissemination of our transgressive conversations.

Thus, on the one hand, URACCAN's young people are able to produce community television programs of the rituals and dances of the diverse Indigenous and Creole groups on Nicaragua's Atlantic Coast; these embodied cultural expressions captured on video can also serve as counter-hegemonic curricular material in URACCAN classrooms and coastal communities. The website created by Checo Valdez's community-based mural production course, Pintar Obediciendo,[26] offers its graduates a way to share the murals that are popping up on walls in Munich, Toronto, San Salvador.

Without the simultaneous translation equipment (and committed translators!), it would have been very difficult to enter into transnational bilingual dialogue. Without the audio and video recordings, we would not now be producing a collective book, both a Spanish and an English edition, integrating multiple voices from transcriptions, and including a DVD of short videos that will bring the projects alive, beyond the written text. But what are we losing? What, in the end, do we carry forward deep within us? Our email and webcam conversations are only possible because of our shared embodied exchanges. Nothing can replace that contact or the deep human relationships that have been forged during our annual encounters and our visits to each other's contexts. And yet we hope to share our projects and the exchange with a broader public, across many other geographic and cultural spaces. This is also made possible by these new media tools. We are creative transgressive cyborgs—finding our way through this morass by experimentation, reflection, and rethinking of our priorities.

Another tension within the group stems from the fact that we come from both NGOs and university contexts, and so feel comfortable with different kinds of languages depending on our institutional locations and practices as activists, artists, academics. There are, on the one hand, conferences and chapters, like this one, that are directed to more academic discussions and can be alienating to some partners.[27] Yet we have agreed that our collective book is to be geared to a broader activist public, requiring a more popular narrative approach, with multiple examples of practice in both verbal and visual form (such as the short videos on a DVD inserted into the book).

It is important to acknowledge that our attempts at communicating across (at least) two languages (as well as differences of social location, education, gender, race, class, North/South dynamics) are at the core of our exchange, perhaps the most difficult but also the richest dimension of the transnational project. We have worked to identify words and concepts that can't be translated from Spanish into English or from English into Spanish; they point the way to the distinct histories and specific contexts that have shaped each of us and that inform our work. "Community arts," for example, is not a term used in Central America, where "popular communications" might more likely be used to refer to grassroots forms and processes of media and art-making for social change; they are similar but not the same. In our discussions about "colonization" and "decolonization" at our third annual gathering in Chiapas in 2006, we struggled to find common terminology for how historical forms of domination and resistance are practiced today; we also debated our own understandings of "art," "education," "research," and "politics."

Over the three years of the exchange, we have been developing a genealogy of terms that are central to our diverse and common practices. We have deliberately framed this exercise as a process of constructing a genealogy, rather than a glossary, precisely because we are not interested in agreeing to precise definitions; rather we are seeking to understand the specific historical contexts out of which the terms have arisen and what diverse meanings they have taken on from one place and time to another. Our efforts to understand each other have been accentuated as each collaborator's chapter for the collective book is translated; in fact, the translators themselves have helped us to identify the "untranslatable" terms.

We collaborators in the VIVA! project have to recognize as well that we are still working in two colonial languages; while there are intriguing differences between them, there are even more pronounced differences between them and the Indigenous languages represented by two of our partners, in particular, a Kuna in Panama and a Miskitu in Nicaragua. In both cases, we have to be careful to not fall prey to what Marie Battiste and James (Sa'ke'j) Youngblood Henderson call "the Eurocentric illusion of benign translatability," a dominant cultural assumption that worldviews can be translated. Such an assumption has often gone hand in hand with benign neglect in the face of the extinction of up to half of the world's six thousand Indigenous languages. Our experience has confirmed what the Supreme Court of Canada declared in 1990, that "Language is more than a mere means of communication, it is part and parcel of the identity and culture of the people speaking it" (Battiste and Henderson 2000: 79–80). This notion, as well as Battiste and Henderson's caution about "cognitive imperialism," keep us probing, listening, and trying to walk in each other's shoes.

What implications does this questioning have for collaborative trans-national research on community arts and embodied practices? How do we engage these contradictions in a way that recognizes the limits and particular values of each? How do we appropriate technologies in a way that doesn't reproduce dominant relations? How do we juggle the multiple languages we are working with and the audiences we are engaging? How do we communicate across language differences that reveal distinct worldviews? These are questions we would like to further probe with other transnational activist/scholars.

Insider/Outsider Collaboration

The final cross-cutting tension addresses aspects of our collaboration, both between artists/animators and participants in local projects as well as project partners in the transnational gatherings and productions. While we recognize that power relations constantly shape our interactions in North/South, university/community, professor/student, artist/participant, funder/recipient terms, the ways in which we move between positions of insider and outsider are complex and constantly changing. Tuhiwai Smith suggests that the conventional notion of distinctions of the outside researcher and inside subject, for example, is based on positivist notions of objectivity and neutrality. Participatory action research, on the other hand, turns upside down the insider/outsider dichotomy, transforms subjects into researchers, and, at its most transparent, advocates self-reflexivity to constantly monitor our shifting roles and relationships.

A crisis in 2006 accentuated certain insider/outsider dimensions of our North/South partnerships in the VIVA! project. In late May of that year, an attack by the Mexican military on Indigenous people claiming their territory in Atenco caught two young participants from the Mexican mural project team in the crossfire as "free media" journalists; one was arrested, beaten, and sexually assaulted by police and deported to her native Chile. The flurry of emails that alerted our network to the details reminded us starkly that the risks of alternative media and community arts work are greater for some than for others, what VIVA! collaborator Heather Hermant calls a "hierarchy of risks."[28] In Canada, at least in the social movement contexts of our projects, we are rarely in real political or physical danger. Those on the front line of life-and-death situations not only risk more but also possess a kind of "epistemic privilege"[29] in understanding the potency of combining grassroots media/art with political struggle.

A less dramatic difference, though endemic in our roles as academics collaborating with activists or artists, is the university/community divide. In Canada, there has been a shift toward legitimizing and funding collaborative research that will benefit communities. But academic agendas and methods often still dominate in what turn out to be somewhat unequal partnerships.[30] Our community artist partners in Toronto remind us that while we are paid to do this kind of work, they survive on piecemeal grants, with little time to dedicate to the critical reflection, writing, and exchange so central to the VIVA! project. In overseeing the book project, I often find myself in an uncomfortable nagging role, asking people to do something that may not be a priority for them. We dance around our insider/outsider roles as we move in and out of each other's contexts; academia can be alienating for activist partners, and university researchers are viewed with suspicion by community participants—even when the process is participatory and arts-based.

Collaboration is messy, agendas can conflict, our work rhythms don't always jive—whether institutionally or culturally or emotionally based. Why do we do it? Because even the tensions—inevitable in our attempts to (re)integrate art, academics, and activism—are real and compelling, and, if engaged honestly, can be ultimately creative.

But is there not a basic contradiction in the arguments I have put forth? Does our framework of creative tensions ultimately reproduce the dichotomous thinking that we claim to challenge? Popular education as a practice shaped by Latin American activists was built upon positivist European and Marxist dialectical analyses of history, even though it has been interrogated and reshaped in recent decades by feminists, people of "color," environmentalists, and Indigenous peoples. Nonetheless, as we revisited our tensions in Panama in 2005, some found the framework limiting in its dualistic form. After three days of hearing about and analyzing the local projects, we engaged in a process of *sistematización*; out of this grounded theorizing emerged a new model in the form of a spiral, which resonated more with non-Western visions that most inspire us.[31]

From Pairs of Tensions to Spirals of Processes

Our analysis could be synthesized in two interrelated spirals: one (figure 8.3) that envisioned the *substantive* core of our collaborative research as historical and cultural reclamation, and within that a focus on transformative processes of ethical representation and artistic creation, all of which are aimed at fomenting popular education and art for social change.

The second spiral (figure 8.4) articulates the key features of our collectively crafted *methodology*: an integral or holistic approach (ecological, interdisciplinary, body/mind/spirit), promoting intergenerational dialogue (between students, interns, and youth participants with elder partners), and engaging intercultural and equity-related tensions (both within our projects and within our transnational collaboration).

The spiral, of course, conjures up a completely different universe story than the creative tensions. But for now, perhaps we will sit with these two different worldviews, side by side, since our practice as well as our hemispheric dialogue is clearly in the interstices within and between them. Our bodies and the ground we stand on carry the stories of multiple layers of mapping and remapping the "Americas."

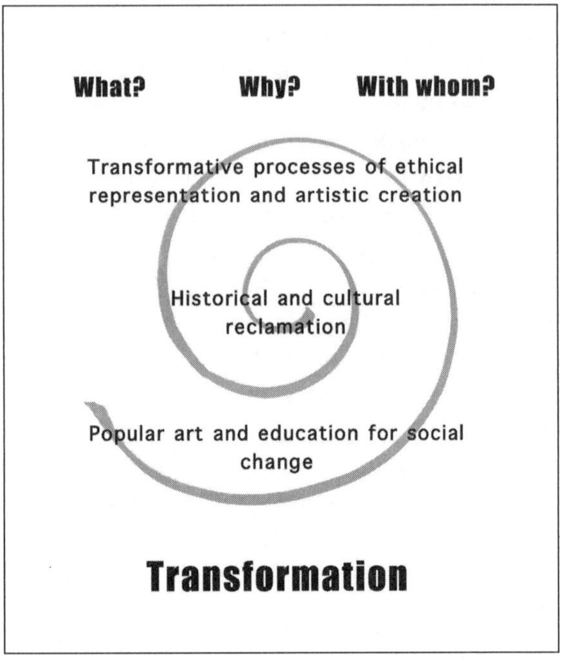

What? Why? With whom?

Transformative processes of ethical representation and artistic creation

Historical and cultural reclamation

Popular art and education for social change

Transformation

Figure 8.3 Spiral model of VIVA! project's, substantive focus and methodology.

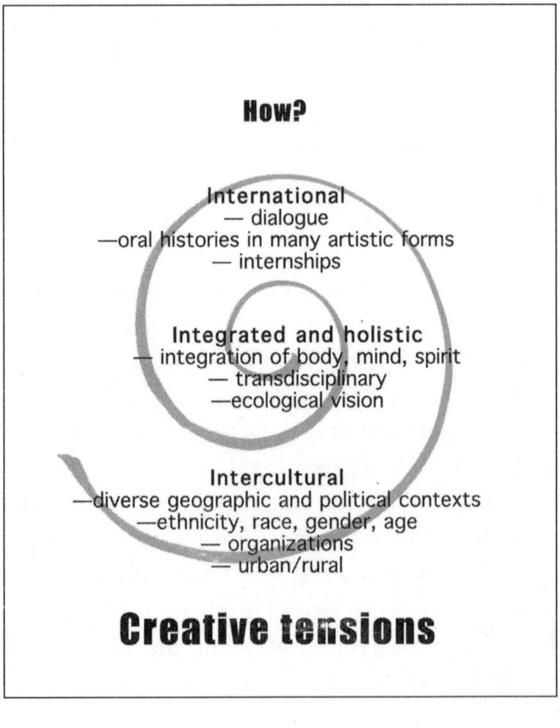

How?

International
— dialogue
—oral histories in many artistic forms
— internships

Integrated and holistic
— integration of body, mind, spirit
— transdisciplinary
—ecological vision

Intercultural
—diverse geographic and political contexts
—ethnicity, race, gender, age
— organizations
— urban/rural

Creative tensions

Figure 8.4 Spiral of key methodological components of the VIVA! project.

Notes

1. For a fuller introduction to the VIVA! project, see its website, www.vientos.info/ viva, and the forthcoming book, *VIVA! Community Arts and Popular Education in the Americas*; both English and Spanish editions are in production and are due out in late 2010.

2. We have chosen this name for our transnational project because it is understandable in both Spanish and English and reflects cross-fertilization among activists in the South and the North. It is at the same time a recognition of those who have given their lives to a cause, a celebration of struggle, a call to action.

3. While popular education has become known in the North mainly through the pioneering pedagogical theories of Brazilian educator Paulo Freire, its emerging practice was very much shaped by grassroots organizing by poor communities (and liberation theology) in the 1960s in response to poverty, military dictatorships, and U.S. hegemony in the region. Related concepts with different histories are emancipatory or liberatory education, transformative learning, critical pedagogy, radical adult education, among others. In Canada, we have adapted the term as an overall frame that draws from specific practices by equity-seeking groups: indigenous education, antiracism education, feminist pedagogy, labor education, global education, queer pedagogy, popular environmental education, among others.

4. The fertile space at FES is evident in the recent publication of a collection of essays by eighteen former graduate students whose work challenges the separation of art, activism, and academics. See Deborah Barndt, ed., *Wild Fire: Art as Activism* (Toronto: Sumach Press, 2006).

5. Latin American scholars have challenged cultural studies for not giving "sufficient importance to social movements as a vital aspect of cultural production." See the landmark volume, Sonia E. Alvarez, Evelyn Dagnino, and Arturo Escobar, eds., *Culture of Politics, Politics of Culture: Re-Visioning Latin American Social Movements* (Boulder, CO: Westview Press, 1998).

6. The eight local projects serving as case studies in the VIVA! project include:
   1. Kuna Children's Art Project in Kuna Yala, Panama: Centro de Acción y Educación Social Panameña (CEASPA);
   2. Bilwivisión Community Television Station run by youth in Bilwi, Nicaragua: Universidad Regional Autónoma de la Costa Caribeña de Nicaragua (URACCAN);
   3. Pintar Obediciendo, community-based mural production workshop in Mexico City: Universidad Autónoma Metropolitana (UAM);
   4. Tianguis Cultural (Cultural Marketplace) in Guadalajara, Mexico: Instituto Mexicano para el Desarrollo Comunitario (IMDEC);
   5. ArtsBridge Program in Los Angeles, California: UCLA World Arts and Culture Department;
   6. Telling Our Stories in Toronto, Canada: Catalyst Centre;
   7. The Personal Legacy Project, Diane Roberts, Montreal/Toronto/ Vancouver;
   8. Jumblies Theatre in Toronto, Canada: Faculty of Environmental Studies, York University.

7. Transnational social justice activism, in particular initiatives that promote

alliances between Indigenous and non-Indigenous peoples, also challenge the male/female dualism upon which Western feminism has been built.

8. There's a double edge to the racism here, because obviously the sculptor used a European woman as the model for the smaller, browner Indigenous woman.

9. Cajete emphasizes the spiritual and psychological importance of dreaming, as central to art, education, and ceremony.

10. See Uma Narayan and Sandra Harding, eds., *Decentering the Center: Philosophy for a Multicultural, Postcolonial, and Feminist World* (Bloomington: Indiana University Press, 2000). Both Shari Stone-Mediatore and Lorraine Code in their respective essays laud Chandra Mohanty's refusal to dichotomize the local specific analysis and the broader analysis of global forces shaping the local. I adopted a similar approach to my study of women workers in the NAFTA Food Chain: *Tangled Routes: Women, Work, and Globalization on the Tomato Trail* (Lanham, MD: Rowman & Littlefield, 2002).

11. Artists such as Judy Chicago, Judy Baca, and Suzanne Lacy pioneered more collective feminist art-making processes. See Suzanne Lacy, *Mapping the Terrain: New Genre Public Art* (Seattle, WA: Bay Press, 1995) and the more recent: Jayne Wark, *Radical Gestures: Feminism and Performance Art in North America* (Montreal & Kingston: McGill-Queen's University Press, 2006). For a more global perspective on feminist practices, see Pilar Riano, *Women in Grassroots Communications: Furthering Social Change* (Thousand Oaks, CA: SAGE Publications, 1994).

12. Diana Taylor (2003) found echoes of this dynamic among the Nahuatl in colonial Mexico: an *ixiptlatl*, referring to the integration of the spiritual being and the physical being, was always constructed as temporary, the "constant making and unmaking pointing to the active role of human beings in promoting the regenerative quality of the universe" (39).

13. "It is a paradox that a feminism that has insisted on a politics of a historicized self has rendered that self so secularized, that it has paid little attention to the ways in which spiritual labour and spiritual knowing is primarily a project of self-knowing and transformation that constantly invokes community simply because it requires it." Jacqui Alexander, *Pedagogies of Crossing: Meditations on Feminism, Sexual Politics, Memory and the Sacred* (Durham, NC: Duke University Press, 2005), 15.

14. See Ronald Wright, *A Short History of Progress* (Toronto: Anansi Press, 2004) for convincing evidence that certain past Indigenous civilizations have, in fact, self-destructed due to a lack of ecological consciousness, depleting natural resources that led to their downfall.

15. Thanks to Margo Charlton, Heather Hermant, Maggie Hutcheson, Laura Reinsborough, and Diane Roberts for the island retreat and the Kits beach rant!

16. Organizational affiliations, in contrast with individual academic collaborators, also translate into potential turnover of staff, and thus shifting participation. Three of the original partners have left their organizations and thus the project; over the first two years, we integrated four new partners.

17. We think these issues are important ones to discuss in transnational feminist networks, and they resonated with other coauthors when we first met in Minnesota in 2006, and shared our "creative accounting" strategies.

18. Diane Roberts, during VIVA! project meeting, May 2006.

19. We have called "sticky moments" those situations that emerge and cause us discomfort, often because they are tapping really important issues that we have avoided but need to address. The challenge is to name them, to go into instead of flee the discomfort, and to work through the underlying reasons that they seem "sticky."

20. There is an ongoing and challenging conversation with Latin American partners about the different constructions of race, ethnicity, and gender in a context where "mestizaje" and "machismo" have been dominant cultural developments. In Bilwi, Nicaragua, for example, the production team of the community television station includes young people of Miskitu, Creole, and mestizo origins, in fact, most have two or more of these ethnicities in their ancestry. As the regional autonomy law enshrines the "right to self-identification," however, most of them choose to identify themselves as Miskitu.

21. Thanks to Diane Roberts for her comments on this section and for keeping this conversation alive and critical, challenging us to wrestle with this internal contradiction.

22. Thanks to Heather Hermant for articulating some of the nuances of the contradictory role white women play in the emerging field of community arts.

23. We are committed to making the VIVA! project totally bilingual, an ongoing, labor-intensive and expensive proposition. For us, it is more than an issue of equalizing participation (four Latin American partners don't speak English, one North American partner doesn't speak Spanish), but a deeper belief that collaborative knowledge production must draw from the distinct epistemologies that are so embedded in language.

24. Our website is part of a "free media" network, Drupal, which emphasizes access and democratic use; each new tool offers us a chance to consider how we use it in ways that counter its dominant exclusionary, individualistic, and commodified uses. However, one of the contradictions of this "free" server is that there is little technical support available.

25. Haraway built her cyborg myth on the premise that "most American socialists and feminists see deepened dualisms of mind and body, animal and machine, idealism and materialism in the social practices, symbolic formulations, and physical artifacts associated with 'high technology' and scientific culture. Donna J. Haraway, "A Cyborg Manifesto: Science, Technology, and Socialist-Feminism in the Late Twentieth Century," in *Simians, Cyborgs and Women: The Reinvention of Nature* (New York: Routledge, 1991), 154.

26. Valdez has adapted the Zapatista mandate of "mandar obediciendo" or "lead by taking direction from the people" to his approach to community mural production; "pintar obediciendo" means, literally, "to paint by obeying," but we have translated it more loosely as "painting by listening."

27. Thanks to Heather Hermant and Diane Roberts for raising this issue as they read drafts of this chapter.

28. Heather Hermant elaborated this idea during our VIVA! meeting, December 2006, Chiapas, Mexico.

29. I have adapted the notion of "epistemic privilege" from Uma Narayan, "Working Together Across Difference: Some Considerations of Emotions and Political Practice," *Hypatia* 3(2) (1988): 31–48.

30. Niks suggests, in fact, that there is less money now available for community groups to do their own research, as they are forced into collaboration with academic partners. Marina Niks, "The Politics of Collaborative Research Between University-Based and Non-University-Based Researchers," unpublished doctoral dissertation, University of British Columbia, 2004.

31. The spiral can be found in many ancestral practices of diverse origins; consider, for example, the Celtic tri-spiral, which can be traced back to the Druids in what is now known as the United Kingdom. Of political significance to VIVA! partners, however, is the fact that the spiral also echoes the Zapatista symbol of the *caracol*, referring simultaneously to the conch shell, which was a major form of popular communications among Indigenous peoples in Chiapas, and the snail shell (which we have adopted as a symbol). The *caracol* is the name given to the seat of autonomous government established by the Zapatistas in the liberated zones of Chiapas, Mexico.

Works Cited

Alvarez, Sonia E., Evelyn Dagnino, and Arturo Escobar, eds. 1998. *Culture of Politics, Politics of Culture: Re-Visioning Latin American Social Movements.* Boulder, CO: Westview Press.

Antillón, Roberto. 2002. *Para Construir Conocimiento a través de la Sistematización de la Práctica Social.* Guadalajara: IMDEC.

Barndt, Deborah, ed. 2006. *Wild Fire: Art as Activism.* Toronto: Sumach Press.

Barndt, Deborah. 1991. *To Change This House: Popular Education under the Sandinistas.* Toronto: Between the Lines.

Battiste, Marie, and James (Sa'ke'j) Youngblood Henderson. 2000. *Protecting Indigenous Knowledge and Heritage: A Global Challenge.* Saskatoon, SA: Purich Publishing.

Cajete, Gregory. 1994. *Look to the Mountain: An Ecology of Indigenous Education.* Skyland, NC: Kivaki Press.

hooks, bell, and Amalia Mesa-Bains. 2006. *Homegrown: Engaged Cultural Criticism.* Cambridge, MA: South End Press.

Kane, Liam. 2001. *Popular Education and Social Change in Latin America.* London: Latin American Bureau.

Kapoor, Ilan. 2002. "The Devil's in the Theory: A Critical Assessment of Robert Chambers' Work on Participatory Development." *Third World Quarterly* 23(1): 101–117.

King, Thomas. 2003. *The Truth About Stories.* Toronto: Dead Dog Café Production and CBC.

Loomba, Ania. 2005. *Colonialism/Postcolonialism.* New York: Routledge.

Luke, Carmen, and Jennifer Gore. 1992. *Feminisms and Critical Pedagogy.* New York: Routledge.

Maguire, Patricia. 1987. *Doing Feminist Participatory Research.* Amherst, MA: Center for International Education.

McKenzie, Christine. 2002. "Popular Communications: Negotiating Contested Terrain on Nicaragua's Caribbean Coast," unpublished MES paper, Faculty of Environmental Studies, York University.

Nuñez, Carlos. 1998. *La Revolución Ética.* Guadalajara: IMDEC.

Nuñez, Carlos. 1994. *Educar para Transformar, Transformar para Educar.* Guadalajara: IMDEC.

Reid, Colleen. 2004. "Advancing Women's Social Justice Agendas: A Feminist Action Research Framework." *International Journal of Qualitative Methods* 3(3). Retrieved 10 April 2007 from http://www.ualverta.ca/~iiqm/backissues/3_3/html/reid.html

Reinsborough, Laura. 2006. "Sistematización: A Guide to Critical Reflections for Community Art Work." Unpublished zine.

Ress, Mary Judith. 2006. *Ecofeminism in Latin America: Women from the Margins.* Maryknoll, NY: Orbis Books.

Roberts, Diane. 2008. "The Lost Body—Recovering Memory: A Personal Legacy." Forthcoming in *VIVA! Art, Education and Politics in the Americas.* Bluefields, Nicaragua: URACCAN University. Unpublished manuscript.

Strega, Susan. 2005. "The View from the Poststructural Margins: Epistemology and Methodology Reconsidered." In Leslie Brown and Susan Strega, eds., *Research as Resistance: Critical, Indigenous and Anti-Oppressive Approaches.* Toronto: Canadian Scholars' Press. 199–235.

Taylor, Diana. 2003. *The Archive and the Repertoire: Performing Cultural Memory in the Americas.* Durham, NC: Duke University Press.

Tuhiwai Smith, Linda. 1999. *Decolonizing Methodologies: Research and Indigenous Peoples.* New York: Zed Books.

Young, Robert. 2003. *Postcolonialism: A Very Short Introduction.* Oxford, UK: Oxford University Press.

(**9**)

Envisioning Justice

The Politics and Possibilities
of Transnational Feminist Film

RACHEL SILVEY

Interstitched: **A Collaborative Transnational Feminist Film**

Visual images are politically unwieldy. Transnational feminist collaborative film and video makers are aware that our work is framed by, and often unintentionally complicit with, the very power relations that we seek to disrupt and even modestly reformulate. Yet we continue to want to carry out this work in order to participate in a form of praxis that in its best moments aligns "the medium (inexpensive,[1] debased, nonprofessional), the message (woman, as subject, needs to be constructed), and the ideology (the personal is political; process over product)" of transnational feminism (Juhasz 2003: 72). Collaborative film teams that work across national borders deliberately provoke questions about the ramifications of multiple axes of difference and inequality, and we invite dialogue about the exclusions and political tensions associated with doing ethnographic "fieldwork," making film, teaching with film, and the power of the filmic gaze. I am interested here in exploring the implications and possibilities for transnational feminist alliance-building and pedagogy in film-making and teaching through film.

With migrant workers and migrant rights activists in Indonesia, as well as students in both Indonesia and the United States, I have been working on a film titled, *Interstitched.* The film is a short documentary that asks viewers, initially assumed to be mostly undergraduate university students in the United States., to begin to critically analyze the politics of representing migrant women workers in the global South and in Indonesia in particular. It is inspired by transnational feminist theoretical work on representation and alliance-building (Alexander and Mohanty 1997; Mohanty 1991; Katz 2001; Spelman 1988; Moghadam 2005; Swarr and Nagar 2003; Pratt 2004; Sangtin

Writers and Nagar 2006). Its goals are to encourage viewers to consider both the construction of national, gendered, and racialized patterns of labor exploitation, and how students' own lives are connected to these issues. It focuses on these themes through attention to local labor relations, immigrant rights, the consumption of globally traded commodities, discourses of victims and saviors, and the power relations manifest in image production, circulation, and reception. Viewers are also asked to consider the networks of activism emerging transnationally to combat migrant factory labor abuses, and the roles that both students and workers are playing in resisting and transforming the conditions under which migrant women labor in both Indonesia and the United States.

This film project fits into long-term work I have done with Indonesian women workers, anti-sweatshop student activists, and immigrant factory workers in the United States. But film and video are new media for me, and engaging with them has pushed my collaborators and me to confront old questions about power, positionality, collaborative praxis, and transnational feminism from new angles. Specifically, while our previous projects have sought explicitly to engage issues of transnational inequality (e.g., Silvey 2002; 2003), none of my collaborators ever expressed interest in using the research in the direct service of their political goals. In this earlier, more standard written-format research, the research process had always involved the coidentification of themes with collaborators and deliberative, ongoing discussions about the politics of various methodological approaches (Acker et al. 1991), but ultimately the written research product had been most obviously valuable to my own career.[2] In contrast, when I suggested making a film that would mobilize images and stories of Indonesian workers and activists, many migrant workers, labor movement leaders, and students expressed great enthusiasm about the potential for such a film to contribute to their visions and enactments of justice.

While these collaborators (discussed in detail further on) held multiple, often competing perspectives on how to define justice and how it should best be achieved, there was strong consensus about the importance of building networks of opposition to the gendered violence and exploitation that travels transnationally too smoothly, and the vital role that film and video can play in strengthening transnational opposition movements (see also Hesford 2005; Juhasz 2001). Indeed, not only did all collaborators in both the United States and Indonesia express enthusiasm for the film project, but also they insisted that it was part of the responsibility of foreign researchers to move beyond written, published research products to participate with them in collecting, deploying, and distributing moving images of the transnational spaces and subjects associated with migrant labor and activism. Some argued that film would be a far more effective and accessible medium than writing for raising awareness of the systems shaping the conditions of migrant laborers' lives, work, and activism.

These collaborators thus cast the film project as politically vital work. They worked with me from the beginning of the planning stages of the project to make the end product relevant in some way to all our various goals. In addition, we expressed a shared commitment to making the film production process itself as collaborative, reflexive, and equitable as possible. The work has been difficult in part because sharing these principles has required that we do the hard work of continually and explicitly confronting the inequalities and differences in our incomes, social locations, agendas, and audiences. Most basically, not only do Indonesian factory workers produce material goods for higher income consumers, often located in the global North, but in "field research" they also often produce the raw materials for the knowledge produced in the northern academy, a process that then repositions northern scholars as experts of the knowledge produced about research subjects in the South. Similar relations of inequality and potential exploitation exist between NGOs and the people whose interests they ostensibly represent (Sangtin Writers and Nagar 2006). Given these structural inequalities embedded in production relations, what sorts of spaces remain for producing films that may in some measure nonetheless contribute to emancipator efforts? Is it possible to make a film that provides a critical lens onto the politics of representing "sweatshops" and the overseas migrant domestic labor program without reproducing in practice some aspects of the very representations and relations of inequality we oppose? What different problems and possibilities does film represent relative to academic writing for transformational, radical alliance-building?

In the film project, a central goal has been to work through such questions together and to persistently examine our relationships to one another as we make the film. As Nagar et al. (2003: 356) put it,

> The challenge for postcolonial and feminist geographers, then, is to conceptualise border-crossings that are committed to forming collaborative partnerships with academic and non-academic actors in "other" worlds, in every sense of the term—partnerships in which the questions around how power and authority would be shared cannot be answered beforehand, but are imagined, struggled over and resolved through the collaborative process itself.

We have faced entrenched power differentials and misunderstandings through our work, and we have confronted a number of unexpected differences in the ways we approach our political priorities. In exploring these differences, in our best moments, we have developed expanded senses of our intended audiences and political agendas, as well as broadened views of our transnational affinity groups. In the most difficult moments, we have been overcome with anger toward one another and defensiveness about the value of our own positions and work. As discussed in the following section, questions about "the politics of representation" have been at the core of some of the most initially agonizing and ultimately productive debates.

The Challenges of Collaborative Representations

There were several reasons that the film project seemed worthwhile from my location. As a faculty member in a North American university, I spend the majority of my time doing research and teaching undergraduate students in the university, so my work needs to serve students in some capacity. Second, the film seemed important because most students in the United States know remarkably little about other parts of the world, and they are even less conscious of the myriad ways that they and the United States are systematically connected to political-economic processes in other parts of the world. By presenting the film to large introductory human geography courses, the aims were to fill this educational gap and to push U.S. students to understand some of the interdependencies linking global neoliberalizing pressures on all laboring bodies, with particular attention to the racialized gender politics of inequality. I also hoped the film would disrupt some of the stereotypes and inaccuracies that pervade representations of immigrant factory working women, particularly the victim narrative that flattens and objectifies women's issues. In that the film was conceived as a deliberately transnational project, it was also aimed at pushing viewers to challenge the fetishism of the "other" as exotic and vulnerable laborer. And, it sought to disrupt notions of the individual subject as the primary agent producing inequality (as consumer) and/or holding the keys to liberation (as activist). Geographically, I hoped the film would move beyond conceptions of "here" and "there" as hermetically sealed oppositions.

The film production began in collaboration with Akatiga, an independent, non-governmental self-described "social analysis" group focused on labor issues, agrarian change, and the politics of development in Indonesia. I had worked with Akatiga on previous projects, and together we had been involved in labor organizing and research with communities of factory workers who also expressed interest in planning the film project. We began with what seemed to me to be largely compatible overlapping goals in mind. One goal, mine especially, was to contribute to the development of critical visual literacy (hooks 1992), such that our work would help hone the skills necessary for thinking through images in relation to their political ramifications, subtexts, and contexts of production and consumption. In the planning stages, everyone expressed interest in and support for a critical engagement with the politics of filmic images, and together we committed to a production process that would strengthen our alliance. This commitment involved ongoing discussion and negotiation of all our interests.

Akatiga, founded in 1987, was staffed in 2002 during the making of the film by highly educated Indonesian people who have built their institution and their professions around labor issues and agrarian politics. They were initially funded through two Indonesian universities working with Dutch researchers and funds, and have more recently received funding from a variety of donors, including the International Labor Organization, Oxfam, the Ford Foundation, and the Indonesian government's Office of the Ministry of Environment. According to Okol, the woman from Akatiga who was most interested in and involved with the film, Akatiga has carefully selected the institutions from which it will accept funds. They have refused to work directly with some funders because they do not want their work to be dictated by these large multilateral lending institutions and their agendas.[3] Okol expressed her hope that our partnership would help both Akatiga as well as America academics resist such funding pressures. Her perspective is in agreement with Benson and Nagar (2006: 582), who point out that such alliances between NGOs and academics, though they require "endless scrutiny and self-critique," can be effective elements of resistance to the dictates of funding agendas.

Okol and others at Akatiga argued that their organization's most important task is to address the fact that women workers are facing overwork, underpayment, harassment, and other forms of violence every day (see also Peake and de Souza, chapter 5 in this volume, on the centrality of material concerns driving the movement). These are the stories, Okol insisted, that need to be publicized to a wide and diverse audience. Okol pointed out that Akatiga wants its work to put pressure on the state, employers, and international regulatory institutions to develop better regulations and protections for the rights of workers. As a group, they want to enlist the support of foreign academics in pressuring state and supranational regulatory institutions such as the International Labour Organisation to develop conventions focused on the protection of migrant workers' human rights. Akatiga's mandate is thus in strong alignment with other NGOs, such as the Asian Migrant Centre in Hong Kong, that address migrant workers' rights (Gibson et al. 2001).

Despite disagreements within Akatiga over the best strategies for overcoming labor problems, the organization's analytical consensus is that the continued abuse of workers is rooted in the lack of political will on the part of the state and international actors. Thus, it was quite clear to Okol that foreign academic expertise, location in foreign universities, and English-language fluency should be mobilized to put pressure on states and international actors.[4] Okol's views of Akatiga's audience, and the clarity with which she saw the foreign academic's role, led to an expanded vision of the film's intended audiences. She helped us all understand that for the film to be effective in contributing to workers' rights, it had to reach more than the American undergraduate students whom we, and especially I, had initially identified as the primary intended audience.

Then Muna, a factory worker and labor activist involved in producing the film, voiced her ideas and described the images that she thought should be included prominently in the film. Specifically, Muna hoped that the film would include what she called the "success stories" of former factory workers who have worked abroad. She wanted the film to include images of the wealth they had earned, the fashionable clothing they had purchased, and the international travel they had experienced. She said that her coworkers were proud of this part of their migration history and wanted it to be featured in the film. Muna's interest in sharing such a narrative fit well with my sense of a key part of what U.S. students needed to learn. That is, students in the United States often subscribe to the stereotype of factory workers as a homogeneous group primarily and solely defined by their victimization, and Muna's emphasis on the "success stories" could help dispel this myth.

Okol and the NGO with whom she worked, Akatiga, did not view the inclusion of Muna's "success story" as particularly necessary or productive. In particular, Okol argued that in order to develop support for workers' rights, it was vital that workers' victimization remain at the center of the film. As Doezema (1998: 42–43) puts it, "it is easier to gain support for victims . . . than for challenging structures." Muna, however, hoped that the film would include more than a story of exploitation. In expressing her dissatisfaction with the victim narrative she joins the many feminist scholars who have argued that a sole focus on exploitation not only oversimplifies the more complex lives of workers, but also serves to reexploit and discursively colonize them (Mohanty 2004).

Because Okol and Muna held different ideas about what the film should represent, it was crucial that the group address this tension. Okol and Muna explored their interest in deleting one another's preferred narrative. Okol argued that it was necessary for NGOs to provide interpretations of workers' narratives because "workers tend to lack extra-ideological analyses of their situation, and it's the NGOs job to educate them, even if sometimes we disagree about strategies." Both Okol and Muna asked me to identify as the arbiter in the debate about the direction of the film, but I did not see it as my role to try to resolve the tensions between Okol and Muna. Indeed their difference of opinion was a key part of film's story and process. Fortunately, we remained in agreement that a film—or several different short films, as Okol suggested—should still be made, but we faced a number of difficult questions.

Would it be possible to represent key elements of Okol's and Muna's concerns in ways that satisfied both of them by placing representational concerns in their relational transnational contexts of power and history? In doing so, would it be possible to shift the film's analytic gaze toward understanding the political tensions of experience (Mohanty 1991)? Should the film expand its analytic gaze to include greater attention to students and foreign researchers as subjects of the film, contextualized in relation to the corporatizing academy? Would such an expanded focus better reflect the project's goals of reflexive, relational work and analysis of the systemic production of inequality? In grappling with such questions, the film might be able to illustrate the historically specific production of our variously positioned visions for the film. By placing the politics of representation and knowledge production at the center of planning for the film, I hoped to be able to open up some political space for everyone involved to think about the various forms and purposes of the knowledge and images it would be possible to create together (Benson and Nagar 2006).

Okol and Muna remained skeptical, however. The politics of representation as an analytic entry point was less relevant to their work than what they saw as more basic, material questions of workers' rights. My interest in framing their diverse approaches to workers' rights as a question of representation was, from their perspective, really just my own agenda. Indeed, this approach faced the danger of positioning the U.S.-based film-maker as the analyst in possession of the comprehensive, more "global" perspective, able to incorporate and synthesize what would be represented as the more local, particular views of Okol and Muna. It could also lead to a film that would reinforce the U.S. student's view of him/herself as the subject who "lives in the capital of the world. [In northern academic institutions, t]he student is encouraged to think that he or she is there to help the rest of the world. And he or she is also encouraged to think that to be from other parts of the world is not to be fully global" (Sharpe and Spivak 2003 622).[5] At the project's outset, one goal had been to upset such assumptions among students, but we were finding that even in our attempts to teach against the grain, our film as product might unintentionally reinforce the social hierarchies and structural inequalities we hoped it would confront. While everyone applauded Okol's suggestion that we make several films in order to address this problem, we had neither the funding nor the time to pursue multiple film projects that year.

Nevertheless, we all agreed that we would commit to making additional films in the future, and it was this agreement—that no single film could completely and equally encapsulate all of our interests, and that we would continue to work together over time to make films that addressed our different (and always evolving) priorities—that allowed us to move forward with our work. We collected and edited over one hundred hours of tape over the course of a little more than a month, and these parts of the process involved making decisions that were at least as politically complex as the film-planning process. All original footage was collected in the Indonesian language, which required that the U.S.-based group needed to complete transcriptions and produce subtitles. The first draft of the U.S.-based version has been completed and viewed by U.S. students.

Reception and Revision

Transnational research emphasizes interactions and relationships between places, as it seeks to move beyond the analytic limitations of research focused on single sites bounded within the nation-state (Mitchell 2004). Rather than locating engagement between U.S. students, researchers, Indonesian migrants, U.S. immigrants, and migrant-rights NGOs solely within a regional or national political economy, a transnational approach asks how the regimes of governance and economies that connect these various subjects and their spaces produce particular practices and experiences. A central goal of the film project was to illuminate these linkages, and in doing so to contribute to finding common cause across geographic and social differences.

However, the structural systems of inequality that infuse research and education projects, and the complicated politics of translation and trans- mission, were further underscored when the film was complete and we presented it in the United States. American students interpreted the film in several particularly problematic ways. First, despite our editorial intentions to the contrary, students viewed the activist agenda as in conflict with the migrants' interest in consumption. "Why," one student asked, "do migrants want to buy expensive blue jeans?" Students judged migrants for their consumption practices. One student said, "They [migrants] shouldn't waste their money on shopping; they should save their money for organizing." In these moments, students revealed their subscription to a liberal conception of the ethico-political subject in which consumption is not a right but rather an ultimate freedom reserved for certain citizens with high incomes. In this way, the film left intact students' senses of themselves, their own actions and privileges, as separate from, rather than related to, the struggles of migrant workers. In addition, students' responses suggested that they had maintained a sense of moral superiority that in their minds gave them the right to judge the choices of the subjects of the film.

Students' misunderstandings initially led me to see the film project as a failure. In particular, despite our efforts to make a collaborative film, the visual medium seemed especially prone toward reinforcing a mechanics of domination. Specifically, voyeurism inheres in the documentary form in that it "depends on the power of the gaze to construct meanings for the writer and the reader of 'the people'" (Rabinowitz 1994: 51). However, in discussions after the viewing, students began to shift their gaze, ultimately working toward making their own film about their own global imbrications in networks of consumption and production and transnational relationality. These students are also now working to find funding to translate their film into Indonesian and distribute it both in the United States. and among our collaborators and fellow students in Indonesia.

The students' follow-up film begins with the questions, "What historical relations of inequality permit us to be making this film? . . . What pressures exist in our immediate university environment that are common to students and workers in Indonesia, and how can we work together to try to transform these?" Following the work of transnational feminists (see Benson and Nagar 2006), students have delved into reflexive work that has prompted them to expand their vision from a sole focus on individual difference toward shared projects of alliance-building. Their project's subject is neither the Indonesian workers, nor immigrant workers in the United States, nor even themselves, but rather the systems of labor control and economic restructuring that are affecting everyone, albeit in very distinct, unequal ways. They focus on individual experiences and interviews not in order to fix the gaze on the vulnerability nor even the agency of an individual subject, but rather to reveal the subjective specificities and contours of the more broadly shared conditions. I have hoped to help them to follow Swarr and Nagar (2003) in seeking to "conceptualiz[e] new frameworks that explore the mutually constitutive struggles for resource access and material survival on the one hand," and in this case, the possibilities for film on the other hand.

Overall, the collaborators in Indonesia tended to think that the money that had been spent on the film would have been better used for their own research and activist agendas. This was a disheartening realization to all of us, and it pointed to the intractability of the divides of difference, position, and victimization as these played out in our various agendas and audiences for the film. While such struggles are common to all transnational feminist collaborations, they are painful for feminist documentarians in particular ways. Specifically, as Juhasz (2003: 76) writes, "any collaboration that takes place through acts of representation will also remain painful for all participants: makers, subjects, and viewers. For every documentary—like every prison—is an arrangement founded on violence and disequilibrium." And, I would add, every transnational feminist film project is founded on lived spatial separations combined, always incompletely and often awkwardly, with a commitment to working toward shared political goals through visual images that we hope will help to bridge some of the distance. Okol and Muna did not see the American film as providing a bridge that was immediately valuable to them, but they remained committed to completing their own research and activism in the service of what they view as workers' more pressing issues.

Revaluing Transnational Feminist Film Work

In my first draft of this reflection on the film project, I concluded that the effort was largely a failure. Not only had the process been fraught with conflict, but the film we made in the United States had been misunderstood by students and deemed irrelevant by our collaborators in Indonesia. Moreover, all of us had participated in this work as a side project, taking time away from our regular work, channeling funds from other projects to cover the costs, and accepting that the film work would not provide any immediate material or professional gain. The process was exhausting, expensive, and time-consuming, and the film itself was unsatisfying to almost everyone we cared to reach.

But several lessons for our transnational feminist praxis have emerged as a result of this reflection, and they have led me to revalue the project as a step along the way to better collaborative work. First, it is necessary to value the process over the product, and to understand that no final film product can satisfy everyone completely, nor could any single project fully and equally encompass the goals, desires, and interests of everyone involved. We can learn from one another and contribute to one another's work through the making of multiple films and offshoot projects, all of which serve as testimony to the worth of the initial project as a piece of a much larger conversation. Second, it became clear that we could and must remain committed to our work together well beyond the completion of the film. Indeed, maintaining and continuing the relationships over time, and working through and with our struggles within them, has proved to be the aspect of our alliance that has proved the most valuable in and of itself.[6] If we had placed value solely on the film itself, as indeed we all initially had, we would not have deemed the project a success. It is only in retrospect that we have come to see our alliance-building as strengthened through facing the impossibility of fitting all of our interests neatly into one set of filmic images and one overarching storyline.

Each of the participants in our collaborative project faces particular material constraints and institutional contradictions that came to light as we struggled to define our priorities for the film. Such transnational feminist praxis work is not accommodated by any of our primary workplaces, whether the factory, the NGO, or the academy. Indeed, in order to participate in this work, each of us has had to find creative, temporary escapes from our specific institutional pressures and expectations, as well as a longer-term commitment to trying to change these institutions. For North-based academic feminists, this means both working with people involved in transformative politics in the South, while simultaneously challenging academic structures, norms, and practices in the corporatizing universities where we are employed. One crucial task of radical transnational feminist praxis, then, is to hold ourselves responsible for this translocal activist work and demand accountability from us along these lines. This may not always seem the most important work to collaborators who live and work in other worlds, nor will our collaborators' agendas always seem the most crucial to political allies in the North. But if we can continue to work in persistent dialogue with one another, and support one another's efforts to effect feminist transformation via multiple political entry points over time, then perhaps we will all begin to understand our coimplication in one another's work in new ways. If this is the measure of success, then the film project was indeed a beginning, and in seeing it as such, we can be encouraged to persevere.

Notes

1. Video production is far less expensive than filmmaking, but films too have grown increasingly affordable for many activists with the advent of digitized cinema. Many collaborative filmmakers advocate for contributing the media equipment to the movements with whom they work, so that the cameras and projectors can be used for movement work beyond the making of any initial film project.

2. But see the discussion in Benson and Nagar (2006) about the importance of valuing and legitimating research processes and products beyond academic publications.

3. See Sangtin Writers and Nagar (2006) for analysis of the NGOization process, as it both encourages and delimits justice-oriented alliances.

4. Once when speaking with an NGO activist collaborator, I suggested that I might be able to sponsor some of her colleagues as graduate students, find fellowship funding for them, and support them in obtaining advanced degrees at the U.S. university where I work. She became irritated and said, "But that's not all we need to do. There is so much more." She went on to explain all the political entry points she saw as more crucial than increasing access to advanced education, and in so doing pointed out the presumptuousness and limitations of my offer.

5. I thank a graduate student in Richa Nagar's seminar for bringing attention to the imperialist positioning intrinsic to this framing.

6. Valuing the struggles and relationships themselves did not come quickly to me or my collaborators, as I discuss in the conclusion of this chapter. My understanding of the film's worth has deepened for me through the process of focused critical reflection in writing this chapter on the film project. Reframing the value of the film alliance as process has been enabled by the transnational feminist praxis (TFP) workshop, follow-up exchanges with TFP participants, and the writing and revision of this analysis. I thank Amanda Swarr, Richa Nagar, and the participants in the workshop for making this growth possible. I am also indebted to Professor Karen Ho at the University of Minnesota for the incisive critical commentary she provided in her discussion of this chapter, and to Richa Nagar and Geraldine Pratt for their sharp engagements with the political/intellectual efforts herein. I remain responsible for any remaining shortcomings.

Works Cited

Acker, Joan, Kate Barry, and Johanna Esseveld. 1991. "Objectivity and Truth: Problems in Doing Feminist Research." In Mary Fonow and Judith Cook, eds., *Beyond Methodology: Feminist Scholarship as Lived Research*. Bloomington: Indiana University Press. 136–151.

Alexander, Jacqui, and Chandra Talpade Mohanty, eds. 1997. *Feminist Genealogies, Colonial Legacies, Democratic Futures*. New York: Routledge.

Benson, Koni, and Richa Nagar. 2006. "Collaboration as Resistance? Reconsidering Processes, Products, and Possibilities of Feminist Oral History and Ethnography." *Gender, Place and Culture* 13(5): 581–592.

Doezema, Jo. 1998. "Forced to Choose: Beyond the Voluntary v. Forced Prostitution Dichotomy." In Kamala Kempadoo and Jo Doezema, eds., *Global Sex Workers: Rights, Resistance, and Redefinition*. New York and London: Routledge. 34–50.

Gibson, Katharine, Lisa Law, and Deirdre McKay. 2001. "Beyond Heroes and Victims: Filipina Contract Migrants, Economic Activism and Class Transformations." *International Feminist Journal of Politics* 3(3): 365–386.

Hesford, Wendy. 2005. "Kairos and the Geopolitical Rhetorics of Global Sex Work and Video Advocacy." In Wendy S. Hesford and Wendy Kozol, eds., *Just Advocacy? Women's Human Rights, Transnational Feminisms, and the Politics of Representation*. New Brunswick, NJ, and London: Rutgers University Press. 146–173.

hooks, bell. 1992. *Black Looks: Race and Representation*. Boston: South End Press.

Juhasz, Alexandra. 2003. "No Woman Is an Object: Realizing the Feminist Collaborative Video." *Camera Obscura* 18(3): 71–96.

Juhasz, Alexandra, ed. 2001. *Women of Vision: Histories of Feminist Film and Video*. Minneapolis and London: University of Minnesota Press.

Katz, Cindi. 2001. "On the Grounds of Globalization: A Topography for Feminist Political Engagement." *Signs: Journal of Women in Culture and Society* 26(4): 1213–1234.

Kempadoo, Kamala, and Jo Doezema. 1998. *Global Sex Workers: Rights, Resistance, and Redefinition*. New York: Routledge.

Mitchell, Katharyne. 2004. "Transnationalism in the Margins: Hegemony and the Shadow State." In Peter Jackson, Philip Crang, and Claire Dwyer, eds., *Transnational Spaces*. London: Routledge. 122–146.

Moghadam, Valentine. 2005. *Globalizing Women: Transnational Feminist Networks*. Baltimore, MD: Johns Hopkins University Press.

Mohanty, Chandra Talpade. 2004. *Feminism without Borders: Decolonizing Theory, Practicing Solidarity*. Durham and London: Duke University Press.

Mohanty, Chandra Talpade. 1991. "Cartographies of Struggle: Third World Women and the Politics of Feminism." In Chandra Talpade Mohanty, Ann Russo, and Lourdes Torres, eds., *Third World Women and the Politics of Feminism*. Bloomington: Indiana University Press. 1–47.

Nagar, Richa, in consultation with Farah Ali and Sangtin Women's Collective. 2003. "Collaboration Across Borders: Moving beyond Positionality." *Singapore Journal of Tropical Geography* 24(3): 356–372.

Pratt, Geraldine. 2004. *Working Feminism*. Philadelphia: Temple University Press.

Pratt, Geraldine. 2005. "Abandoned Women and Spaces of the Exception." *Antipode* 37(5): 1052–1078.

Rabinowitz, Paula. 1994. *They Must Be Represented: The Politics of Documentary*. London and New York: Verso.

Sangtin Writers and Richa Nagar. 2006. *Playing with Fire: Feminist Thought and Activism Through Seven Lives in India*. Minneapolis: University of Minnesota Press.

Sharpe, Jenny, and Gayatri Chakravorty Spivak. 2003. "A Conversation with Gayatri Chakravorty Spivak: Politics and the Imagination." *Signs: Journal of Women in Culture and Society* 28: 609–624.

Silvey, Rachel. 2003. "Spaces of Protest: Gendered Migration, Social Networks, and Labor Protest in West Java, Indonesia." *Political Geography* 22(2): 129–157.

Silvey, Rachel. 2002. "Sweatshops and the Corporatization of the University." *Gender, Place and Culture* 9(2): 201–207.

Spelman, Elizabeth V. 1988. *Inessential Woman: Problems of Exclusion in Feminist Thought*. London: Women's Press.

Swarr, Amanda Lock, and Richa Nagar. 2003. "Dismantling Assumptions: Interrogating 'Lesbian' Struggles for Identity and Survival in India and South Africa." *Signs: Journal of Women in Culture and Society* 29(2): 491–516.

Continuing Conversations

CRITICAL TRANSNATIONAL FEMINIST PRAXIS CONTRIBUTORS

As a nontraditional "ending" to this volume, we present a set of reflections authored by the contributors in partnership with Piya Chatterjee, who was invited by SUNY Press to serve as a reviewer for our manuscript. Coincidentally, Piya had been invited and planned to participate in the workshop, Towards a Transnational Feminist Praxis, in September 2006 but was unable to attend. As part of her evaluation for SUNY Press, Piya wrote a set of comments that sparked critical conversations among the contributors and resulted in our invitation to Piya to join us as a coauthor of this final chapter.

This commentary served as a basis for subsequent written reflections by several contributors on our participation in this project, while initiating further conversation about authors' engagement with questions of agency and processes of institutionalization in our work. These written reflections of Danielle Bouchard, Piya Chatterjee, Jigna Desai, Karen de Souza, Diane Detournay, Richa Nagar, Linda Peake, Rachel Silvey, Amanda Lock Swarr, and Hui Niu Wilcox (listed alphabetically) were interwoven by Amanda and Richa and then circulated to the whole group for further comments and revision. What follows here is a product of this dialogue. Our goal here is not to present a balanced overview or assessment of all of the chapters in the volume. Rather, this dialogue represents some contributors' attempts to return to the task of asking difficult questions about goals, agendas, and visions of transnational solidarities as facilitated and constrained by specific institutional spaces and practices.

Knowledges, Locations, and Solidarities

In the past decade and a half, "transnational feminisms" have become increasingly legitimated within feminist academic writing and research in the global North. This legitimation and institutionalization is embedded within, and informed by, the larger social/structural shifts compelled by globalization and its imperial histories and geographies. As such, the concept of the "transnational" and its coupling with "feminisms" can lose the specificities of its production and its politics within particular spaces and sites—not the least of which is the northern academy. The transnational becomes a wide net that catches all, and, in so doing, can lose the traction that is so important in understanding or illuminating the various investments, contradictions, and relations of power embedded in diverse feminist projects to which it is so intimately linked. In that light, the transnational is in danger of becoming an empty metaphor for academic feminist theories—signifying everything and nothing.

The authors of *Critical Transnational Feminist Praxis* grapple with the genealogy of the transnational and its usage in two decades of feminist knowledge production in the global North. For instance, the volume discusses two canonical texts (Nagar and Swarr); the deployment of the transnational in curricular content in U.S. and Canadian women's/gender studies such that the transnational is either placed elsewhere or positioned Eurocentrically or within the U.S. as theoretically normative (Alexander and Mohanty); the manner in which transnational feminisms feed into the still-problematic construction of "difference" in the neoliberal academy (Desai, Bouchard, and Detournay); the simultaneity of historically and geographically specific transnationalisms (Pratt et al.); and the grounded geopolitics located between theorizing in the North and the involvement of women in the global South (Peake and de Souza). In different ways, all of the essays in this volume engage the now familiar methodologies and theorizing offered by feminist writers around issues of positionality, self-reflexivity, and accountability—but they parse these almost totemic modes of feminist inquiry against the fault lines of a heteronormative, patriarchal, and capitalist geopolitics and everyday "sites" of transnational feminist knowledge production. In so doing, they help to advance the critical project outlined by Alexander and Mohanty in this volume—to destabilize the "cartographic rules" that draw rigid boundaries around neoliberal academies and construct the "community" as a hyper-racialized homogeneous space, while also normalizing the spatial location of the northern academy as the epitome of knowledge production. Such destabilization necessarily requires acute attentiveness to connectivities among multiple, though unequally organized, geographies, temporalities, and interests so that we do not lose sight of the key political questions that reside at the heart of this project (Alexander and Mohanty, this volume): What are the relationships between the politics of location and the politics of knowledge production? And how can transnational feminist solidarities shift the dominant rules about who is legitimized to make sustainable claims about these links?

Agency and Accountability

Several authors reflect, in critical ways, on the possibilities and limitations of agency within the political economy of the academy. For example, Rachel Silvey, in placing the politics of representation and knowledge production at the center of planning for the film *Interstitched*, attempts to open up political space for everyone involved to carefully consider the various forms and purposes of knowledge that it would be possible to create together. Silvey's aim is not so much to look for easy answers or successful strategies, but to "illustrate the historically specific production of our variously positioned visions for the film" (198). The collaborative film project becomes a vehicle to explore how the regimes of governance and the economies that connect various subjects and their spaces produce particular practices and experiences (199).

In reflecting on her work in this volume, Silvey underscored the inseparability of the intellectual and political goals of such work from the emotional labor that goes into forging and nurturing collective dialogues. For her, the collective work of creating this volume translated into the sense of possibility within the agony that inevitably comes with research that is committed to social justice, providing tools with which to grapple with sorrow, intractability, immobility, and depression. Silvey acknowledges that these feelings have persisted:

Indeed, much of this work has heightened my sensitivity to the frustrations and conflicts that inhere in transnational feminist work. In particular, I have been freshly (and ultimately productively) haunted by questions related to "race," nation, neocolonialism, and my position as a North American researcher in Indonesia. And perhaps this is as it should be. We must be (indeed it is our job to be) haunted—and motivated—by the myriad forms of global inequality and our negotiated positions within them.

What is agency coming to mean in relation to the "transnational"? For me, there are both openings and closures of women's agency that come along with the transnational. These don't necessarily add up to a greater or lesser degree of agency nor do they cancel one another out. On the one hand, it is very exciting for both me and my collaborators to be able to consider making a film together for people in both Indonesia and the United States. This is a possible geography into which our work can enter that was unavailable to us even fifteen years ago. In addition, we are aware—and this gives our agency a twist of a particular kind of consciousness—that this geography is not innocent, nor can it be understood in a dehistoricized vacuum. We know, and we explore, the sedimented histories of inequality that have characterized the U.S.-Indonesia relationship, and indeed we find the common elements of this understanding to drive and direct our work together. In this way, these two meanings of the transnational—as both empirical context (i.e., we are able to work across borders in new ways because of accelerated global travel, communication, etc.) that enables the everyday practice of human agency as working together, and as conceptual tool (i.e., it provides a vocabulary with which we can meet each other to talk about our differences, the colonial, imperial, and neoimperial relations that structure and limit our agency) that also enables and enriches our agency as thinking subjects in dialogue with one another. For me, these two aspects of the transnational enhance and enrich the practical and theoretical (indeed the praxis) possibilities for feminist agency. Moreover, they provide the opportunity to think about agency as potentially a collective rather than simply an individual human capacity.

The problematics of agency, geography, and academic locations are inseparable from questions of accountability. Rather than promoting a unified idea of accountability, contributors to this volume bring nuance to their discussions of multifaceted responsibility even as they are acutely aware of the ways in which locations of North-based feminist academics "figure prominently in the consolidation of Empire, the corporatization of knowledge, and the operation of the national security state" (Alexander and Mohanty, 30). Several chapters end with a call for responsibility and accountability. For Pratt et al., this concern is centrally linked with the assumptions that structure our knowledge. Our responsibility, then, is to thoroughly "scrutinize how [our] geographical imaginations have been shaped by [our] institutional and national contexts, and the ways that they [we] may (despite [our] best intentions) see 'like the state,' whether this be by absorbing and reproducing Russian-doll models of care and responsibility, overgeneralizing the reach of knowledge developed in the global North, erasing the global South, or conceiving places outside the global North through tropes of poverty and underdevelopment" (Pratt et al., 84).

Deborah Barndt and her collaborators frame their call for accountability in the language of participatory action research (PAR) and the practice of *sistematización* as methods for exploring community arts projects. While PAR has become increasingly constrained by mainstream development paradigms and funding practices, Barndt sees its intent as congruent with a commitment "to promote critical and collective self-reflection within popular education and community arts processes aimed at stimulating collective action for social change" (171). The VIVA! project reminds us that participatory research originated within popular education networks and work toward reclaiming it is integral to the three-pronged process of research, education, and action associated with Freirean-shaped popular education (171). Accordingly, Barndt sees process/product, aesthetics/ethics, cultural reclamation/cultural reinvention, spiritual/political, and body/earth in dialectical rather than dichotomous tension with one another, tensions that cannot be resolved but must be acknowledged and engaged creatively (172). In struggling with these dialectics, and in shifting their communication and collective analysis to the embodied realm, the VIVA! partners imbue traditional PAR, as well as the field of women and development, with new meanings, while asking themselves difficult questions about appropriation and languages.

A similar but differently articulated concern undergirds the work of the Sangtin Writers who write in a context where those in power "expect to hear our rage and screams when . . . women's bodies are cut or burned alive" but not when they "refuse to separate the murders of women in our community from the larger political economy of displacement and dispossession in our villages" (140). The Sangtin Writers critique the ways in which a complex political and cultural economy at local and global scales becomes associated with the ghettoization and bureaucratization of feminism and empowerment, and they point out the ways in which a compartmentalization of poverty and violence along the lines of gender helps to sustain the existing caste- and class-based structures of privilege and deprivation. For them, "the durability and the value of a collective community-based struggle . . . must also be assessed on the basis of whether all the members of an alliance can participate fully in the processes of making, revising, and deploying the coproduced knowledge, and in developing rigorous structures of accountability that allow people from all fields—the farms, the disciplines, and the villages of "intervention"—to evaluate the relevance of that knowledge in their own lives and journeys" (141).

Scrutinizing Praxis

This brings us to another key intervention of this volume: what does it mean to "collaborate" in a feminist manner across national and other borders of difference and power? How can we think about "praxis" as the center of how we engage and understand collaboration across borders? Even as the authors seek to reconceptualize transnational feminist collaboration, each of them troubles the claims toward collaboration as a panacea for northern-based feminist academics—and what it might mean to work coevally with "other" knowledge producers in sites located outside metropolitan centers. In placing their varied kinds of practices (and praxis) under scrutiny, the contributors draw the sharp-edged contours of collaboration while negotiating and balancing the contradictions of transnational solidarities and commitments.

The collection explores cartographies of knowledge, power, collaborations, and solidarities, even as the authors resist the idealization of any one model or cartography. Indeed, as Pratt et al. remind us, the realization that our research "is a transnational practice; and it is a very small part of a much larger political project," is a fundamental challenge to the individualism of the academy, a system that rewards and celebrates "solo feminism" (Pratt et al., 84). Locating our projects and investments in a wider world of collectives and collaborations can liberate us from the tendency to idealize a model of collaboration based only on the ideals of closeness, proximity, and intimacy and make us more open to the ways in which collaborations may differ from project to project and how the terms of collaboration must be rethought as circumstances change, a point echoed in a number of chapters, including Bullington and Swarr (chapter 4).

For these two authors, collaboration is necessarily messy and fraught with difficulties even as it creates new spaces to challenge academic expectations through its agenda, form, and content. As Bullington and Swarr reflect on their collaborations with one another, with other academics, as well as with South African activists, they participate in a dialogic exchange that is intended to disrupt the expectation of smooth coauthorship or easy relationships in favor of conversations that uncover nuances and problematics of the collaborative process. They take seriously the idea that collaborations are always shifting and paradoxical. Together, they scrutinize their own research process as a means to produce specific grounded analyses of intense relationships formed over more than a decade in different locations in South Africa and their own personal negotiations with communities in conflict and with histories of distrust. Instead of being cowed by the challenges of transnational feminist partnerships, Bullington and Swarr address the complicated relationships of trust that they have built in marginalized communities with activists who believe that the authors' labor and presence as researchers will help advance the political struggles to which they have collectively committed.

Risks, Im/possibilities, and Struggles

Hui Niu Wilcox of Ananya Dance Theatre further questions the relation-ships between agency and collaboration in terms of the dichotomous North-South relationships that both compel and repel us. Reflecting on this volume, she muses:

Where does agency reside when collaboration takes place? Ideally, we would like that all parties involved exercise an equal degree of agency. But it is also important to acknowledge that agency is always constrained by the structures and institutions that we operate within. Discussion of the privilege of the white academics does not mean that their agency is not compromised; it just means that their agency is compromised in different ways. Between the researcher in the North and the activist partner in the South, the former seems to be the one that initiates projects and sets agenda (as far as research is concerned). I agree that the researcher always has more to gain and less to risk (Desai et al., Barndt). Should we just come to terms with this inevitable unequal relationship, or is there anything anybody can do to change this dynamic?

The essays offer glimpses of the kind of tenacity and optimism that is required in the fractured and contested terrain of such social praxis. The dialogical production of the essays imparts an immediacy and honesty that takes these reflections beyond angst-ridden navel-gazing. For example, Peake and de Souza note the constant tension around what it means to produce knowledges for "theory" when women in organizations such as Red Thread are battling for daily survival. As their chapter points out, many of the preoccupations of "transnational feminisms" are based in the North; even travel to the North can take away from the immediate needs of organizing and feed into academic feminist preoccupations in extractive ways—in a kind of academic feminist colonization. These two authors' struggles with intersections of location, knowledge, and power lead them to pose a series of crucial questions including: What do women in the South—placed in different points in organizational hierarchies—stand to gain *and lose* from transnational feminist exchanges? And how much of themselves are northern-based feminist academics willing to put on the line, given that they work in institutions that reward obedience and status quo, and that widely discourage the convergence of action and research (Peake and de Souza, 119)?

The Sangtin Writers challenge the privileges of dominating academic and NGO-based feminisms by exploring the writing and dissemination of knowledges through three fields that, they underscore, cannot be separated; the traffic between languages and "between the lettered and unlettered" intersect in complex ways with the politics of NGOization where "poor rural women" become a category excised from the integral connections to class/caste/religious violence. The authors argue for a knowledge-action linkage in which shifts in grassroots organizing, movement-based critiques of the developmental state, and (re)alignments of social differences and power become organic and integral parts of knowledges produced through reflexive activism and public self-critique.

At the same time, the question of how these praxiological knowledges traffic in and out of certain locations, and how they are valued, is of critical concern. That is, when these knowledges are produced and circulated through the neoliberal university in the global North, how are they valued or marginalized? How do we understand and confront the devaluation of "praxis" in knowledge production? For Silvey, one answer to these questions is the concept of justice, which, she suggests, might smuggle imperial relations of inequality into "collaboration," as might human rights rhetoric. But because these concepts are never free of their social contexts and the meanings that people ascribe to them, they can also be—and indeed are being—reclaimed and invested with political force for anti-imperial work. Silvey pushes for ways to build alliances that facilitate social justice and oppose the neoliberalizing tendencies of the academy.

One way to begin this process would be to pay more attention to what binds our work together, whether it be transnational, postcolonial, or women of color feminist, and a bit less attention to what divides us. I argue this not as a naïve invocation of global sisterhood, but rather as a plea for working together despite, and indeed because of, our differences. Some of this work will be more analytical and textually based, while some will be more immediately and directly involved with people's everyday lives and struggles, and we can work toward connecting these various entry points rather than opposing them to one another. We can argue for diverse forms of scholarly achievement, and we can actively support the organizing strategies and work of students, faculty, and university service workers who might otherwise be marginalized.

Openings, Closures, and Commitments

In formulating their reflections for this final chapter, Desai, Detournay, and Bouchard address the discontinuities that arise within the space of this volume:

Transnational feminism's relationship to collaboration emerges as deeply contested from this set of conversations, and there is no easy or unqualified celebration of collaborative practice as a formula for destabilizing boundaries between academia and its research subjects, or intellectual knowledge production and activism. Indeed, collaboration is rife with complicated and fraught questions about how such engagements forward and contribute to the agendas of activists, and how these subjects are represented within the academy. While the contributions to this volume focus on the struggles that occur within the practice of transnational feminist collaboration, our own piece attempts to take a step back and look at the intellectual histories and trajectories that collaboration fits into and within. As a result, we are led to ask a set of questions concerning how a certain institutional and academic lineage enables, and calls forth, collaboration. First, how do we understand the relationship between the terms "transnational feminism" and "collaboration"? How does this collection participate in offering a particular narrative and agenda for transnational feminism? What role does the invocation of "collaboration" play in constituting specific models of political and intellectual community? Furthermore, rather than just allowing us to "move across" implicitly preexisting identities and boundaries, how might the invocation of "collaboration" do the work of actually constituting these identities and boundaries (in ways that both replicate and resist disciplinary and institutional interests)?

At the same time that collaborative praxis works to interrogate and dismantle oppositions between theory and practice, it might also be productive to recognize the ways in which these categories also structure and legitimate the meaning of collaboration. In other words, the call for "undoing" this opposition also hinges upon it. In this sense, it is not enough to name transnational feminist praxis as a formation that is inherently unstable and internally diverse. Rather, we need to ask difficult questions about how its meaning is shaped by the terms of our conversation, how these terms have a lineage of their own, and how it might perform certain kinds of work for a globalizing academe.

The critiques offered by Desai, Bouchard, and Detournay remind us how efforts to carve out new openings often simultaneously create new closures. However, Rachel Silvey suggests that these critiques are not incompatible with visions of transnational feminist praxis offered here more broadly.

Indeed, I think all of the contributors in the volume are aware of the dangers posed by the politics of representation in relation to the transnational, and none of us sees transnational feminist praxis as a panacea or an ultimate solution to any of the struggles in which we are differently engaged. Rather, I view transnational feminist praxis as offering a set of politically reflexive lenses that can help us continue to engage the haunting, impossible challenges thrown up in the face of working for justice across difference.

An engagement with such "haunting, impossible challenges" leads Hui Niu Wilcox to observe that many of the collaborations in this volume are between white feminist researchers from the North and organizations/individual advocates from the South. She notes,

The dominant model (white academics + disadvantaged communities of color in the South), if not explicitly addressed, reinforces the existing hierarchical binary that equates subjectivity/center with whiteness/Westernness/Northernness and otherness/margin with otherwise. I was especially struck by Karen de Souza's comment about how academic projects such as this often fail to facilitate connections between activist communities. It's a poignant and important realization. What is really at stake? Producing a network of scholars and scholarly knowledge or producing a network of activists? Theoretically, these two should not be posited against each other, but in reality, with all of us burning out in our institutions, we all know too well what the priority is.

For Piya Chatterjee, the problematic binary "that equates subjectivity/center with whiteness/Westernness/Northernness and otherness/margin with otherwise" gets translated into a parallel set of concerns. Chatterjee urges us to consider the ways in which critiques of geopolitical issues attend to the question of ethno-racial and class positionings of feminist activists and scholars who are based in the northern academy but who do complex transnational alliance work both within the North, and in various kinds of national/ethno-racial spaces in the global South. She points out that many of the authors in the volume attend to some of these questions directly or obliquely, but we need to engage these "fault lines of feminisms, geopolitics, and race more sharply." This engagement, furthermore, is undergirded by inevitable questions of translation. As Chatterjee asks, "How do we, for example, translate ethno-racial categories and realities of the North to the same in the global South? For what audience, and to what purpose? And how do various acts of translation (including mis/non/presumed translations) around perceived ethno-racial/class differences then make possible, or imperil, efforts of solidarity building?"

Grappling with some of the same questions of translation and solidarity building, Omise'eke Natasha Tinsley, Ananya Chatterjea, Hui Niu Wilcox, and Shannon Gibney argue that forms of dance must be "deconstructed and reconstructed in keeping with the shared narratives that are created by the women together, in intersection with their diverse cultural and political histories, their shared histories of struggle and resistance, and their shared articulation of dream" (149). Yet, this shared articulation refuses to homogenize and collapse specificities. Rather, it struggles "to make a community of singularities . . . singularities that roil and clash and teem with life like the spaces where currents meet" (164). But retaining singularities while articulating a shared dream might make collaboration harder rather than easier, for it requires that we immerse ourselves in the materialities of our metaphors. As the dancers note in their reflections about *Duurbaar: Journeys into Horizon*:

> it would have been one thing to build on water as a metaphor for femininity, to splash a little across our costumes; it was quite another to immerse ourselves in the materiality of it and it was hard. but this piece was an act of solidarity with other women who work with water and a statement of the need to imagine transforming this work, and *so to be water with the women of ananya dance theatre was never ever easy.* and it was never supposed to be. (152)

In balancing several registers of language and theorizing, the authors combine conventional academic rhetoric and argument with epistolary, "split text" forms that separate out different voices, and a stream-of-consciousness style format. In addition, "embodiment" structures the various elements of this collection. Hui Niu Wilcox suggests that this book is one of the most embodied academic works she has encountered:

Embodiment is implied in a few of the chapters: when Linda Peake and Karen de Souza refer to "embodied interaction," when Barndt vividly recounted her embodied experience in the middle of a jungle, when Geraldine Pratt mentions her pleasurable experience in role playing, and when Bullington and Swarr candidly discuss their visceral experience of research collaboration (being caught in between fistfights and all). Embodied ways of knowing is explicit in the piece on Ananya Dance Theatre, because it's about dance, after all, but when the body is not made explicit in our "normal" academic writings, we end up falling into the trap of scriptocentrism as discussed by Barndt. Another trap is to associate the other with the body in the [global] South, and the knowing subject as the mind in the [global] North.

I would like us to think about the extent to which our agency as researchers in the North and in the South is constrained by the ways in which our material bodies are tied to our different institutions. Border-crossing is an embodied act that demands us to think about ethics. Our bodies and embodied practice are also important sources of knowledge, despite the constraints they experience. Working/dancing with Ananya Dance Theatre has permitted me vantage points that I would have not been privy to. But how much of this embodied knowledge is lost or muffled in the process of translating it into academic texts? Omise'eke is a brilliant translator in that sense; but I struggle so much to put embodiment on paper—partly due to my lifelong academic training to erase the body.

Along with embodiment, the authors of *Critical Transnational Feminist Praxis* recognize the significance of the intimate and affective in feminist collaborations and solidarities—the emotional work of building and sustaining relationships that is so hard to speak about in conventional academic forms and yet is so integral to the knowledges created. As noted in the introduction to this volume, all the essays, in some form or another, were critiqued by other authors and the balance, coherence, and "smoothness" of each piece—in situ and together—makes evident this "internal" editorial collaboration. The resultant intellectual partnerships have produced efforts and relationships that are personal and political, and successful and unsuccessful. In engaging the paradoxes of embodiment and scholarly writing, of collaboration and conflict, of agency and constraint, we have begun the collective process of simultaneously defining, producing, and unsettling transnational feminist praxis without compromising a shared commitment to engender new convergences among locations, knowledges, and solidarities that demystify and challenge the northern academy as the pinnacle of knowledge production.

About the Editors and Contributors

Editors

AMANDA LOCK SWARR is Assistant Professor of Women Studies at the University of Washington. She holds a PhD in Feminist Studies from the University of Minnesota and was Mellon Postdoctoral Fellow at Barnard College of Columbia University from 2003–2005. Amanda has been working with South African activists since 1997 on questions of (trans)gender rights, LGBT justice, and HIV/AIDS treatment access. She has also been collaborating and writing with Sam Bullington since 1995 and Richa Nagar since 1996. She has published articles in *Signs*, *The Journal of Homosexuality*, and *Feminist Studies*, and her current book project is entitled *Sex in Transition: Apartheid and the Remaking of Gender and Race*. Amanda's activist passions center on medical equity and justice and sexual violence/self-defense.

RICHA NAGAR is Professor of Gender, Women and Sexuality Studies at the University of Minnesota (USA) and a founding member of Sangtin Kisaan Mazdoor Sangathan in Sitapur District of Uttar Pradesh (India). She has coauthored *Sangtin Yatra: Saat Zindagiyon mein Lipta Nari Vimarsh*, *Playing with Fire: Feminist Thought and Activism through Seven Lives in India*, and *A World of Difference: Encountering and Contesting Development*. Richa's academic research on gender, race, and communal politics among South Asian communities in postcolonial Tanzania and her subsequent work have resulted in numerous articles and essays. Since 1996, her research, organizing, and creative writing (in Hindustani) have focused mainly on collaborative efforts that seek to reconfigure the political terrain and processes associated with "empowerment" projects aimed at "the poor." Richa was a resident fellow at the Center for Advanced Study in the Behavioral Sciences at Stanford in 2005–2006.

Contributors

M. JACQUI ALEXANDER's work has focused extensively on the relations between nationalism and sexuality and on the ways in which heterosexualization works as a verb to organize nation-building projects across both neoimperial and neocolonial formations. Her most recent book, *Pedagogies of Crossing: Meditations on Feminism, Sexual Politics, Memory and the Sacred* is a critical illustration of these links that both reformulate dominant notions of modernity and shore up the utility of transnational feminist frameworks. Other recent work has wrestled with the sacred dimensions of experience and the significance of sacred subjectivity. Under the auspices of a Guggenheim fellowship she has continued work on the embeddedness of Kongo epistemology within metaphysical systems in the Caribbean. Alexander serves on the editorial boards of *Feminist Review*, *Signs*, and *Dawn* (Canada); she has lectured extensively in the United States, Canada, Europe, Latin America and the Caribbean, and Africa. She is a member of the Caribbean Association for Feminist Research and Action. Alexander is Cosby Endowed Chair in the Humanities at Spelman College and Professor of Women and Gender Studies, University of Toronto.

DEBORAH BARNDT has struggled for four decades to integrate her artist, activist, and academic selves. From engagement in U.S. civil rights, antiwar, and women's movements (1960s) to doctoral research on Freirean pedagogy in Peru (1970s), from training literacy teachers in participatory photo-story production in revolutionary Nicaragua (early 1980s) to organizing multisectoral workshops of activists in diasporic Toronto, Canada (late 1980s/early 1990s), her work has been informed by feminist methodologies, transnational analysis, and praxis-orientation. Since the mid-1990s, she has been teaching popular education, gender and development, and community arts in the Faculty of Environmental Studies at York University in Toronto. As a photographer, she has exhibited widely, and has published ten books, including *To Change This House: Popular Education under the Sandinistas* and *Tangled Routes: Women, Work and Globalization on the Tomato Trail*, as well as edited volumes *Women Working the NAFTA Food Chain: Women, Food and Globalization* and *Wild Fire: Art as Activism*.

DANIELLE BOUCHARD is an Assistant Professor of Women's and Gender Studies at the University of North Carolina at Greensboro. Her research interests include feminist theory, postcolonial studies, critical studies of disciplinarity and interdisciplinarity, and theories of language. She is currently working on a book manuscript that critically examines the centrality of the concepts of interdisciplinarity and globalism to the contemporary U.S. university and their reconsolidation of the university's mission around longer-lived racial, sexual, and national formations. Her work has appeared in *Quarterly Review of Film and Video*, *Contretemps*, and will be included in an upcoming issue of *Differences*.

SAM BULLINGTON is an Assistant Professor in the Department of Women's and Gender Studies at the University of Missouri. Sam has been engaged in ongoing relationships with South African communities for the last decade and involved in a variety of collaborations with Amanda Swarr during the same period. His research examines how the institutional and social legacies of apartheid inform nation-building and progressive politics in contemporary South Africa, and he is a founding member of the University of Minnesota's chapter of Universities Allied for Essential Medicines.

ANANYA CHATTERJEA envisions her work in the field of dance as a "call to action" with a particular focus on women artists of color. She is Associate Professor in the Department of Theater Arts and Dance and Director of Dance at the University of Minnesota, Minneapolis. She is also the Artistic Director of her company, Ananya Dance Theatre, a dance company of women artists of color who work at the intersection of artistic excellence, social justice, and community building (www.ananyadancetheatre.org). Ananya believes in the integral interconnectedness of her creative and scholarly research and in the identity of her art and activism. Her book, *Butting Out! Reading Cultural Politics in the Work of Chandralekha and Jawole Willa Jo Zollar*, was published by Wesleyan University Press in 2004. Ananya has recently performed in Osaka (Dance Box Festival), Jakarta (Indonesian Dance Festival), Kuala Lumpur (Sutra Dance Theater), and Minneapolis (Southern Theater). She has recently been recognized as one of the "21 leaders for the 21st century," among the "7 who will not be stopped," by Women's E-News, a national women-centered news organization (http://www.womensenews.org/21leaders2007.cfm).

PIYA CHATTERJEE is Associate Professor in the Department of Women's Studies, University of California–Riverside. She has published *A Time for Tea: Women, Labor and Post/Colonial Politics on an Indian Plantation* (Duke University Press 2001 and Zubaan Books, India, 2003) and has written on pedagogy, women's organizing, and labor issues. She has been involved in rural women's grassroots organizing in West Bengal since 1999.

JIGNA DESAI is an Associate Professor in the Department of Gender, Women, and Sexuality Studies at the University of Minnesota. Her research interests include Asian American, postcolonial, queer, and diasporic cultural and cinema studies. Her book on the emergence and formation of a South Asian diasporic cinema in the United States, Canada, India, and the United Kingdom was published by Routledge Press in 2004. *Beyond Bollywood* analyzes the complex relationships between diaspora and nation in the current moment of globalization through contestations over gender and sexuality in South Asian transnational public cultures. She is currently working on a manuscript on the globalization of Bollywood.

DIANE DETOURNAY is a graduate student in Feminist Studies at the University of Minnesota. Her research interests include postcolonial and feminist theory, as well as critical approaches to studies of empire and liberalism.

SHANNON GIBNEY is a creative writer, journalist, and activist who lives in Minneapolis. A 2005 Bush Artist Fellow, she has won many awards for her writing, which has appeared in numerous journals and publications. Shannon has an MFA in fiction from Indiana University, and an MA in twentieth-century African American literature from the same institution. She was Executive Director of Ananya Dance Theatre 2004–2006, and is still an active member of the community. For more information on Shannon, or to read her work, visit www.shannongibney.net.

CHANDRA TALPADE MOHANTY is Professor of Women's and Gender Studies and Dean's Professor of the Humanities at Syracuse University. Her work focuses on transnational feminist theory, cultural studies, and antiracist education. She is author of *Feminism Without Borders: Decolonizing Theory, Practicing Solidarity* (Duke University Press 2003 and Zubaan Books, India, 2004); and coeditor of *Third World Women and the Politics of Feminism* (Indiana University Press 1991) and *Feminist Genealogies, Colonial Legacies, Democratic Futures* (Routledge 1997). She is a member of the national advisory board of *Signs, A Journal of Women in Culture and Society, Transformations, The Journal of Inclusive Pedagogy and Scholarship, Feminist Africa* (South Africa), *Asian Women* (Korea), and the *Caribbean Review of Gender Studies*. She has worked with three grassroots community organizations, Grassroots Leadership of North Carolina, Center for Immigrant Families in New York City, and Awareness, Orissa, India and is series editor of Comparative Feminist Studies for Palgrave/Macmillan.

LINDA PEAKE is a geographer with an interest in feminist geographies of race, class, sexuality, and gender, antiracist geographies, and methodologies. She has been working with Red Thread in Guyana since the early 1990s on a range of research projects including the impact of structural adjustment, women's reproductive health, domestic violence, sex work, and most recently, trafficking. One of her interests in these projects has been to work on developing postcolonial research practices and investigate sites of knowledge production outside the academy. She is the Managing Editor of *Gender, Place and Culture: A Journal of Feminist Geography* and Director of the Centre for Feminist Research at York University in Toronto, Canada, where she is also Professor of Geography.

GERALDINE PRATT is Professor in Geography at the University of British Columbia and has collaborated with the Philippine Women Centre for the last fifteen years. The Philippine Women Centre of BC is a community-based organization that carries a vision of an empowered community whose members share a common interest in the issues and problems relating to their reality as marginalized women and immigrants in Canada; a common desire to preserve and increase awareness of their shared historical, political, and cultural roots in a diverse society; and a common willingness to uphold the principles of human rights, equality, peace, and development and freedom for all Filipino women, wherever they may be. Ugnayan ng Kabataang Pilipino sa Canada or Filipino Canadian Youth Alliance has been conducting grassroots organizing among young Filipinos in Canada since 1995. Ugnayan represents the dynamism of Filipino youth and their desire to struggle for the empowerment and genuine development of the community by educating, organizing, and mobilizing Filipino youth.

REENA is a founding member of Sangtin Kisaan Mazdoor Sangathan in Sitapur District of the Indian state of Uttar Pradesh. Her activist work began as an instructor in a women's literacy center in a large NGO in Sitapur in 1998. In 2003, she was invited to become a board member of Sangtin and she soon emerged as an able mobilizer in sixty villages of Sitapur District. Reena founded a women's dairy cooperative in the Kunwarapur Village of Mishrikh Block and is currently working to integrate that dairy with the movement building activities of Sangtin Kisaan Mazdoor Sangathan, or the Sangtin Peasants and Workers Organization. She works on issues ranging from rural girls' education, women's participation in *panchayats*, violence against women, and rural people's right to livelihoods, minimum wages, and information. Reena has traveled throughout Uttar Pradesh and several states of India to participate in forums and dialogues on these subjects.

RACHEL SILVEY, Associate Professor of Geography, University of Toronto, focuses on the politics of migration and transnationalism with attention to the ways in which Indonesian people's spatial mobility is produced and controlled. She is interested in developing connections between critical political economy, migration studies, and transnational feminist theory in order to explore how and why specific geographies and meanings of markets and modernities are forged and interpreted in Indonesia. Her projects center on the cultural and economic politics of development, the gendering of labor migration, and the role of the state in shaping local and transnational spaces of work. Her most recent work also examines the Indonesian-Saudi migration of domestic workers, migrants' rights NGOs, and debates about gendered modernity and liberalism in contemporary Indonesian Islam.

RICHA SINGH, also a founding member of Sangtin Kisaan Mazdoor Sanga-than, stepped into the world of activism in 1991 as a member of the office staff in a prominent women's NGO in the Varanasi District of Uttar Pradesh. She soon emerged as a mobilizer and district-level coordinator, which first took her to Saharanpur and then to Sitapur in 1996. As a district coordinator of a large NGO, Richa participated in critical dialogues on violence against women and on formal and informal education on both regional and national platforms. The coauthorship and publication of the book *Sangtin Yatra* in 2004 gave Richa a new life and direction, and marked the beginning of her full-time immersion in movement-building with peasants and workers of Sitapur District to build and strengthen Sangtin Kisaan Mazdoor Sanga-than, which is currently focusing on the issues of access to irrigation waters, minimum employment guarantee scheme, and right to information of the rural poor.

KAREN DE SOUZA is a founding member and since 1990 has been the co-coordinator of Red Thread, a Guyanese women's organization formed in 1986 whose mission is to organize with other women, beginning at the grassroots, crossing race and other divides, and enabling them to transform the material conditions and underlying power relations that shape their daily lives. She has a long history of being engaged in various acts of citizenship and processes of democratization.

SURBALA is one of the founding members of Sangtin, now Sangtin Kisaan Mazdoor Sangathan, and a coauthor of *Sangtin Yatra/Playing with Fire*. Since 1996, her work has focused on mobilizing and movement-building in sixty villages of Sitapur District. After working in a prominent women's NGO for five years, Surbala left her job to provide full-time leadership to Sangtin. She also organized young women and girls who do chikan embroidery in the villages of Sitapur. She works on issues ranging from violence against women, casteism, and communalism, and informal education and literacy missions to rural people's right to livelihoods, minimum wages, and information. Surbala has traveled extensively throughout Uttar Pradesh and in several states of India and the United States of America to participate in critical dialogues on these subjects.

Born in San Francisco and raised on the Pacific, OMISE'EKE NATASHA TINSLEY joined the University of Minnesota's English Department as a professor of Caribbean and Afro-Atlantic women's literature in 2005. While earning her BA in French, and PhD in Comparative Literature at the University of California, Berkeley, she studied ballet and Afro-Brazilian dance and performed and taught hip-hop. She is thrilled to have recently joined Ananya Dance Theatre's charged, joyful community of women of color in the City of Lakes.

HUI NIU WILCOX holds a PhD in Sociology, and teaches in the Department of Women's Studies at the College of St. Catherine in St. Paul, Minnesota. She writes, "Juggling teaching, research, dancing with Ananya Dance Theatre, and parenting, I try to strike a sustainable balance among all these passions through integration. ADT's work inspires me to study race, gender, and politics of cultural representation and production. I have also introduced ADT to my students and colleagues in exploring intersectionality, symbolic protest, and embodiment. I wrote my piece in response partly to many white women's criticism of ADT's politics, and partly to my undergraduate students' difficulty in understanding intersectionality and multiplicity in the context of transnational feminism. This lack of understanding results from pedagogical and curricular loopholes. Thus, I would like this piece to be read as a political statement of Ananya Dance Theatre, as well as a pedagogical reflection about how we can transform thinking about privilege and oppression."

Index

Note: Page numbers in *italics* indicate illustrations; those with a *t* indicate tables.